The French at War, 1934–1944

SEMINAR STUDIES IN HISTORY

The French at War, 1934–1944

NICHOLAS ATKIN

An imprint of **Pearson Education**

Harlow, England · London · New York · San Francisco · Toronto · Don Mills, Ontario · Sydney · Tokyo
Singapore · Hong Kong · Seoul · Taipei · Cape Town · Madrid · Mexico City · Amsterdam · Munich · Paris · Milan

PEARSON EDUCATION LIMITED

Head Office:
Edinburgh Gate
Harlow
Essex CM20 2JE
Tel: +44 (0)1279 623623
Fax +44 (0)1279 431059

London Office:
128 Long Acre
London WC2E 9AN
Tel: +44 (0)20 7447 2000
Fax: +44 (0)20 7240 5771
Website: www.history-minds.com

First published in Great Britain in 2001

The right of Nicholas Atkin to be identified as author
of this work has been asserted by him in accordance
with the Copyright, Designs and Patents Act 1988.

ISBN 0 582 36899 5

British Library Cataloguing-in-Publication Data
A CIP catalogue record for this book can be obtained from the British Library

10 9 8 7 6 5 4 3 2 1

Typeset by 7 in 10/12 Sabon Roman
Printed in Malaysia, LSP

The Publishers' policy is to use paper manufactured from sustainable forests.

To Charlotte and Benjamin

CONTENTS

INTRODUCTION TO THE SERIES

Such is the pace of historical enquiry in the modern world that there is an ever-widening gap between the specialist article or monograph, incorporating the results of current research, and general surveys, which inevitably become out of date. *Seminar Studies in History* is designed to bridge this gap. The series was founded by Patrick Richardson in 1966 and his aim was to cover major themes in British, European and World history. Between 1980 and 1996 Roger Lockyer continued his work, before handing the editorship over to Clive Emsley and Gordon Martel. Clive Emsley is Professor of History at the Open University, while Gordon Martel is Professor of International History at the University of Northern British Columbia, Canada, and Senior Research Fellow at De Montfort University.

All the books are written by experts in their field who are not only familiar with the latest research but have often contributed to it. They are frequently revised, in order to take account of new information and interpretations. They provide a selection of documents to illustrate major themes and provoke discussion, and also a guide to further reading. The aim of *Seminar Studies in History* is to clarify complex issues without over-simplifying them, and to stimulate readers into deepening their knowledge and understanding of major themes and topics.

LIST OF ABBREVIATIONS

AD	Alliance Démocratique
AF	Action Française
AMGOT	Allied Military Government of Occupied Territories
BCRA	Bureau Central de Renseignement et d'Action
BEF	British Expeditionary Force
CDJC	Centre de Documentation Juive Contemporaine
CDLs	Comités de Libération
CDLL	Ceux de la Libération
CDLR	Ceux de la Résistance
CF	Croix de Feu
CFLN	Comité Française de la Libération Nationale
CFTC	Confédération Française du Travail Chrétien
CGEGS	Commissariat Général à l'Education Générale et Sportive
CGQJ	Commissariat Général aux Questions Juives
CGT	Confédération Générale du Travail
CGTU	Confédération Générale du Travail Unitaire
CHDGM	Comité d'Histoire de la Deuxième Guerre Mondiale
CIMADE	Comité Intergouvernemental auprès des évacués
CNR	Conseil National de la Résistance
COs	Comités d'Organisation
COMAC	Comité d'Action Militaire
CSAR	Comité Secret d'Action Révolutionnaire
CSP	Centre Syndicaliste de Propagande
DCRs	Divisions de Corps Ramassés
DGEN	Délégation Générale à l'Equipement National
FFI	Forces Françaises de l'Intérieur
FNSP	Fondation Nationale des Sciences Politiques
FR	Fédération Républicaine
FTP	Franc-Tireurs et Partisans Français
GMR	Groupes Mobiles de Réserve
GPRF	Gouvernement Provisoire de la République Française
IHTP	Institut d'Histoire du Temps Présent
JAC	Jeunesse Agricole Chrétienne

JEC	Jeunesse Etudiante Chrétienne
JOC	Jeunesse Ouvrière Chrétienne
LFC	Légion Française des Combattants
LVF	Légion des Volontaires Français contre le Bolchevisme
MLN	Mouvement de Libération Nationale
MOI	Main d'Œuvre Immigré
MP	Milices Patriotes
MRP	Mouvement Républicain Populaire
MSR	Mouvement Social Révolutionnaire
MUR	Mouvements Unis de la Résistance
NRF	Nouvelle Revue Française
NSDAP	Nationalsozialistische Deutsche Arbeiterpartei
OCM	Organisation Civile et Militaire
OS	Organisation Secrète
OSS	Office of Strategic Services
PCF	Parti Communiste Français
PNP	Parti National Populaire
POPF	Parti Ouvrier et Paysan Français
PPF	Parti Populaire Français
PQJ	Police des Questions Juives
PSF	Parti Social Français
RNP	Rassemblement National Populaire
SAP	Sections d'Affaires Politiques
SFIO	Section Française de l'Internationale Ouvrière
SNI	Syndicat National des Instituteurs
SOE	Special Operations Executive
SOL	Service d'Ordre Légionnaire
SS	Schützstaffel
STO	Service du Travail Obligatoire

AUTHOR'S ACKNOWLEDGEMENTS

I have incurred several debts in writing this book, not all of which can be acknowledged here. I must, however, thank Professor Gordon Martel, the general editor of *Seminar Studies in History*, who first invited me to undertake the project and who was supportive throughout. Heather McCallum, and her team at Pearson Education, have carefully seen the book through to production. My students Giacomo Lichtner and Matthew Peaple offered valuable comments on a first draft. Dr David Laven of the University of Reading, Dr Simon Kitson of the University of Birmingham, Dr Martin de Lisle, and Charles Williams (Lord Williams of Elvel), corrected mistakes and sharpened my ideas. As well as reading the text, Dr Kay Chadwick of the University of Liverpool and Dr Frank Tallett of the University of Reading advised on some of the translations. Professor Julian Jackson of the University of Swansea kindly let me see his authoritative work on the Occupation before its publication. As a work of synthesis, the present volume is grateful to the scholarship of those numerous authors who have written about Vichy; its shortcomings are my own. My greatest thanks are to my family: my wife Claire, daughter Charlotte, and son Benjamin, who arrived just as this volume was being completed.

PUBLISHER'S ACKNOWLEDGEMENTS

We are grateful to HarperCollins Publishers for permission to reproduce extracts from *The Call to Honour, 1940–1942* by Charles de Gaulle translated by Jonathan Griffin, and *Paris in the Third Reich: A History of the German Occupation, 1940–1944* by David Pryce-Jones.

In some instances we have been unable to trace the copyright owners of material and we would appreciate any information which would enable us to do so.

CHRONOLOGY

1934

6 February	Right-wing leagues demonstrate in Paris
7 February	Resignation of Daladier government
9 February	Communist counter-demonstrations in Paris
12 February	General Strike
27 July	Socialists and Communists agree on pact for joint action

1935

18 January	Gamelin becomes commander-in-chief
14 July	Radicals agree to join Communist and Socialist pact

1936

12 January	Publication of Popular Front programme
24 January	Resignation of the Laval government
25 March	Unification of Socialist and Communist unions
5 May	Election victory of the Popular Front
7 June	Matignon Agreements
18 June	Suppression of right-wing leagues
21 June	Croix de Feu becomes Parti Social Français
27 September	The *franc* is devalued

1937

22 June	Resignation of Blum government

1938

29–30 September	Munich Agreements
4 October	Parliament approves Munich Agreements
1 November	Paul Reynaud becomes minister of finance
12 November	Reynaud publishes decree laws

1939

28 July	Promulgation of Daladier's *Code de la famille*
23 August	Signing of Nazi–Soviet Pact

27 August	Introduction of censorship in France
1 September	Germany enters Poland
3 September	Britain and France declare war on Germany
26 September	French Communist Party outlawed
8 October	Arrest of Communist deputies

1940

20 January	Communist deputies stripped of parliamentary immunity
20–22 March	Daladier resigns as prime minister; replaced by Reynaud
10 May	German offensive in Belgium, Holland and Luxemburg
13 May	German armour breaks through at Sedan
15 May	Surrender of Dutch army
18 May	Pétain made deputy prime minister
19 May	Weygand becomes commander-in-chief in place of Gamelin
27 May	Belgium capitulates
5 June	De Gaulle appointed under-secretary of state for war
9 June	French government quits Paris
10 June	Italy joins the war against France
11–13 June	French cabinet meetings in the Loire
14 June	Germans arrive in Paris; cabinet leaves Tours for Bordeaux
16 June	Reynaud resigns; Pétain takes over as prime minister
17 June	Pétain makes his first radio broadcast; Edmond Michelet writes his protest in Brive
18 June	De Gaulle issues his appeal from London
21 June	A handful of deputies leave France on the *Massilia* bound for North Africa
22 June	Franco–German Armistice
27 June	Laval included in government
28 June	Churchill acknowledges de Gaulle as 'head of the Free French'
3 July	French fleet anchored at Mers-el-Kébir bombed by the British
10 July	National Assembly votes full powers to Pétain
11 July	Constitutional Acts are ratified making Pétain 'head of the French state'; at Paris, Châteaubriant publishes *La Gerbe*
17 July	Public jobs are debarred to all those with a foreign father
20 July	Pétain gives his speech on the causes of the defeat
22 July	All naturalisation certificates issued since 1927 are reviewed
27 July	Déat proposes a single party
30 July	Vichy creates a Supreme Court of Justice; founding of the Chantiers de la Jeunesse

2 August	De Gaulle condemned to death by a military tribunal in Clermont-Ferrand
13 August	Vichy dissolves freemasonry
26–29 August	French Cameroons and much of French Equatorial Africa rallies to de Gaulle
29 August	Establishment of the Légion Française des Combattants
September	Founding of the journal *Liberté*
6 September	Pétain sacks most parliamentarians in his cabinet
7 September	General Weygand becomes *délégué général* of North Africa
17 September	*L'Œuvre* appears in Paris; rationing introduced for key foodstuffs
23 September	Gaullist forces attack Dakar
27 September	Jews in the southern zone debarred from going back to the occupied zone
October	Beginnings of Ceux de la Libération/Défense de la France
3 October	First *Statut des Juifs*
11 October	Vichy law regulating the employment of women in the public sector
20 October	Trade unions abolished and corporations instituted
22 October	Laval meets Hitler at Montoire
24 October	Pétain–Hitler meeting at Montoire
27 October	At Brazzaville de Gaulle establishes the Conseil de Défense de l'Empire
30 October	Pétain's message on collaboration
November	Mouvement de Libération Nationale launches its manifesto, first issue of *Liberté*
11 November	Paris students celebrate Armistice Day with a demonstration in Paris
December	Beginnings of Organisation Civile et Militaire and Libération Sud
2 December	Peasants' Charter
13 December	Dismissal and arrest of Laval
14 December	Flandin appointed as Laval's replacement; Marcel Déat arrested in Paris

1941

17 January	Ministers and high-ranking civil servants obliged to swear an oath of loyalty to Pétain
22 January	Creation of the Conseil National
1 February	Déat founds the Rassemblement National Populaire
9 February	Darlan made deputy prime minister

7 March	Reappearance of *Je Suis Partout*
29 March	Creation of the Commissariat Général aux Questions Juives
11 May	Darlan–Hitler meeting at Berchtesgaden; first Vichy celebration of Joan of Arc day
14 May	First round-up of Jews in Paris
15 May	Creation of the Front National
23 May	Paris Protocols signed
26 May	Beginnings of the miners' strike in Nord-Pas-de-Calais
2 June	Second *Statut des juifs*
3–6 June	Refusal of cabinet to ratify Paris Protocols
8 June	British and Free French troops attack Syria
22 June	Germany invades the USSR
14 July	First issue of *Défense de la France*
17 July	Pucheu appointed minister of the interior
18 July	Creation of the LVF Légion Française des Volontaires contre le Bolchevisme
22 July	Law on the aryanisation of Jewish property
26 July	Assassination of Marx Dornoy
12 August	Pétain delivers his speech on 'an ill wind'
14 August	Oath of loyalty extended to other public servants
20 August	Second round-up of Jews in Paris, opening of camp at Drancy
21 August	Möser shot by 'Fabien'
27 August	Assassination attempt on Laval and Déat
24 September	Founding of the Comité National Français
4 October	*Charte du Travail* published
20 October	General Weygand dismissed as High Commissioner of North Africa
22–23 October	Execution of hostages at Nantes and Châteaubriant
1 November	Mouvement de Libération Nationale and Liberté combine to found Combat
7 December	Pearl Harbor attacked by Japan
12 December	Service d'Ordre Légionnaire founded

1942

20 January	Conference at Wannsee on the 'Final Solution'
19 February	Riom Trials commence
March	Founding of Francs-Tireurs et Partisans
3–4 March	Allied bombing of Boulogne-Billancourt, Paris
26 March	Laval–Pétain meeting

27 March	First French Jews sent to Auschwitz
28 March	Sauckel told to recruit French labour
15 April	Suspension of the Riom trials
18 April	Reinstatement of Laval in government
6 May	Darquier de Pellepoix becomes head of the CGQJ
18 May	Germany demands French skilled workers for its war effort
29 May	Jews in the Occupied zone obliged to wear the Yellow Star
22 June	Speech of Laval introducing the *Relève*
16 July	Vél d'Hiv round-ups
18 July	Creation of *Légion Tricolore*
29 July	Free French become Fighting French
18 August	Failed Anglo-Canadian raid on Dieppe
25 August	Germans introduce conscription in Alsace-Lorraine
26–28 August	Start of first round-ups of Jews in the non-occupied zone
4 September	First measures of the Service du Travail Obligatoire
8 November	Allied invasion of North Africa
11 November	Germany occupies the southern zone
14 November	Darlan sides with the Allies
18 November	Constitutional act number 12 gives full powers to Laval
26 November	French fleet scuttled at Toulon
24 December	Assassination of Darlan
26 December	General Giraud appointed commander-in-chief in North Africa

1943

17 January	De Gaulle and Giraud meet at Anfa, Morocco
26 January	Creation of the Mouvements Unis de la Résistance
30 January	Founding of the *Milice*
17 February	Inauguration of the second stage of Service du Travail Obligatoire
1 March	Demarcation Line disassembled
24 March	First *milicien* killed by the Resistance
27 May	First meeting of the Conseil National de la Résistance
30 May	De Gaulle arrives in Algiers
3 June	Constitution of the Comité Française de la Libération Nationale agreed at Algiers
21 June	Arrest of Jean Moulin
8 July	Likeliest date of Moulin's death
11 July	Allies invade Sicily
25 July	Fall of Mussolini

31 July	De Gaulle sole president of the Comité Française de la Libération Nationale
8 August	Capitulation of Italy
5 September	Liberation of Corsica
8 September	Germany occupies the former Italian zone
18 December	Pétain accepts German restrictions on his government's freedoms

1944

1 January	Darnand put in charge of internal security
6 January	Henriot becomes secretary of state for information and propaganda
20 January	Introduction of special court-martials for resisters
27 January	*Milice* allowed to operate in the northern zone
20 March	Execution of Pucheu at Algiers
16 March	Déat becomes secretary of state for labour
26 March	*Miliciens* and German troops attack *maquis* on the Glières Plateau
26 April	Pétain visits Paris
3 June	Comité Française de la Libération Nationale becomes Gouvernement Provisoire de la République Française
6 June	D-Day landings
10 June	SS massacre inhabitants of Oradour-sur-Glane
14 June	De Gaulle arrives at Bayeux
20 June	Assassination of Jean Zay
28 June	Assassination of Philippe Henriot
7 July	Assassination of Georges Mandel
15 August	Landing of Allied troops in Provence; final convoy of deportees leaves France
20 August	Pétain leaves Vichy
25 August	Germans surrender in Paris
26 August	De Gaulle in Paris
8 September	Pétain and Laval established at Sigmaringen

1945

26 April	Pétain gives himself up to the French authorities
8 May	Germany surrenders
10 May	Deportees and POWs begin to return to France
July	Trial of Pétain in Paris
October	Trial and execution of Laval

1946

20 January	De Gaulle resigns as leader of the Provisional Government
10 September	Paul Touvier sentenced to death *in absentia* by a court in Lyon
13 October	Referendum endorses the constitution of the Fourth Republic

1947

4 March	Second death sentence pronounced on Touvier by court in Savoy

1951

5 January	First amnesty for crimes under the Occupation
23 July	Death of Pétain

1953

6 August	Second amnesty law

1954

14 April	Last Sunday in April officially declared National Day of Memory for Victims and Heroes of the Deportation
9 October	Karl Oberg and Helmut Knochen sentenced to death in Paris, later commuted to life imprisonment (released in 1962)

1958

1 June	De Gaulle becomes prime minister
28 September	Constitution of the Fifth Republic

1964

18–19 December	Jean Moulin's remains interred in the Panthéon
26 December	Parliament agrees law on 'crimes against humanity' with no statute of limitations

1970

9 November	Death of de Gaulle

1971

April	Release of *Sorrow and the Pity*; Pompidou reduces Touvier's sentence

1972

	Release of Robert Paxton's *Vichy France*

1973

9 November   Touvier charged with crimes against humanity by a court in
                    Lyon

1978

28 October   Interview with Darquier de Pellepoix in *L'Express* in which he
                    claims only lice were gassed at Auschwitz

1983

19 January   Maurice Papon charged with 'crimes against humanity'

1987

4 July   Klaus Barbie sentenced by a Lyon court to life imprisonment
                    for 'crimes against humanity'

1989

24 May   Touvier arrested in Nice

1992

16 July   Fiftieth anniversary of the Vél d'Hiv round-ups; Mitterrand
                    declares 16 July a day of national mourning but will not
                    accept any responsibility on the part of the French state in the
                    round-ups

1993

8 June   Shooting of René Bousquet while waiting trial for 'crimes
                    against humanity'

1994

20 April   Paul Touvier condemned to a life sentence for 'crimes against
                    humanity'

June   Fiftieth anniversary of the Liberation; President Mitterrand
                    later makes public his Vichy connections

1995

16 July   President Chirac acknowledges the responsibility of the
                    French state for the round-ups

1998

2 April   Maurice Papon condemned for 'crimes against humanity' and
                    given a ten-year jail term

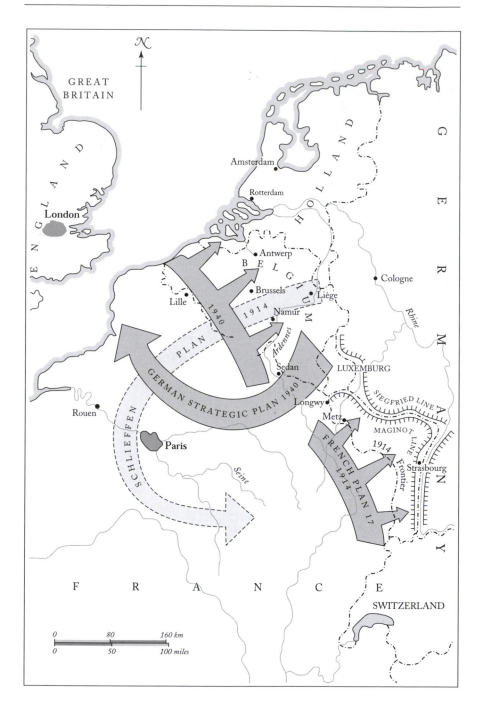

Map 1   French and German strategies in 1914 and 1940
Source: Alistair Horne, *To Lose a Battle* (Penguin, 1973)

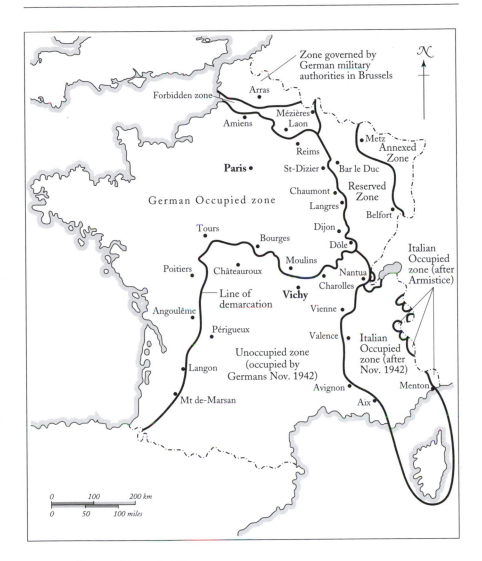

Map 2 Zones of Occupied France

PART ONE   THE CONTEXT

CHAPTER ONE

INTERPRETING THE VICHY REGIME

THE VICHY SYNDROME

On 10 May 1940, German forces, having overrun much of Eastern Europe, turned westwards and began their invasion of Belgium, Holland and Luxemburg. The Allies anticipated a long campaign; instead, it was over in seven weeks, within which time France itself had been defeated. On 16 June, Paul Reynaud, the French prime minister, tired of political infighting and despondent at the desperate nature of the military situation, resigned and handed over power to the 84-year-old Marshal Pétain, who had brought France victory at Verdun in 1916. If Reynaud had hoped that this old man would repeat his earlier triumph, he was to be sorely disappointed. Deeply pessimistic, politically ambitious, naive about true German intentions and anxious to avoid further bloodshed, the marshal soon negotiated an armistice with Germany, signed on 23 June [*Doc. 8*], the terms of which divided France into two principal zones. The larger of the two areas, governed by the Germans, sprawled over northern and western France (Map 2). The Unoccupied zone remained in French hands, although its independence was always questionable, and its title *la zone libre* ('the free zone') quickly invited ridicule. Nonetheless, it was there that, in July 1940, Pétain set up a new government at the little spa town of Vichy. Entrusted with extensive personal powers, voted by the National Assembly meeting at the town's casino on 10 July, he oversaw the destruction of the Third Republic, entered into a policy of collaboration with Germany, and launched an ambitious programme of internal reform known as the National Revolution. While this project of renewal had its progressive side, it also possessed a sinister streak, persecuting minorities, including Communists, freemasons and Jews. As repression intensified, French men and women were forced to make a series of agonising 'choices'. A small minority threw in their lot with the Germans and gravitated to the collaborationist organisations which flourished in Paris and the occupied zone. An even smaller group attempted the difficult journey to London to serve with General de Gaulle, or elected to join the resistance organisations which were emerging on metropolitan soil. Most waited on events, a phenomenon known as *attentisme*, retaining a loyalty to Pétain, but not necessarily to his government. However, following the steady intensification of measures against Jews, the loss of successive French colonies to Gaullist forces, the occupation of all of France in November 1942 and the introduction of compulsory work service in Germany, the Service du Travail Obligatoire (STO), early the following year, it became increasingly difficult to maintain such a position. As civil disorder spread, Vichy refined its instruments of repression, setting up the hated *Milice*, a paramilitary gang of cut-throats and n'er-do-wells, whose function was to hunt out resisters. At the time of the D-Day landings on 6 June 1944, the country was nearly at war with itself. In the event, the purges (*épuration*) that accompanied the Liberation, were not as bloodthirsty as many had feared, permitting France to undertake the massive task of reconstruction, although this job of rebuilding would not assuage the wounds opened up during the war years.

Given the sheer drama of the Vichy period, its innate importance, relevance to the present, and ties with the Holocaust, it is no surprise that the Occupation has attracted intense interest. Yet writing about the so-called *années noires* ('dark years') has not proved easy, at least for French writers. In the words of Henry Rousso, Vichy has resembled a *syndrome* in the nation's psyche, a terrible 'neurosis' that has to be prodded over and over again in the desperate quest for a 'cure' which will restore the 'well-being' of the nation's conscience (Rousso, 1989). Through his own analysis of this introspective process, Rousso has made a profound contribution to our understanding of the ways in which the French have recalled this most terrible episode in their past. He has further established a series of phases, now accepted as orthodoxy (Munholland, 1994), through which the historiography of Vichy has passed, each period exemplifying how, in France, past and present frequently intermingle. There was first, writes Rousso, a period of 'unfinished mourning' (1946–54) when few authors were prepared to tackle the Occupation. Then came a time of 'repressions' (1954–71) where the myth-makers got to work, creating the legend of *la France résistante*. This image was brutally shattered in the early 1970s 'the broken mirror' (1971–74), to be succeeded by an era of 'obsessions' (1974–80s) when the Occupation seemed ever present. Vichy watchers have since struggled to classify the subsequent evolution of the *syndrome* as historians become ever more eclectic in their chosen areas of research (Munholland, 1994).

THROUGH MOURNING TO REPRESSION, 1946–69

In the early years of the Fourth Republic (1946–58), the French public and politicians were principally preoccupied with the task of political and economic reconstruction and were anxious to expedite the remaining trials of the *épuration*. With the exception of the Communists, ever eager to embarrass the establishment, few French people had any great desire to revisit the Occupation years. In particular, they wished to avoid confronting the treatment of the Jews. In this era, Rousso's time of 'unfinished mourning', it was left to former Vichy ministers to give their version of events. Some of these commentaries, notably those of Henri du Moulin de Labarthète (Pétain's private secretary from May 1940 to April 1942) and Jérôme Carcopino (one of the regime's six ministers of education) were remarkably candid (Du Moulin de Labarthète, 1946; Carcopino, 1953). For the most part, however, former Vichy officials, among them Paul Baudouin and Yves Bouthillier, were desperate to rehabilitate their political reputations and take advantage of recent amnesty laws. Hence, they produced memoirs that were little more than *apologias*: deferential to the marshal; economical with the truth; vague on such events as the deportation of French workers and Jews; and insistent that France would have suffered more had it not been for the protection afforded by the 'shield' of the Pétain government (Baudouin, 1948; Bouthillier, 1950–51). Significantly, it has been posthumous memoirs, notably those of Joseph Barthélemy, one-time minister of justice, published in the 1980s, that have proved the most revealing, highlighting the early autonomy that Berlin permitted Vichy (Barthélemy, 1989).

In the 1950s, as France attempted to come to terms with the loss of empire in Indochina and Algeria, and struggled to achieve political stability at home, the memory of the Occupation came to be 'repressed' and distorted by a series of myth-makers. In 1954, Robert Aron, a right-wing author who had flirted with fascism in the 1930s, produced his *Histoire de Vichy* (Aron, 1954). A mammoth undertaking – based on oral testimony, documents of the High Court and unpublished memoirs – this was the first serious study to appear on the Occupation. As a Jew, Aron had been forced to flee wartime France, yet he retained a sense of debt to those high-ranking Vichy officials, notably Jean Jardin, who had protected him from the regime's antisemitic legislation, and was disconcerted by the way in which the Fourth Republic had subsequently punished Pétainist officials. Accordingly, he tailored a sympathetic portrayal of the regime: a 'benevolent' Vichy of the marshal which did its utmost to counter German demands, and an 'evil' Vichy of Laval which was only too ready to meet Berlin's requests. In a further balancing act, again designed to assuage the wartime memories of the French, he measured criticism of Vichy for undertaking its National Revolution with harsh words for the Resistance which, he later maintained in his history of the *épuration*, had arbitrarily murdered some 30,000 people at the time of the Liberation [*Doc. 26*]. No statistics were included on the persecution of Jews and other minorities (Aron, 1959).

As Rousso relates, if Aron had attempted to offer France 'retrospective dignity' by underplaying Vichy's villainy, then his efforts were surpassed by

Charles de Gaulle who, in 1954, published the first volume of his war memoirs, *L'Appel, 1940–1942* (De Gaulle, 1954). Still smarting from the fact that his services had been rejected at the Liberation, and careful to keep his political options alive given that the Fourth Republic was in serious difficulties, the general had an agenda of his own. Largely ignoring events in Vichy, which he condemned as an illegitimate regime, de Gaulle recalled the history of wartime France almost exclusively from the vantage point of London and Algiers. The message was transparent: France owed its wartime deliverance not to the marshal, who had cynically taken advantage of the defeat, nor to the Communists, who had exploited their role in the internal Resistance for revolutionary purposes. Instead, salvation derived from the actions of the general himself who, through his 'call of honour' in June 1940, had incarnated French sovereignty and maintained the republican tradition. As Rousso surmises, if France 'was to merit, in retrospect, the glory of having defeated the occupying power, then he who embodies the essence of France (i.e. de Gaulle) must once again preside over the country's highest destiny' (Rousso, 1989: 245). His chance came in 1958 when the crisis over Algerian independence ushered in the Fifth Republic under his presidency.

De Gaulle's interpretation of events received unexpected endorsement from members of the historical profession. With French settlers in Algeria seemingly intent on denying the wishes of both the Arab separatists and Paris, and with many Vichyites returning to public life in metropolitan France, it appeared that the new Fifth Republic was far from secure. In this situation, historians of the Comité d'Histoire de la Deuxième Guerre Mondiale (CHDGM), a semi-official body founded in 1951 and led by the eminent historian and former resister Henri Michel, uncovered a political purpose. Despite being a Socialist, Michel shared a common design with de Gaulle in that both men wished to portray the Resistance as a valiant struggle which embodied republican legitimacy that was now manifest in the Fifth Republic, thus fending off any revival of Pétainism. In his many accounts of clandestine activities in wartime France, notably his 1962 study *Pensées de la Résistance*, Michel readily acknowledged that resisters had been a minority (Michel, 1962), but maintained that they had only been able 'to operate because of the support of the nation' (Gildea, 1995: 65). As Gildea elaborates, the logic of this argument was clear: 'the Resistance had recreated national unity, and in turn imparted the grace of having participated in the Resistance to the nation as a whole' (Gildea, 1995: 65) Slowly but surely, the myth grew that France had been a 'nation of resisters'.

From an academic standpoint, it was difficult to sustain this illusion. In their extensive researches into wartime France, researchers of the CHDGM discovered an elaborate mosaic of French reactions to the occupier and, in 1966, Michel himself published *Vichy: Année 40*, a brilliant study that underscored the initial popularity of Pétain's government although, significantly, the book only covered the first year of the Occupation (Michel, 1966). Meanwhile, historians belonging to the Centre de Documentation Juive Contemporaine (CDJC), released extensive documents authenticating Vichy's involvement in the Holocaust (Kaspi, 1976). As Rousso adds (Rousso, 1989: 250), individual scholars – Jacques Duquesne on French Catholics (Duquesne, 1966), Jacques Delarue on the black market (Delarue, 1968), Jacques Delperrié de Bayac on the *Milice* (Delperrié de Bayac, 1969), Eberhard Jäeckel on collaboration (Jäeckel, 1966) – were also challenging 'resistancialist' orthodoxy. For the most part, however, their findings were confined to scholarly circles, and had little resonance among the public at large. Nor was it likely that opinion would take much interest in the scholarship of anglophone historians, notably Geoffrey Warner's brilliant biography of Laval (1968), which has never appeared in French translation, and Richard Griffiths' astute life of Pétain (1970).

ORTHODOXIES AND OBSESSIONS, 1971–85

Ultimately, it was not a book but a film, Marcel Ophuls' 1971 *Le Chagrin et la pitié* (*The Sorrow and the Pity*), that 'cracked the mirror' of 'resistancialist' mythology, fundamentally challenging what Gildea terms the 'redeeming, unifying, heroic story of the war years', carefully elaborated by Aron, de Gaulle and others (Gildea, 1995: 65). There had, of course, been films about the 'dark years' before, yet these had been comedies, romanticised accounts of the Resistance, or tales of everyday life under the Occupation (Rousso, 1989: 232). Most dramas had shied away from the issues of collaboration, deportation and the nature of Vichy itself. Ophuls' film was different. This was a documentary, some four hours in length, which chronicled the daily life of the people of Clermont Ferrand, their experiences purportedly held similar to those of most French men and women during the Occupation. Interspersing interviews with archive footage, the film dented the notion of 'a nation of resisters'. Both active resisters and collaborators had been a minority at Clermont; the majority had been decidedly craven, waiting on events and retaining an abiding faith in Pétain, behaving in a manner they were now deeply reluctant to acknowledge. Especially disturbing were the revelations about French antisemitism. In one of the most memorable scenes in the film, two distinctly uncomfortable secondary-school *professeurs* deny any knowledge of the fate of their fellow Jewish teachers, only for their testimony to be called into question by subsequent footage of the antisemitic images that had been rife in wartime Clermont (Rousso, 1989: 102) [*Doc. 27*].

Not surprisingly, *The Sorrow and the Pity* angered the French establishment. Initially shown on German television, it was kept off French screens until 1981, and could only be viewed in a small art-house cinema in the Latin Quarter of Paris. Yet, following the student demonstrations of May 1968, de Gaulle's resignation from the presidency in April 1969, and the general's death in September 1970, public attitudes towards the Occupation began to change, especially among a younger generation who had not lived through 'the dark years'. In 1972, President Pompidou was visibly taken aback at public protests over his secret pardoning of the war criminal Paul Touvier the previous year. At long last, it seemed that the French people, or at least certain sections of public opinion, was ready to confront the past.

It was in this context that, in 1972, an American historian Robert Paxton published his *Vichy France: Old Guard and New Order, 1940–1944* (Paxton, 1972). Although frostily received by most French scholars, who were suspicious of Paxton for being both young and foreign and thus not able to appreciate the complexities of the Vichy years, this was a truly remarkable study that has since become the starting-point for any real understanding of the Occupation. Through his deft handling of German archives, Paxton built on Jäeckel's earlier work to demonstrate how the impetus for collaboration had come from the French not from the Germans. In so doing, he demolished the double-game argument deployed by Pétain and his followers, who suggested the marshal had been engaged in secret negotiations with the British. In addition, Paxton dedicated far more attention than previous historians to Vichy's domestic reforms, and revealed how the National Revolution had been an exclusively French experiment drawing on a series of indigenous political ideologies, among them traditionalism, Catholicism, Maurrassianism, Orleanism, and positivism. All in all, the National Revolution had amounted to a wholesale attempt to overturn French institutions, predating the reforms that would overtake France in the 1950s. In this way, Paxton maintained, Vichy represented not a 'break' but a 'continuity' in French political life. Turning to the dark side of the Occupation, Paxton further revealed how Vichy's antisemitism had been homegrown, owing little to German pressure. Eventually this persecution troubled consciences and, in 1942–43, public support for Vichy began to wane. Historians have since proved that the regime lost its popularity as early as January 1941, yet endorse Paxton's claim that Resistance was never anything more than the work of a minority. Paxton controversially suggested that few men and women, maybe one in ten of the population, engaged in active resistance, a figure that is difficult to substantiate. Equally controversial was his overall conclusion that Vichy never constituted a 'shield' and 'spared France little'. Such a hypothesis cannot, of course, be scientifically tested, and now historians stress the very real restraints under which Vichy operated. Yet most agree that Pétain's government did little to protect the French people.

In the 1970s, as the image of a 'nation of resisters' was broken, Vichy became an 'obsession', especially among Jewish historians. Worried by the re-emergence of a xenophobic right in the form of Jean-Marie Le Pen's Front National and troubled by the refusal of former Vichyites, especially Louis Darquier de Pellepoix, head of the Commissariat Général aux Questions Juives (CGQJ), to acknowledge the horror of their crimes (notably in an interview Darquier gave to *L'Express* magazine in 1978), Jewish writers such as Ganier Raymond and Serge Klarsfeld were keen that Vichy's role in the Holocaust should at long last be established as an historical fact (Raymond, 1975; Klarsfeld, 1982). It was in the wake of their findings that, in the 1980s, France witnessed a series of trials in which former Vichyites were tried for 'crimes against humanity', although it was a German, Klaus Barbie, who in 1987 first experienced the wrath of belated French justice. Elsewhere, scholars were also eager to demonstrate the repressive and xenophobic nature of the Vichy regime, taking advantage of the gradual opening of state archives. Claude Lévy, Jean-Pierre Azéma, Pascal Ory and Rousso dissected the world of the Paris collaborationists (Lévy, 1974; Azéma, 1975; Ory, 1976; Rousso, 1987), while the diplomatic historian Jean-Baptiste Duroselle unravelled the pusillanimous nature of Vichy foreign policy (Duroselle, 1981). Yet, despite this 'obsession', not all French historians were eager to explore their national past. It is telling that, during this phase of 'obsessions', much of the best history on the Occupation was written by anglophone writers: Paxton, along with the Canadian Michael Marrus, on the Jews (Marrus and Paxton, 1981); W.D. Halls on Vichy's educational and youth policies (Halls, 1981); H.R. Kedward on the resistance (Kedward, 1978); and Bertram Gordon on collaboration (Gordon, 1978). The extent to which the French public was prepared to accept new historical scholarship was also questionable. As Rousso reminds us, during the 1980s, the most popular French historian of the Occupation was the journalist Henri Amouroux who, in 1976, began his *Grande Histoire des Français sous l'Occupation*, a multi-volume work that easily outsold its competitors (Amouroux, 1976). Written in a conversational style, but based on formidable research, it was the soothing nature of Amouroux's conclusions that appealed. Echoing the earlier conclusions of Aron, Amouroux saw faults in the wartime behaviour of his countrymen, but conveniently blamed many of the calamities of the Occupation on the inescapable tensions of wartime (Rousso, 1989: 257).

ALLTAGSGESCHICHTE

In 1990, the Institut d'Histoire du Temps Présent (IHTP), the successor to the CHDGM, organised a major international conference to commemorate the fiftieth anniversary of the defeat and Occupation (Azéma and Bédarida, 1992). There had been conferences on Vichy before, notably that organised

in 1970 by the Fondation Nationale des Sciences Politiques (FNSP), yet
none had been on this scale (FNSP, 1972). Significantly, most of the con-
tributors were French, although anglophone historians including Paxton,
Kedward and Sweets were present. Also significant was the fact that few
subjects, if any, were regarded as taboo. Indeed, in the 1990s, the fas-
cination with the Occupation has continued unabated, a far cry from the
1950s and 1960s when only a select band of writers dared tackle so
sensitive a topic.

Analysing the evolution of the Vichy *syndrome* in the 1990s, historians
have attempted to add a further phase to Rousso's periodisation. Azéma has
suggested that recent scholarship has been marked by an attempt to moderate the 'harsh judgements' that initially appeared in the wake of Paxton's
original research (Azéma, 1992; Munholland, 1994: 803) Undoubtedly,
historians today are more alive to the constraints under which Vichy
operated. Nor has there been any shortage of books attempting to rehabilitate the reputations of the marshal's government. In 1991, the Gaullist
historian and politician François Dreyfus attempted to update Aron in the
light of recent scholarship, although his use of that scholarship proved
extremely selective (Dreyfus, 1990). Rather, it appears that in recent years
historians of the Occupation have unconsciously emulated their counterparts working on Nazi Germany by becoming increasingly interested in
Alltagsgeschicte, the 'history of daily life'. Having exhausted the high
politics of Franco-German relations, having explored the numerous
intrigues that dominated Vichy's corridors of power, having established that
the Pétain government was responsible for the deportation of French
workers and Jews, researchers have gone on to explore life from the bottom
up, developing the lines of enquiry on public opinion first established by
John Sweets and Pierre Laborie (Sweets, 1986; Laborie, 1990). Denis
Peschanski on propaganda (Peschanski, 1990), Dominique Veillon on the
economics of austerity (Veillon, 1990, 1995), Françoise Muel-Dreyfus on
the experiences of women (Muel-Dreyfus, 1996) – these are now the fashionable areas of enquiry. In so doing, historians have unveiled the pluralism of
Vichy, the continuities between the 1930s and 1940s, and the impotency of
many of Vichy's policies at a local level where public opinion soon became
disenchanted with the regime.

As the Occupation has steadily become one of the most researched
episodes in French history, writers are rapidly running out of new areas to
investigate. As I have had occasion to argue before, the historian of Vichy
has come to resemble a skilled physician, well aware of the physiology of
the Pétain regime: 'Yet, like a cancer specialist, the historian has struggled
to devise a cure which will heal the divisions within France' (Atkin, 1999:
263). In the manner of a dreadful illness, the Vichy *syndrome* still unsettles
and frightens both the French establishment and public. Recent revelations

about the internal quarrels within the Resistance, notably the ambiguous role played by de Gaulle's close lieutenant Jean Moulin (Cordier, 1989–93; Péan, 1998), the trials of Vichy functionaries such as Touvier, Bousquet and Papon, and the astonishing confessions of the socialist president, François Mitterrand, who admitted to a Vichy past (Péan, 1994), have demonstrated how the 'dark years' continue to cast a shadow over France. Some argue that it is time to forgive and forget; others still take refuge in the 'resistancialist' mythology of de Gaulle and Aron, conveniently blaming the horrors of the Occupation on the actions of maverick individuals such as Touvier and Papon. Such attitudes will probably never disappear. Yet so long as the Front National remains one of the largest neo-fascist parties in Europe (perhaps rivalled only by Jörg Haider's Freedom Party in Austria), and is prepared to discriminate against ethnic minorities and deny Vichy's complicity in the Holocaust, it is critical that the Occupation should remain in the spotlight.

PART TWO   ANALYSIS

CHAPTER TWO

THE THIRD REPUBLIC, 1934–40

Although historians generally acknowledge the durability of the Third Republic in its pre-1914 phase, it is often viewed as a politically unstable and economically backward regime during the interwar years: the final débâcle of June 1940 was an accident waiting to happen. Yet to accept these censures wholesale is to accept Vichyite propaganda. Whether the Republic was in a state of terminal decline by June 1940 remains questionable and most authors now agree that it was failings on the battlefield, not the alleged imperfections of French politics and society, that brought about collapse. That said, there is little doubt that the interwar years were an agonising period for the French. While the 1920s had been relatively successful, *bourgeois* self-confidence was fragile and was easily shattered by the onset of a Depression in 1931–32 which refused to go away. The irony is that confidence was returning at the moment when France went to war.

THE REPUBLICAN CONTEXT

The Third Republic was founded in September 1870 amid the rubble of Louis Napoleon's Second Empire (1852–70). The new regime was envisaged as a temporary affair until the quarrelsome monarchists could reconcile their differences and effect a restoration. In the event, they continued to squabble, and the Republic went from strength to strength. By crushing the Paris Commune of 1871, by putting their own people into positions of civil authority, by introducing a raft of vaguely progressive social measures, by exploiting the instruments of modernisation such as the primary school and railway, and by prudent housekeeping, high tariffs and minimal state interference in the economy, the moderate Republicans of the 1880s persuaded the majority of French men and women, especially among the peasantry, that the regime was a tempered and tolerable one. As such, it was able to weather all kinds of political storms: financial crises such as the Panama Canal and Union Générale scandals; a Bonapartist pretender in the shape of General Boulanger; and, most famously, the Dreyfus Affair, a

15

political maelstrom sparked by the serious miscarriage of justice in which the unfortunate captain Alfred Dreyfus was wrongly convicted of spying. War was a more serious business. If Joffre had not held his lines at the battle of the Marne in September 1914, it is likely that, after another Armistice, a Fourth Republic would have emerged to govern whatever territory the Germans were prepared to leave the French. Small wonder, victory in 1918 was received with relief; for many politicians, it was a vindication of the political system that had existed in France for some 40 years.

The Constitution of the Republic, devised in 1875, provided for what political scientists term a *régime d'assemblée*, that is a system in which the legislature, in the shape of the National Assembly, ruled on behalf of the people. The National Assembly itself was bicameral, consisting of a con-servative-orientated Senate, whose members were elected by universal male suffrage for a seven-year term of office, and a Chamber of Deputies, far more varied politically, which was elected every four years, once again by an all-male electorate. Although the Senate frequently blocked legislation from the lower house, it was the Chamber that held real power. According to many historians, this was the root of France's political problem. Because French party discipline was loose and because alliances between parties were constantly shifting, it was difficult for a prime minister to sustain a working parliamentary majority. Thus ministerial instability was rife. During the interwar years, France had 42 governments: most lasted around six months; one clung on for a day. Nonetheless, historians have emph-asised that a change of cabinet did not mean a general election, and have pointed to the impressive continuity of government personnel. One cure for this ministerial instability, prescribed by several conservatives in the 1930s, among them André Tardieu and Georges Mandel, was a more powerful presidency. However, the 1875 Constitution, keen to thwart any future Bonaparte, shied away from creating a strong executive arm of government; this proved an unexpected blessing in the 1920s when the president, Deschanel, out of touch with reality, lived in a tree rather than the Elysée. Perhaps the most serious consequence of cabinet instability was that it blocked progressive reform. During the 1930s France was awash with ambitious schemes for renewal which were continuously frustrated by parliamentary procedures. This partially explains why, in its short lifetime, Vichy was impetuous enough to initiate so much legislation, despite the unpropitious circumstances of occupation.

Although in the 1930s politicians of all parties became exasperated with the political system that served France so badly, the majority remained committed to liberal democracy. As Richard Vinen reminds us, the parlia-mentary right was dominated by two groups: the Fédération Républicaine (FR) and the Alliance Démocratique (AD) (Vinen, 1996: 6). The first of these bodies, established in 1903, was fiercely nationalistic, was wedded to every dot and comma of the Versailles treaty, was protective of Church concerns, and was generally orthodox in financial matters, suspicious of all state spending. Dominated by 'political dynasties', continues Vinen, and drawing heavily on the support of the wealthy *bourgeoisie*, it won 1,233,360 votes in the 1932 elections and returned some 60 deputies to parliament. The Alliance Démocratique, created in 1901 and headed by Pierre-Etienne Flandin, later to play a cameo role at Vichy, also mobilised the *bourgeois* vote, yet was more restrained in its conservatism, retaining its anticlerical baggage of the early 1900s. The centre was dominated by the Radical Party which, as Serge Berstein explains, was established in 1901 to protect the Republic against the anti-Dreyfusards (Berstein, 1988: 55). While the Radicals professed to be defenders of the revolutionary tradition, they were only daring in their approach to constitutional, educational and religious matters: they remained fierce anticlericals, determined to maintain the strict religious neutrality of the French state. In social affairs, they were cautious, reflecting the interests of their key supporters: the peasantry, small shop-keepers, minor civil servants and the liberal professions. Unburdened by any real ideological baggage, the Radicals adapted well to the ebb-and-flow of Republican politics, and often commanded a number of portfolios in any cabinet. They performed handsomely in the 1932 elections, collecting over 2 million votes and winning 157 seats to become the dominant party in the Chamber. Far less pragmatic were the 'real' parties of the left: the Socialists, the Section Française de l'Internationale Ouvrière (SFIO), founded in 1905, and the Parti Communiste Français (PCF), which broke away from the SFIO in 1920 to become part of the Moscow-sponsored Third International (Comintern). During the 1920s, the Communists had the upper hand, but by 1932 could only muster ten seats in parliament and some 796,630 votes, whereas the Socialists won nearly 2 million votes and 97 seats. Both parties were Marxist and overwhelmingly working-class in origin, yet the SFIO was happier to play the parliamentary game and took up a number of so-called *bourgeois* issues such as anticlericalism. By contrast, the PCF, under the strict surveillance of Moscow, was committed to revolutionary politics and preferred to build up its support in the factories rather than in the Chamber. The right also possessed its extra-parliamentary representatives. The growth of the leagues will be discussed later in the context of French fascism, yet some mention should be made of the Action Française (AF) which, until the 1930s, remained the dominant voice of the extreme right. Anti-parliamentarian, intensely xenophobic, and pro-monarchist, the AF had little to do with elections. It was instead a 'publicistic' phenomenon, spreading its message through its newspaper and the writings of its leading ideologue Charles Maurras, writings that were widely read among priests, army officers, intellectuals and the respectable *bourgeoisie*.

The majority of French men and women, however, had little time for political extremes. It is sometimes said they lived in a 'stalemate society', a sleepy and predominantly rural world in which peasants, shopkeepers and members of the middle class remained loyal to the Republican ideal (Hoffmann, 1974). Such an interpretation has much to commend it, but should not disguise the subtle shifts that were taking place. Demographically, the French population was getting older, but was not getting bigger. Throughout the interwar years, the population remained just under 40 million strong, despite the efforts of successive governments, both right and left, to boost the birth rate. Historians have never fully comprehended the reasons for this stagnation, but usually point to 'a Malthusian mentality' among French families which often restricted themselves to one child, a decline in the number of young male adults following the devastation of the First World War, and the impact of the Depression which discouraged people from marrying (Berstein, 1988: 5–6). It was, however, a population on the move. In 1931, for the very first time, the numbers living in towns surpassed those in the countryside. By 1936, two-thirds of France was urban-based, giving rise to considerable concern among conservatives about the disappearance of rural values, a theme that would be enthusiastically taken up by Vichy. In truth, most towns were small in size, retaining strong links with the countryside. As Eugen Weber writes, 'one family in three lived on a farm or in a village and consumed the produce of its fields' (Weber, 1994: 37). Although France was not without its large-scale agrarian enterprises, especially in the Nord, the Paris basin and the Centre, most rural families owned a small-holding, often without running water and electricity, and remained rooted to traditional farming methods; in 1939, continues Weber, France only possessed some 35,000 tractors. Small wonder, then, that French peasants have been characterised as parochial and backward-looking, their lives ruled by the seasons as much as by Paris.

As befitting a country as geographically diverse as France, regional variations within the rural world were pronounced. Urban France was even more diverse. As Berstein writes, this included some 14 million *bourgeois*, an ever-expanding and extremely eclectic group, comprising the *grande bourgeoisie*, bankers, large-scale industrialists, property-owners, and the so-called *patronat*; a *moyenne bourgeoisie* of businessmen, professionals and civil servants; and a *petite bourgeoisie* of shopkeepers, artisans and white-collar workers (Berstein, 1988: 10–20). Additionally, the towns housed some 13 million workers. Although in the interwar years, France saw the rise of large-scale industries, such as chemical plants and car factories (Renault, Peugeot and Citröen), these were concentrated in specific areas – the Nord-Pas-de-Calais, Paris, the Rhône and Meurthe-et-Moselle – and only employed 21.8 per cent of the work force. The vast majority, some 58.4 per cent, were engaged in small-scale enterprises, counting fewer than 100 employees. At least, the majority were employed. Unemployment was rare in the 1920s. Yet there was no denying the fact that working conditions were grim. While 'real wages' rose some 17 per cent during the 1920s, most workers were housed in ugly suburbs on the outskirts of towns and cities, such as Clichy in Paris. There, distant from the costly leisure activities that were spawning in the city centres, they toiled long hours, possessed few trade union rights, and were seemingly forgotten by successive governments which were reluctant to pass social reform. Already, it is apparent why the Popular Front would be welcomed with such enthusiasm. Already, it is possible to see a political system increasingly out-of-touch with the people it was supposed to serve. Already, it is possible to see why Vichy was so scared of the potential power of the working class and the left.

DECADENCE AND DEPRESSION

The 1920s had been a successful decade for France. Buoyed by the victory of 1918, Paris had become the hub of international affairs, even though the diplomacy of the Quai d'Orsay did not always get its own way. Economic reconstruction had been relatively painless, and the Republican system had emerged out of the 1914–18 conflict more or less intact, capable of containing the left-wing threat which raised its head in the shape of the PCF. The 1930s were different: an agonising, uncertain, and crisis-ridden decade. Many commentators began to talk of a 'decadence' that had gripped French institutions and society. On the international stage, France seemed powerless when confronted by the rise of international fascism and the ever-present threat of Bolshevism. Politically, the republican system was more unstable than ever, incapable of sustaining progressive reform and buffeted by political extremism. Economically, France appeared caught in a Depression out of which there appeared to be no escape. Demographically, the French population failed to grow, its ranks swelled only by unwelcome foreigners: Jews, Spanish Republicans and refugees. In religious matters, the Catholic Church agonised over declining religious attendances, and arrived at the frightening conclusion that France had become a *pays de mission*, a missionary country ready for rechristianisation. And, despite the vibrancy of French cultural life, especially the cinema, among conservatives at least, there was a fear that France was being swamped by all things American – jazz, the cinema, advertising, candy bars and cigarettes. In his apocryphal *Scènes de la vie future*, based on his visits to the USA, the influential novelist Georges Duhamel painted a bleak vison of a depersonalised, egotistical and materialistic future that awaited France should it follow the American model (Duhamel, 1930).

In many ways, it was the onset of the global Depression that set the tone for the 1930s. This economic crisis was unusual in several aspects.

First, it had a delayed impact. Whereas Germany and the USA were immediately hit by the Wall Street Crash of 1929, France was not affected until 1931. Part of this delay was due to the enormous gold reserves which France had stored up since the stabilisation of the *franc* in 1926. It is also said that French industries, in comparison to their German, British and American counterparts, were small and largely self-financing; they were thus insulated from some of the fluctuations in the international markets. Second, the Depression in France endured much longer than it did else-where. While much of the industrialised world had by 1935 escaped the worst effects of the economic downturn, France was still in the midst of the crisis. It is a telling statistic that industrial production would not reach its 1929 level until after 1945. Historians are generally agreed that the crisis endured because of the unwillingness of successive governments to devalue the *franc* in the manner of sterling (1931) and the dollar (1933). Saddled with an overvalued currency, French industries could not compete abroad, yet in the minds of many, devaluation equalled the breakdown of social structures. Third, the Depression was odd in that its impact was gradual rather than dramatic. Although unemployment reached 1 million in 1935, this was never as high as in the USA and Britain. Those in work benefited from a fall in prices, although the working class was resentful that employ-ers sought to reduce wages. Large businesses also proved able to ride out the slump. Worst hit were immigrants and women, who were forced out of jobs, and the so-called *classes moyennes*: small shopkeepers, artisans and peasants. In the countryside, the price of wheat dropped by 40 per cent and that of wine by 60 per cent (Jackson, 1999: 226). It is sometimes suggested that the nature of the crisis helped modernise the French economy by encouraging the growth of new technology and the consolidation of indus-tries into larger, more viable enterprises; in reality, there is little evidence of such a process. If anything, the numbers of self-employed actually rose as they set up fledging businesses to survive the downturn.

Nor was government prepared, or able, to overhaul the nature of the economy. Two answers to the Depression were put forward. The first, championed by the forward-thinking conservative Tardieu, was consti-tutional reform which would strengthen the powers of the executive, but this was too radical for the Radicals who emerged triumphant in the 1932 elections. Their response, the second answer, was to slash government spending and attempt to erase the budget deficit. Such a decision created friction with their Socialist allies within the Chamber. The upshot was political breakdown: no cabinet was able to last for much longer than two months, and no significant reform was passed, beyond a handful of finance bills that did little to cure the economy's ills.

With government at a standstill, power slipped away to extra-parliamentary pressure groups. As Jackson relates, while shopkeepers mobilised in the Fédération Nationale des Contribuables, peasants rallied round the Front Paysan of Henry Dorgères (Jackson, 1999: 226). Most worrying was the re-emergence of the right-wing leagues which had been born in the 1920s, but which had lost support in 1926 when Poincaré took charge of government and re-established confidence in the economy. They included the venerable Action Française, but this was increasingly seen as old-fashioned; 'inaction française' was how Lucien Rebatet dubbed it in 1941 (Rebatet, 1942). Far more active were those veterans leagues which had been set up in the 1920s: the Jeunesses Patriotes of Pierre Taittinger and the Faisceau of Georges Valois. The early 1930s saw the rise of yet more leagues: the Solidarité Française of François Coty and the Parti Franciste of Marcel Bucard. It was, however, the Croix de Feu (CF) of Maurice d'Hartoy, which initially recruited among holders of the Croix de Feu medal, that dominated. In 1931, the CF fell under the control of Colonel de La Rocque, an inspirational figure who, in 1935, increased its membership to some 300,000 and who led the organisation down a political path, setting up a youth section.

The power of these organisations was demonstrated in 1934. At the start of the year, a small-time criminal of east European origin, Serge Stavisky, committed suicide after his scheme to issue bonds for a non-existent pawnshop in Bayonne was exposed. It was a petty scandal but, in the midst of the Depression, was blown out of all proportion by the leagues who alleged that Stavisky's supposed friends in the Radical Party had shielded him from prosecution and that the suicide was really murder. Amid these charges, the Chautemps government fell and Daladier took charge. A forceful figure, the new premier created a cabinet of both right and left, and dismissed Jean Chiappe, the Paris police chief, who had been implicated in the scandal and who had treated right-wing demonstrations with kid gloves. This was the moment the leagues had been waiting for. On 6 February 1934, they assembled in the Place de la Concorde apparently intent on invading the Chamber of Deputies which stood across the river. As the demonstrators marched to the bridge, fighting with police broke out, leading to 15 deaths and leaving some 1,435 wounded, acknowledged to be the most serious political fighting Paris had witnessed since the crushing of the Commune in 1871. The next day Daladier resigned and the conservative Gaston Doumergue, a former president, set up a 'cabinet of national union', including the future Vichy leader Marshal Pétain, as minister of war, and the Radical politician Edouard Herriot.

Like bad pennies, several prominent *liguers* were to turn up at Vichy, lending credence to the left-wing notion that the February demonstrations were an attempted *coup d'état*, a dress rehearsal for the right's move into power in July 1940. This was not the case. It is now known that the rioters were hopelessly disorganised and had no plan of action. Many of the CF supporters, predominantly lower middle-class suburbanites, were more troubled about how they would get home than they were about the fate of democracy. It has further been established that La Rocque was undecided in his attitude towards taking power [*Doc. 1*]. Although he constantly denounced the corruption of parliamentary politics and urged his para-military supporters to be prepared for the moment when they would storm into office, as a soldier he retained a respect for constitutional procedures and was wary of anything that smacked of illegality. In this sense he was similar to Pétain who, throughout the 1930s, was urged to take on dicta-torial powers, possibly by a *coup*. Again, as a soldier, the marshal was wary of anything outside the law, and instead preferred to bide his time waiting for the call to office. La Rocque might have been doing the same. There is speculation that he hoped the February riots would force the Doumergue government to offer him a ministerial portfolio. The call never came. In this sense, the February demonstrations have been interpreted as a protest against the traditional forces of the right as much as they were a rebellion against liberalism.

Historians have since considered whether the paramilitary leagues equated to a form of French fascism. For a long while the debate was dom-inated by René Rémond, who argued that since 1815 the French right had manifested itself in three different guises – Orleanism, Legitimism and Bonapartism (Rémond, 1969). In his view, the leagues equalled a revived form of Bonapartism, or at the very most a pale imitation of Italian fascism. In any case, he suggested, France lacked the essential prerequisites for the rise of a genuine fascism: unlike Germany, it had been victorious in 1918 and possessed, in the shape of Radicals, a centrist party which appealed to the peasants and lower middle class, the *milieu* among which Hitler and Mussolini recruited. A tradition of democracy further existed in France. If a true fascism did emerge, then it was represented by Jacques Doriot, a former Communist, whose ideological indiscipline and general disenchant-ment with the left led him in 1936 to found the Parti Populaire Français (PPF), although even here historians cannot agree whether this organisation was truly fascist before 1940 (Wolf, 1969; Brunet, 1986). Amid much controversy, the Israeli historian Zeev Sternhell suggested that France did indeed possess fascists and that these emanated from the left, drawing on the nationalist syndicalism of such writers as Georges Sorel (Sternhell, 1986). More persuasive are the suggestions of Robert Soucy, who high-lighted the fact that many of fascism's claims to be truly revolutionary, certainly in the Italian case, were extremely dubious: fascism was instead an awkward mesh of traditionalism and radicalism. In that sense, Soucy labelled the CF as fascist (Soucy, 1986). So, too, has Kevin Passmore, albeit for different reasons. In his detailed local study of the CF in Provence, he has suggested that the movement's programme was indeed genuinely radical, even if La Rocque was not necessarily aware of this radicalism (Passmore, 1997).

Whatever the merits of these respective claims and counter-claims, there is a budding consensus, at least among anglophone writers, that France was not immune from fascism. Among French historians, there is still a tendency to discount fascism outside the PPF. Nonetheless, at the time, the French left certainly believed that right-wing extremism was on the march. On 9 February 1934, the Communists took to the streets in a demonstration which again resulted in bloodshed, some six dead and 100 injured. Three days later, workers mobilised in a general strike to uphold the Republic. What these protests demonstrated was the fragmented nature of the French left. Something more was going to be needed if the tide of fascism was to be resisted both at home and abroad.

THE POPULAR FRONT

Paradoxically, the moves for left-wing unity stemmed from the most sectarian of parties: the PCF. Since its foundation in 1920, it had serious reservations about partaking in *bourgeois* politics and, in 1928, steadfastly refused to cooperate with the Socialists. In 1934, the February riots and the rise to power of Hitler forced party leaders to reconsider their isolationism. Importantly, the same view was being reached in Moscow. Recognising Nazi Germany as the Soviet Union's principal threat, Stalin told the PCF to drop the campaign against liberal democracy and rally behind the Republic. So it was that, on 27 July 1934, a pact of unity was signed with the Socialists. The next step was to win over the Radicals who were troubled that they might lose seats to the newly unified left. On 14 July 1935, they too joined the emerging *rassemblement*, as did the rival trade union confederations the Socialist Confédération Générale du Travail (CGT) and the communist Confédération Générale du Travail Unitaire (CGTU) which amalgamated in March 1936. Earlier that year, on 12 January, the Popular Front agreed its programme which provided for the dissolution of the fascist leagues, press freedoms, the nationalisation of war industries, a public works programme, partial state control of the Bank of France and the attainment of world peace through collective security. It was a truly progressive and imaginative platform that had a mass appeal, especially among the working classes who felt ignored by successive governments. It was also a programme to address the problems of the Depression which the savage deflationary policies of the 1935 Laval government had failed to cure. As Douglas Johnson writes, the fact that the Popular Front was more than a temporary electoral alliance, under a dynamic 'new' leader in the shape of the Socialist Léon Blum, gave it further appeal (Johnson, 1970). In this respect, the rallying of the Radicals and Communists was especially significant, and even won votes from the respectable *bourgeoisie*. And, finally, the anti-fascist and republican dimension of the Popular Front struck a resonance among the electorate, many of whom had been alienated by the behaviour of the CF. At the elections of June 1936, the Popular Front parties won an overwhelming majority. While the Radicals' share of the seats dropped from 159 to 116, the number of PCF representatives grew from ten to 72, and the proportion of Socialist deputies rose from 97 to 146. For the first time in its history, the Third Republic possessed a genuinely left-wing government.

It was a government soon in difficulties. A savage right-wing backlash ensued: extremist papers openly mocked Blum for being a Jew and spread unfounded rumours that Roger Salengro, the interior minister, had deserted in the First World War, a slur that led to his suicide. By fulfilling his pledge to disband the leagues, Blum made matters worse. Rather than strengthening democracy, his action brought about a strengthening of the extreme right. The CF responded by transforming itself into a political party, the Parti Social Français (PSF), jettisoning some of its violent imagery and paramilitary organisation. Whether the PSF, in its new guise, was truly fascist is again disputed, but there is no question that its enhanced respectability won support: it had ten seats by 1939. It would have won many more if elections had been held, as planned, in 1940. This is why historians have interpreted Vichy, in part, as a backlash against the Popular Front (Kedward, 1982). Indeed, to many conservatives, the Popular Front was nothing less than a revolutionary government. Business representatives baulked at making concessions to workers in the so-called Matignon Agreements (see below); Catholic leaders were intensely suspicious of the *main tendue* offered them by Blum and were alarmed by the secularism of his government; and the respectable middle classes were dismayed at the emphasis on leisure, in particular the introduction of paid holidays which, for the first time, enabled working-class families to take vacations in fashionable resort towns. Some four years later, the memories of these holidays led many northern workers to head for these destinations as they attempted to escape the German advance.

Greater difficulties were posed by the divisions within the Popular Front. The Communists were never the most faithful of partners. Still hesitant about the legitimacy of partaking in *bourgeois* politics, they chose not to accept seats in the cabinet and sat instead on the sidelines where they readily criticised policy, especially over Spain. Across the Pyrenees, there was likewise a Popular Front government attempting to ward off fascism. Blum's instinct was to intervene on behalf of the Spanish Republicans, just as Mussolini and Hitler were intervening on the side of the Nationalists. Yet several voices deterred Blum from doing so: the French High Command, which had no wish to be involved in such a side-show; the British, who were determined to remain neutral; and Blum's own political instincts, which told him that French involvement might well exacerbate domestic political tension. In the event, his non-involvement won him few friends either on the right or on the left.

These problems, however, were overshadowed by economic difficulties. In contemplation of the left's victory at the polls, improvised strikes broke out among the working class, who were heartened at the prospect of a government which, at long last, seemed concerned about their interests. By the time Blum was sworn in as premier, some 1,800,000 men and women were on strike, and 8,441 factories had been occupied. To resolve this economic chaos, and restore business confidence, Blum chaired a series of meetings between the representatives of capital and labour, which led to the Matignon Agreements: the introduction of a 40 hour week; the right to collective bargaining; the increase of trade union rights; and the provision of paid holidays [*Doc. 2*]. This emphasis on paid holidays, youth hosteling, sports and leisure was to be one of the most enduring legacies of the Popular Front; even Vichy attempted to build on the provision of sporting arenas and school playgrounds. Historians, however, have queried the cost of the welfare programme, arguing that such things as paid holidays should have been delayed. As Macmillan writes, this point overlooks the fact that this was a cabinet intensely committed to helping the working class and that, overall, more money was spent on rearmament than on welfare (Macmillan, 1992: 116). Criticism has also been aimed at the 40–hour week which has been held responsible for stifling production at a time when demand needed to be expanded. This is another contentious argument. It forgets that many factories were exempt from this measure which was often flouted. What seems less contentious is that the Matignon Agreements led to a shortage of skilled labour in key industries, such as aviation, and did nothing to cure the phenomenon of impromptu strikes, even though most workers were back on the factory floor by July 1936 (Vinen, 1996: 21).

By June the next year, the failure to build economic confidence had resulted in a financial crisis which led Blum to take the unpopular measure of deflation. This forced his resignation and effectively the collapse of the Popular Front. While Blum briefly returned as premier in 1937, confidence in government did not return until April 1938 when Daladier took control. He inherited a country seemingly in the grip of crisis and ill at ease with itself. Having come to power to strengthen liberal democracy, the Popular Front had failed in its task. Rather, it had succeeded in hardening the bitter divisions between right and left, bringing about a radicalisation of politics. Many of the battlelines between right and left which would emerge during the Occupation, had already been drawn.

DALADIER AND THE COMING OF WAR

For some historians, the measures of the Daladier government foreshadow those of Vichy, and undeniably there are superficial similarities. Tired of political infighting and economic chaos, the new prime minister believed that a firm hand was necessary, and moved the Radicals in an authoritarian direction. Yet as Elizabeth du Réau argues, in so doing he did not relinquish a faith in parliament or in the Republic (Du Réau, 1993). He sought instead to re-energise liberal democracy; paradoxically, as Jackson argues, in its last months of existence the Republic was fitter than it had been for many years (Jackson, 1999). For this achievement, Vichy rewarded Daladier by putting him on trial at Riom, charged with entering a war for which, it was alleged, France was inadequately prepared.

To bring about French recovery, Daladier ensured that he was invested with decree powers, enabling him to rule almost at will. In social policy, he inaugurated the *Code de la famille* which attempted to boost the birth rate by providing mortgage interest rate relief for those with larger families. In religious matters, the government moved closer to the Church and enjoyed cordial relations with Cardinal Verdier, archbishop of Paris, who was hopeful that some of the worst excesses of institutionalised secularism could be curbed. In economic affairs, Daladier appointed the right-winger Paul Reynaud as his finance minister, who rescinded a good deal of the Popular Front progressive legislation, most famously the 40-hour week. When the CGT replied by ordering a general strike, this was brutally crushed by the government which had little respect for civil liberties. In 1939 internment camps were set up for Spanish and East European refugees, camps that would be used for a sinister purpose under Vichy (Caron, 1999). After the Nazi–Soviet pact of August that year, Daladier proscribed the PCF and debarred its members from parliament, in many respects a mistaken policy as the Communists had a well-established reputation of standing up to fascism.

It was in foreign policy that Daladier showed his resolve most clearly. Since the First World War, France had viewed security against Germany as its top priority, yet was uncertain how best to accomplish this end. The left trusted in the League of Nations and collective security. The right, which was in power, took a much tougher, cynical stance. In the years immediately after 1918, it insisted on the strict enforcement of the Versailles settlement, the payment of reparations in full and the maintenance of military alliances with the newly created Eastern European states. When, in 1923, Germany defaulted on reparations, French and Belgian troops went into the Ruhr to extract payment at gunpoint, but only succeeded in sparking off condemnation abroad and left-wing criticism at home. This forced a reconsideration of foreign policy which, under the capable direction of the experienced diplomat Aristide Briand, became more conciliatory towards Germany: both countries signed the Locarno Treaty of 1925 which agreed to respect the borders of 1919 and both subscribed to the Kellogg–Briand Pact of 1928 which denounced war as an instrument of policy. Underpinning this new vision of international harmony was a strong defensive policy that united left and right, and led to the building of the Maginot Line, a huge network of fortresses on France's eastern frontier.

As Jackson argues, the *Briandiste* consensus was not to last for long, thanks largely to the provocation of Hitler, who was eager to reverse the Versailles settlement (Jackson, 1999). In March 1936, he ordered the remilitarisation of the Rhineland, a clear breach of the 1919 settlement, yet France did not act. The High Command argued that it was unready to fight; public opinion was against war; Britain believed that Germany was simply reoccupying its 'backyard'; and government was in the hands of Sarraut, a Radical minister, who saw his task as merely holding the fort until the June general elections. Yet, as Adamthwaite has emphasised, the failure to act over the Rhineland revealed to the world that France no longer had the will to stand up for the 1919 settlement (Adamthwaite, 1977). Lacking confidence, Paris drifted into a policy of appeasement towards Germany. There seemed no alternative: France was stuck in a Depression that seemed incurable; rearmament was in its infancy; Gamelin was undertaking an overhaul of military strategy; public opinion was still wary of war after the horrors of 1914–18; political divisions at home were fierce after the Popular Front; and Britain, France's only genuine ally in the West, continued to accommodate the Nazis. Appeasement reached its height at the Munich conference in September 1938. Heartened by the recent *Anschluss* between Germany and Austria earlier that year, Nazi sympathisers and agents in the Czech Sudetenland pressed for this area to become part of the Reich. Earlier meetings between Chamberlain and Hitler proved inconclusive, and war seemed inevitable for France given its 1924 alliance with Czechoslovakia. To resolve the crisis, Daladier and Chamberlain met Hitler at Munich where it was conceded that the Czech Sudetenland should indeed become German, with plebiscites to be held in ethnically mixed areas. The settlement emboldened Hitler who, ultimately, provoked war over Poland in August the next year. Within France, Munich was greeted with jubilation and Daladier was feted as a hero [*Doc. 3*]. In truth, opinion was split into two, a division that cut across traditional loyalties. The *Munichois* (supporters of the deal) included pacifists within the SFIO, much of the centre right who were anxious to free France of its ties with Eastern Europe and rely instead on the empire, and extreme rightists such as Déat who would later become collaborationists. Those opposed included right-wing nationalists, and Socialists, who were determined that no further concessions should be made to Hitler.

Daladier was one of these hardliners. In summer 1939, he dismissed British recommendations that a more conciliatory line should be taken towards Mussolini, who was looking to encroach upon France's North African empire should there be a general European war. Meanwhile, Daladier concentrated his efforts on building consensus at home – hence his conciliatory gestures to the Church – and readying France for war, particularly through rearmament. Whereas in 1938 France was only devoting 8.6 per cent of its national income on its armed forces in comparison to Germany's 17 per cent, the next year this figure had risen to 23 per cent, the equivalent of Berlin's expenditure (Jackson, 1999: 235). Most impressive were the development of new tanks, often better equipped and faster than their German counterparts, and the creation of a new aircraft industry. Taking advantage of the Popular Front's nationalisation programme, Daladier's technocrats, such as Caquot and Dautry, ensured that France was building 330 planes a month by January 1940 rather than 137 per month which had been the case nine months previously. None of this was enough to save Daladier from the vagaries of parliamentary politics, and he was ousted from office on 20 March 1940 by an 'unholy alliance' of pacifists and bellicists, both of whom were unhappy at the way in which he was conducting a war that, for the moment, seemed rooted in Eastern Europe (Jackson, 1999: 232). Yet Daladier had done enough to give the French people some confidence in themselves and their Republic. This would make the sudden defeat of May–June 1940 that much harder to understand.

CHAPTER THREE

THE DEFEAT

When, on 10 May 1940, Guderian's tanks invaded Belgium, Holland and Luxemburg, they built up a seemingly unstoppable momentum, giving rise to rumours that the Germans were somehow 'supermen' (Sartre, 1950). On 13 May the Nazis reached Sedan, that cornerstone of French defences; the following day the Netherlands surrendered; exactly a fortnight later, Belgium followed suit. By 26 May, the order had already been given to evacuate the British Expeditionary Force (BEF) at Dunkirk, where the French army under General Weygand, Gamelin's recent replacement as commander-in-chief (19 May), formed an arc to protect the retreating troops. By 5 June, the day Dunkirk fell, some 338,226 men had been lifted from the beaches, two-thirds of them British. Despite fierce French resistance, on 9–10 June Reynaud and his government left Paris, which the Germans reached four days later. Holding a series of makeshift meetings along the Loire valley, on 11–13 June, the cabinet discussed the possibility of whether to fight on or to sue for an armistice, an option enthusiastically supported by Weygand and Pétain, who had been appointed deputy prime minister on 19 May in an attempt to bolster morale! On 16 June, at Bordeaux, Reynaud resigned and handed over power to his deputy. The next day, the 'Victor of Verdun' announced to the French people that he had set in motion negotiations for an armistice which was signed on 22 June [*Doc. 7*]. With France divided into two main zones, government and deputies made their way to the little spa town of Vichy where, on 11 July, Pétain was invested with full powers.

THE STRANGE DEFEAT

The débâcle was so unexpected, so overwhelming and so traumatic that the French writer Marc Bloch described it as a 'strange defeat' (Bloch, 1946). Like many other commentators, this eminent historian believed that the calamity was due to a moral malaise that had sapped the inner strength of France. Little agreement existed, however, as to where this decadence originated from. The military men, prominent in Pétain's early cabinets, blamed the nation's youth which, it was suggested, had lost the taste for hard work, discipline and abnegation. In a speech of 20 July, the marshal announced that since 1918 the 'spirit of pleasure' had prevailed over the 'spirit of sacrifice'. Catholic leaders echoed these sentiments, placing the blame on the secular culture of French society that had led to dwindling church attendances, depopulation and an excessive taste for material pleasures such as the cinema, dancing and alcohol [*Doc. 9*]. They even saw some good in a defeat which offered the possibility of rechristianising France. 'Victorious', declared Cardinal Gerlier of Lyon, 'we would probably have remained imprisoned in our errors. By dint of secularisation, France was at risk of dying' (De Montclos, 1982: 81). Right-wing ideologues joined this chorus of disapproval. For them, defeat was the product of a parliamentary system which had put party and self before country. Particular blame was attached to the Popular Front government of 1936, and it was with some glee that in 1941–42 Vichy put Blum, Daladier and Gamelin on trial at Riom, charged with having failed to prepare their country adequately for war. For its part, the left argued that the nation had been let down by the middle classes who had preferred Hitler to Blum. De Gaulle, who on 18 June issued his famous appeal to resistance, was almost alone in attributing the collapse to Germany's military prowess.

Inevitably, moral explanations of 1940 have found their way into the history books, but few writers today would accept these interpretations without qualification. After all, how does one produce empirical evidence to measure levels of decadence? In this respect, it is worth remembering that, in the aftermath of the Franco-Prussian war, politicians and commentators as varied as Gambetta and Renan attributed defeat to the modernity of German civilisation. If France had fallen in 1914, it is highly likely that moral answers would have again been trotted out to explain national humiliation. No doubt the military men would have bemoaned the politicisation of the army undertaken by the Radical Party in the early 1900s; no doubt Catholics would have condemned the secular laws that had recently separated Church and state (1905) and banned religious orders from teaching (1904); no doubt partisans of Action Française would have pointed to a Jewish-masonic conspiracy which had allegedly raised its head during the Dreyfus Affair; and, no doubt, the left and trade unions would have chastised the middle classes for their refusal to countenance social reform.

While most historians no longer attribute defeat in 1940 to decadence, they do acknowledge that the public was not as determined to defend the Republic as it might have been. Here, they have pointed to the strength of pacifism, a sentiment which was especially strong among the peasantry, who had felt the brunt of conscription in 1914–18, and, not unexpectedly, among women whose children and husbands had endured the killing fields of northern France and Belgium (Ingram, 1991). Pacifism was also a formidable force among such diverse bodies as the teachers' union Syndicat National des Instituteurs (SNI) and the employers' federation the Comité des Forges. Politicians – a sizeable section of the Socialist Party, Flandin and Laval on the right, and Déat on the extremes – were also noticeable in their dislike of war; some 87 per cent of parliamentarians approved of the Munich Agreements. Nor did the political squabbles that had dominated the 1930s help prepare France for war. While the Daladier government of 1938–39 gave the country a much needed sense of direction, the proscribing of the PCF, which reluctantly came out against war in the aftermath of the Nazi–Soviet Pact of 23 August 1939, was not good for the bolstering of national spirit. Several commentators have remarked that Daladier spent more time persecuting Communists than he did in elaborating anti-German propaganda. The latter task was entrusted to Jean Giraudoux, the writer and playwright, who headed the recently created Department of Information. Given little direction about his new post, Giraudoux subjected his listeners to intellectual discussions about Franco-German culture, for instance the vagaries of the Alsatian dialect, hardly the stuff Goebbels was devising for Paul Ferdonnet, France's Lord Haw-Haw, who was broadcasting on Radio-Stuttgart. Yet perhaps the most debilitating factor for public opinion was the 'phoney war' which lasted from September 1939 to May 1940. During this period, the war in Poland seemed distant, troops grew bored, and the public hoped that fighting might never reach French soil [*Doc. 5*].

None of the above evidence can satisfactorily explain why France was defeated. It merely illustrates why the military disaster came as such a shock to the nation's system. In his groundbreaking study of public opinion, Jean-Louis Crémieux-Brilhac has displayed that – despite political divisions, despite a natural distaste for war, despite inept propaganda, despite the ups and downs of the 'phoney war' – France came to accept that it had to fight (Crémieux-Brilhac, 1990–91). The mood was remarkably similar to 1914 when, as Jackson reminds us, the Third Republic was even less prepared for conflict (Jackson, 1999: 240–1). The difference was, writes Jackson, that Joffre's victory at the Marne in September 1914 gave the nation time to adjust and rally behind the war effort. In 1940 the speed of Guderian's advance gave no time for such a *ralliement*.

MATERIAL FOR VICTORY

The failure of Gamelin or Weygand to emulate Joffre's success at the Marne has led historians to conclude that the defeat of 1940 was essentially a military phenomenon leading to speculation that Germany emerged triumphant because of its superior armaments. This argument will not wash. In terms of men, both sides were evenly balanced: 136 German divisions faced 94 French, 22 Belgian, 12 British and nine Dutch (Stolfi, 1970). In the matter of tanks, France had the edge: 4,188 machines as opposed to Germany's 3,862. Moreover, French tanks were often faster and better armed. Armaments production, under the watchful eye of Dautry, was also proceeding apace, French factories often outstripping their German counterparts. Aeroplanes were a different matter. Despite the valiant efforts of Pierre Cot, France had fewer planes (1,800 against 3,200) which were decidedly inferior to those of the *Luftwaffe*. On the waters, the French navy was formidable, the most advanced arm of the three services. In the event, it endured an unhappy war. To prevent the fleet falling into German hands, on 3 July 1940 the British sank several vessels at Mers-el-Kébir. Following the occupation of the southern zone in November 1942, the French them-selves completed the job, scuttling the fleet at Toulon.

Given the rough parity that existed between French and German forces, it has been further speculated that the real problem was the manner in which Gamelin deployed his forces. This, of course, was de Gaulle's argument. Throughout the 1930s, he had been advocating the creation of a professional army equipped with mobile armour which would be deployed in densely concentrated divisions [*Doc. 4*]. In his broadcast of 18 June, he announced, 'Much more than by their number, it was by their tanks, their planes and their tactics that the Germans beat us.' Such interpretations have recently been called into question. Through his study of national defence in the 1930s, Martin Alexander has shown that de Gaulle was not the only innovator in the French army, and might well have stymied reform by his advocacy of a professional army which unnerved republican politicians who feared it could be used to suppress individual liberties (Alexander, 1993). Aware of such sensibilities, Alexander has displayed that Gamelin himself was an astute moderniser, creating the first mobilised divisions, the so-called DCRs, and ensuring that his men were professionally trained. To believe they were underprepared is to mistake the reservist divisions placed in the Ardennes for the whole of the French army. Nor should their courage be questioned: over 100,000 men were lost in the battle of France, almost the same number 'lost in the first six weeks of war in 1914' (Jackson, 1999: 241).

As Jackson warns us, there is a risk of taking revisionism 'too far' (Jackson, 1999: 239). He cites the telling fact that the first DCR was not created until January 1940; by May, such divisions only counted for 'one-sixth of all French tanks'. Tanks were still regarded as little more than an appendage to the infantry. Nor had Gamelin succeeded in modernising the communications of his army, something vital for the conduct of modern war. Radios were sparse; carrier pigeons were plentiful; even Gamelin's head-quarters relied solely on the telephone. The commander-in-chief might have compounded the situation by undertaking, in early 1940, major structural reforms to the organisation of his High Command, although to be fair the German General Staff was equally, if not more, cumbersome. Whatever the case, it did make it difficult for French armies in the field to communicate with one another and to call up air support when it was needed. It is frequently said that French planes were in the wrong locations at the wrong times, especially the moment when Guderian advanced into the Ardennes.

The failure to make the best of its equipment was unquestionably a factor in the French army's defeat of 1940 although it is not the complete answer. Once again, as Jackson states, 1914 stands as a parallel. Then, too, the French High Command had not fully woken up to the nature of modern warfare, in particular the destructiveness of the machine gun and the use of heavy cannon. The failure of Moltke's initial advance allowed those lessons to be learnt. If France had held in 1940, it is almost certain that Gamelin would have pressed ahead with further modernisation. That the opportunity was denied him points to the principal reason behind the débâcle: defective strategy.

STRATEGY

Drawing on the lessons of the First World War, French strategic thinkers considered that their best option was to engage Germany in a prolonged war on two fronts. Thanks to the Bolshevik Revolution of 1917, an alliance with Russia such as that which existed in 1914 was out of the question; instead, France cemented bilateral agreements with the Little Entente powers of Yugoslavia, Romania and Czechoslovakia (1920–24), as well as signing an alliance with Poland (1921). Meantime, on the western front, French troops would constitute a continuous front. In the north, Griffiths adds, troops would march into Belgium to adopt 'easily defensible positions' among the many rivers and dykes, a policy unchanged in 1936 despite the Belgian government's declaration of neutrality that year (Griffiths, 1970: 221). The Ardennes would more or less take care of itself. Although troops were stationed here, it was thought this rugged and unforgiving terrain would be obstacle enough for any invading army. The border between Luxemburg and Germany was defended by the so-called Maginot Line (1930), a series of underground fortresses similar to those at Verdun, between which troops and tanks could be deployed. Germany would thus be squeezed in a war of attrition in which it would be brought to its knees.

The above strategy has often been criticised for its short-sightedness and defensive nature, yet as Vinen argues, it should be remembered that ultimately Germany was defeated in 1945 precisely because it could not match the economic resources of the Allies (Vinen, 1996: 32). If anything, the strategy concocted by the French was extremely logical. Because of the need to protect its extensive empire and because of its small population in comparison to Germany (40 million as opposed to 67 million), France could not risk an out-and-out offensive strategy which had proved so disastrous in 1914. Defence was the obvious option, and the Maginot Line was, in many respects, eminently sensible. Much criticism has been made for not extending the fortifications along the Belgian frontier, yet this would hardly have made for good Franco-Belgian relations and was, in any case, financially impossible at a time of Depression and technically infeasible given the watery terrain of the Belgian frontier. As Alexander has displayed, the Maginot Line also served economic, political and psychological purposes (Alexander, 1998). The High Command did not overlook the fact that much of the nation's industry and natural resources were concentrated in the eastern regions around Mulhouse; it was thus vital that this area did not fall into German hands as had happened in 1914. Nor was it lost on the High Command that much of the French working class was based there. With memories of the Paris Commune of 1871 uppermost in their minds, the French generals feared that any war on French terrain would equal revolution. As will be seen, this was one of the reasons why Pétain and Weygand were keen on an armistice in 1940. And, finally, it was important to demonstrate to an anxious public that France had taken steps to cut off the most obvious German invasion route.

However logical the above strategy, the inescapable fact is that France lost in 1940. What went wrong? Much blame must be attached to Gamelin. As Alistair Horne records, when the Germans began their invasion of the Low Countries, he dispatched General Henri Giraud's elite Seventh Army to join up with the Dutch in the North, the so-called 'Breda variant' (Horne, 1969) (Map 1). In this way, he believed that the Allies would be linked together and would recognise that their common security lay in holding firm. Two fatal errors had been committed. First, Gamelin had misjudged the principal German invasion route. Instead of coming through Holland and Belgium, the main attack was through the Ardennes. Although troops were defending this area, they were ageing reservists and no match for the tactics of *Blitzkrieg*. Too much trust had been placed in the natural obstacles of the Ardennes forest which had previously been deemed 'untankable'. Second, Gamelin had no real strategic reserve; this, in effect, had been Giraud's Seventh Army, now isolated in the north. To be fair, there were men protecting the Maginot Line, yet Gamelin was unwilling to commit these lest Hitler advanced via Switzerland. The mistakes in strategy, however, were not Gamelin's alone. As Jeffrey Gunsburg has argued, Britain and Belgium both agreed to the Breda plan, despite its shortcomings and despite the fact that the Allies did not possess any real strategic coordination (Gunsburg, 1979). In this sense, Gunsburg persuasively argues, the defeat was not just a French one; it was also an 'allied one'.

With the Ardennes breached, the Germans decided to make for the Channel, cutting off the French and BEF in the north-east. So began the Dunkirk evacuations of 28 May–4 June. Weygand, who it will be recalled replaced Gamelin on 19 May, was left to make a series of defences, along the Aisne and Somme rivers on 6 June, and then along the Seine on 12 June. There was even talk of forming a last-ditch defence in Western France, the infamous Breton redoubt, but by that stage Weygand no longer had any stomach for the fight. Military historians tend to agree that, in all probability, the battle had been lost before he took command.

FROM RETHONDES TO VICHY

The débâcle of 1940 may, ultimately, be ascribed to costly strategic blunders. It owed little to supposed decadence, low morale, the political crisis of the 1930s, or poor military preparations. What has yet to be explained are the reasons why a military catastrophe became a political one. Here, our attention should focus not so much on the alleged weaknesses of French liberal democracy, but on the role of the two military men: Weygand and Pétain.

Despite what is sometimes stated, these two men had not taken up their posts on 19 May with the deliberate intention of overturning parliament. As Richard Griffiths has shown, they rarely met and possessed a strong mutual mistrust which dated back to their squabblings in the First World War (Griffiths, 1970). However, when they did come together in June, their appreciation of the military crisis was remarkably similar. Both considered that France had prepared badly for war. Here the fault lay with the Third Republic which, in Pétain's famous words of 19 June, had provided, 'Too few allies, too few children, too few arms'. Neither man had much faith in Britain as France's key ally, another legacy of the mistrust of the First World War, and both believed it would not be long before London fell. When on 11 and 13 June Churchill visited France and attempted to firm up cabinet morale by talking of guerilla warfare, Pétain dismissed the idea, reminding the visitor that it would not be Britain which suffered in such a scenario. To be fair, the marshal was genuinely concerned about unnecessary loss of life, one of the few redeeming features of his personality, although such compassion did not extend to all sections of French society. This compassion might also have been affected by a pessimism in which Weygand shared. Despite their undisputed patriotism and dislike of the *Boche*, both men had a habit of fearing the worst and, in early June, believed the battle lost. There was no point in taking off for North Africa which was, in any case, an ignoble option. The honour of the army had to be salvaged. The honour of the Third Republic was another matter. Neither man had much respect for parliamentary democracy. Here, Weygand was particularly at fault.

While Pétain spent much of his time in cabinet sniping behind his colleagues' backs, criticising de Gaulle who had become under-secretary of war on 5 June, Weygand frequently spoke on political affairs, condemning French decadence and arguing in favour of an armistice. As commander-in-chief, Griffiths observes, he had no right to broach such matters. Yet both men were intensely political. Contemptuous of parliamentarians, they looked to an armistice as France's salvation. Only such an expedient would save the country from a possible Communist uprising; only such a solution would offer the chance of national *redressement*. As early as 3 June, Weygand had been hawking round a plan for French renewal, a dismal document which prefigured many of the traditionalist traits of the National Revolution. Political they might have been, but both men were seriously naive about the nature of National Socialism. As Reynaud snarled at Pétain, 'you take Hitler for Wilhelm I, an old man who took Alsace Lorraine. Hitler is Genghis Khan' (Reynaud, 1947: 313–16).

Weygand and Pétain's support for ending the war carried much weight with the cabinet which, on 15 June, made the fatal step of accepting the infamous Chautemps proposal: seek out armistice terms and, then, decide whether to accept them. In this way, the principle of an armistice had been agreed. Unable to control his ministers, missing the support of de Gaulle, who was in Britain liaising with Churchill over the proposal for a Franco-British union until the close of the war (an option quickly dismissed by the French cabinet), too easily influenced by the pacifist sentiments of his mistress Madame des Portes, despondent at his failure to enlist US support, and incapable of persuading his colleagues to leave for North Africa, on 16 June Reynaud resigned and advised president Lebrun to call for the marshal who immediately sued for an armistice. In a deliberate snub to the French, this was signed on 22 June in the same railway carriage at Rethondes where Foch had accepted the German surrender in 1918.

Historians have since speculated what might have happened if the French government had left for North Africa (Gordon, 1998: xvii) Some suggest that this would have forced the Germans to have prosecuted their Mediterranean strategy far more forcefully, possibly enlisting the support of Franco, and bringing about the collapse of Britain which would have been cut off from its empire. Others argue that Germany would have been severely overstretched in its attempts to pacify France; resistance there would have quickly rallied round the government-in-exile in Algiers. Moreover, Britain would have been reinforced by both the French fleet and the colonies, a powerful combination that ultimately would have led to Berlin's defeat in the West. Whatever the case, it does not appear that the Pétain government thought either long or hard about any of these scenarios.

To judge from the wavering voice of General Huntziger, the principal French armistice negotiator who was being secretly recorded by the

Germans, it is clear that there was shock at the severity of the armistice terms. They could have been worse. Anxious to consolidate his position and plan the invasion of Britain, frightened of provoking civil unrest in France and unwilling to give the new French government reason to leave for North Africa (a handful of deputies had already left on the steamboat *Massilia* on 21 June), Hitler moderated his proposals. It was a short document drawn up in a hurry, a mere 23 articles, which guaranteed the integrity of the French empire, the reduction of the army to 100,000 men, and the maintenance of the fleet, although this was to be confined to port [*Doc. 8*]. The economic clauses were more severe, insisting upon reparations and the requisitioning of raw materials. Alone in Hitler's Europe, France was allowed a measure of semi-autonomy, and the return of the government to Paris was even foreseen. The most striking feature of the Armistice was the division of France into two principal zones (Map 2). The Occupied zone was the larger of the two, comprising northern France and the Atlantic coast-line. Within this area, the Germans created further zones: an Annexed zone, essentially Alsace-Lorraine, which was incorporated into the Reich; a Prohibited zone of the Nord-Pas-de-Calais, which was governed by the High Command in Brussels and ringed by a *cordon sanitaire* of a forbidden zone; and, finally, a Reserved zone to the west of Alsace-Lorraine in which Prussian farmers were encouraged to settle. Jackson has appositely described this settlement as the 'Balkanisation of France', a clear indication of Hitler's intention to destroy French identity (Jackson, 2001) Theoretically, the French government in the unoccupied south had jurisdiction over the north, yet its authority carried little weight. A Demarcation Line, rigorously policed by the Germans and the French, separated the two main zones. In the words of General Stulpnagel, 'it was a bit in a horse's mouth' which could be tightened whenever the Germans chose. Indeed, in delineating the contours of the new France, Berlin had made sure that it had occupied the most prosperous areas. As Kedward writes, the German occupied areas contained '67 per cent of the population, 66 per cent of cultivated land, over 75 per cent of mining and industry, 97 per cent of the fishing industry, 62 per cent of cereals, and over 70 per cent of potatoes, butter and meat' (Kedward, 1978: 18) While the Unoccupied zone could boast superior yields of wine and fruit, both industry and agriculture in the south were dependent on supplies and trade with the north, ensuing that high un-employment was one of the first problems encountered by the Pétain regime.

The more immediate problem was to find a new home for government as Bordeaux lay in the Occupied zone and, being a port, offered too great a temptation to take flight. Pétainist propaganda would later make much play of the fact that the new government lay at Vichy, a small spa town, in the heart of the rural department of the Allier, conveniently ignoring the fact that this and surrounding areas had repeatedly opted for left and centrist deputies in the Third Republic. In truth, as Michèle Cointet relates, Vichy was selected for its ample hotels, which could accommodate the many ministries, a modern telephone system, its easy rail links to Paris, and the lack of suitable alternatives (Cointet, 1993). It is Cointet, too, who has explained this lack of other options. Despite the Armistice terms, a return to Paris was always out of the question, and Hitler scoffed at a proposal made in November 1940 for government to move to Versailles. Toulouse was considered but was rejected because of the influence that the two influential Radical politicians, the Sarraut brothers, exercised over the town. Maybe it would have been the presence of the free-thinking churchman, archbishop Saliège, that would have proved the more embarrassing. He was outspoken in his denunciations of Vichy's antisemitism and made no secret of his preference for a victorious France under Blum and the freemasons as opposed to a defeated France under the marshal. Lyon was also considered, but again political considerations got in the way, this time its reputation for industrial unrest and the presence of Herriot, the Radical mayor and president of the Chamber of Deputies. Lyon, Cointet reminds us, would later become 'capital of the Resistance'. Marseilles was fleetingly canvassed, but possessed a disreputable image, hardly suitable for a government set on moral regeneration, and would have been unacceptable to the Germans, its seaborne position again an easy route to North Africa. Eventually, government decided on the industrial town of Clermont Ferrand but this proved hopelessly constricted, and was too near Laval's press and radio empire in the Auvergne. So it was that Baudouin proposed Vichy, where ministers started arriving on 3 July.

It was here that Pétain quickly set up characteristically spartan quarters in room 125 on the third floor of the Hôtel du Parc in the centre of the town, soon to become the headquarters of the new *Etat français*. The way ahead for the new French regime was secured in the town's casino where the deputies and senators of the National Assembly gathered, on 10 July, to vote full powers to the marshal (569 for, 80 against). Three constitutional acts, framed by the right-wing jurist and vicious antisemite Raphaël Alibert, were subsequently passed. The first, and most critical, effectively abrogated the Third Republic and appointed Pétain head of state. The second amplified his powers: his right to initiate laws, appoint ministers, approve budgets, and ratify treaties, although he was denied the authority to declare war, something which had to be approved by the legislative assemblies. A third act suspended the National Assembly and foresaw the drafting of a new constitution, a task never completed during the Occupation. A fourth act, dated 12 July, appointed Laval, minister of state since 23 June, as the marshal's successor, his *dauphin*.

When Pétain and his closest advisers had convened in early July, they had seriously doubted that parliament would fall on its sword and hand over the powers they sought. Why was their task so easy? One myth should be immediately dispelled: that Pétain was involved in a long-standing conspiracy to topple the Third Republic. The marshal was unquestionably hungry for power but was a stickler for legal niceties and was not prepared to indulge in a *coup d'état*. His arrogance was such that he considered he had to be called to power, and was prepared to let others do the running for him, notably Laval, who has often been depicted as the architect of the Third Republic's demise. As Geoffrey Warner has shown, despite being a consummate parliamentarian, Laval had come to view liberal democracy as inferior to fascism and an obstacle to his dream of a Franco-German *rapprochement* (Warner, 1968). He held a particular grudge against the Popular Front chamber which had removed him from power. 'This parliament vomited me up', he sneered, 'now I will vomit it up.' So it was that he readily agreed to steer through the destruction of the 1875 Constitution. He used his persuasive skills to the full, buttering up wavering deputies and threatening others with the possibility of a Weygand dictatorship. On the day of the vote, he pulled a series of constitutional tricks, getting the deputies to agree on the need for a simple majority for the approval of the new laws instead of the two-thirds normally required, and taking the government's proposals before other amendments which would, in any case, have given the marshal extensive powers. Yet it should be emphasised that Laval's task was not a difficult one. As Michèle Cointet has again demonstrated, the National Assembly was all too willing to commit *hari kari* (Cointet, 1987). Defeat had discredited the Third Republic which several deputies felt had served them badly by obstructing constructive reform. Deputies and senators were further convinced that the extraordinary nature of the defeat necessitated the handing over of extensive powers to the executive, something that they had been accustomed to doing during moments of crisis. It should also be remembered, whatever Laval might have thought, that this was not the Popular Front chamber of 1936, but a right-leaning parliament. By-elections had brought successive victories for the right, Daladier had taken the Radicals in a rightwards shift, and the Communists were, of course, debarred. Most importantly, the National Assembly had fallen under the spell of the marshal. Given the pacifism that had been momentarily eclipsed during the 'phoney war', a majority of deputies and senators believed that this supreme patriot, in agreeing to the Armistice, had arrived at the only decision possible. Few had any notion of the ways in which this supposedly apolitical soldier would use his powers.

CHAPTER FOUR

VICHY

Vichy poses a series of conundrums to the historian. The regime barely stood still, its cabinets coming and going with greater speed than those of the Third Republic, making the problem of definition extremely complex. The high ministerial turnover also lent confusion to the National Revolution, a seemingly self-contradictory project, which incorporated an eclectic mix of ideological impulses. What the French people made of Vichy, its policies and the circumstances of the Occupation, especially the German presence, depended on two variables: time and place. The unfolding events of the war, both within and outside France, profoundly affected how men and women behaved. So did where one lived. This was, in part, to be expected in a country as diverse as France, yet regional differences were compounded by the creation of the separate zones. It was not what many had hoped for. In the figure of the marshal, the population had looked for safety, protection, reassurance. Ultimately, he was unable to provide any of these things.

THE CULT OF PÉTAINISM

The faded Pétainist *bric-à-brac* that today can be picked up on the book-stalls that line the banks of the Seine in Paris give little inkling of the popularity the marshal enjoyed during the Occupation. His image was everywhere: on coins, banknotes, stamps, crockery and cigarette cards [*Doc. 11c*]. Within town halls, schools and, frequently, behind the altar, his portrait gazed down on proceedings. Children, for whom the marshal had a 'genuine affection' despite having none of his own (Halls, 1981: 14), were encouraged to play a prominent part in this hero worship. Textbooks were written containing the marshal's precepts; Christmas trees were planted in his honour; and children were urged to write and send their drawings to him [*Doc. 11a*]. The archives of the Ministry of Education record that, by February 1941, Vichy had received some 2,200,000 of these pictures. Moreover, this was a hero the people could see and hear. His frail voice, in the words of Arthur Koestler 'like a skeleton with a cough', repeatedly broadcast on the radio, although more people eventually took to listening to the BBC. Pétain also visited the towns and villages of southern France, an exhausting itinerary for a man 84 years of age in 1940. Indeed, the suggestions that the marshal was already senile in the Occupation should be put to rest: dementia would not set in until his postwar captivity. He might have needed shots of amphetamine to get him through the day, but he remained an energetic figure, with a keen nose for business.

This popularity did not appear overnight and owed little to Vichy propaganda. Its roots go back to the First World War when Pétain had shown himself to be a compassionate and able leader. His natural prudence and preference for defensive tactics proved their worth, especially at Verdun in 1916, the most momentous battle ever fought by the French army. His refusal to countenance foolhardy offensives, the affection he held for his men and his willingness to improve the material lot of his troops made him the natural choice to quell the mutinies that broke out in the French army in 1917. It might have been Foch who ultimately possessed the derring-do to hit the Germans in 1918, yet all the French generals who were present at the final defeat of Germany were awarded with a cult status, and many were elevated to the previously neglected rank of marshal. Pétain's standing was further enhanced by the fact that he and Franchet d'Espérey were the only two marshals left alive in 1934. By then, he had exercised a powerful influence over the evolution of French defensive strategy, yet he studiously kept away from the realm of politics, only stepping out of the shadows to accept the Defence portfolio in 1934 and the ambassadorship to Spain in 1939. His arrogance and self-belief were such that he had to be called to office. Calls there were aplenty in the 1930s when the Depression and Popular Front eras unsettled society's calm. From 1935 onwards, the maverick journalist Gustav Hervé ran a series of polls in his newspaper, *La Victoire*, declaring 'C'est Pétain qu'il nous faut'. Still the marshal kept quiet, unwilling to launch a *coup d'état* or stand for the presidency, for him a largely meaningless position. This silence paid dividends in 1940 when it distanced him from the excitable and discredited politicians of the Third Republic. As Paxton records, he was 'the ready-made hero', 'a blank image' to be 'stamped with everyone's concept of a saviour' (Paxton, 1972: 31). His lowly rural origins appealed to the peasantry; his victory at Verdun played well with First World War veterans; his outward Catholicism heartened the Church; and his silence on political matters reassured the left who viewed him as a 'republican general'. Few, other than de Gaulle, knew the 'real' Pétain: a surly, pessimistic soldier, whose defeatism had proved costly in 1918 and fatal in 1940; a man happier in his Paris apartment and house outside Marseilles than in his native Artois; a nominal Catholic and serial womanizer; and a deeply ambitious politician, a republican yes, but a believer in an authoritarian republic under the firm guidance of one man.

Pétain's popularity further emanated from the *exode*, the name given to the mass flight of people, maybe some 8 million in total, who deserted their homes in Belgium and northern France, to escape the German onrush. In May 1940, Lille, a town of 200,000, was reduced to 20,000 inhabitants. Meanwhile, towns in the south mushroomed: Cahors (Lot) grew from 13,000 to 100,000; Brive (Corrèze) from 30,000 to 100,000; and Pau (Basses-Pyrénées) from 38,000 to 150,000. As Kedward has shown, many fled south believing the countryside would provide 'ample food and plenty of living space', myths engendered by the Popular Front 'paid holidays' when numerous workers from the north had first experienced life in the countryside (Kedward, 1978: 7). In the event, they discovered accommodation scarce and prejudices abundant; thanks to the Demarcation Line, their return home proved difficult, leaving many in unfamiliar surroundings. The fear, chaos and discomfort that accompanied the *exode* have been vividly evoked by novelists (Jean-Paul Sartre's *La Mort dans l'âme* and Lucien Rebatet's *Les Décombres*) and filmmakers (René Clément's *Les Jeux interdits*), yet it is the first-hand accounts and the pitiful advertisements placed in local newspapers for lost children (some 90,000 in total) that evoke the horror of this painful episode, and explain why so many turned to the marshal as a saviour [*Doc. 6*]. Through the Armistice, he appeared to have made the only sensible decision and, through his new government, he alone seemed to have France's best interests at heart. By contrast, the Third Republic looked a shameful and uncaring regime. Having put elaborate plans into place for the orderly evacuation of civilians, local administrators had taken flight in May–June 1940, leaving the local populace to fend for itself.

Given the hold of the marshal, it is tempting to believe Henri Amouroux's suggestion that France equated to '40 million Pétainists' in 1940. This is an exaggeration. There were dissenting voices from the very moment of the Armistice, giving rise to a fledgling resistance movement. Vinen has shown how different areas reacted differently to the marshal's appeal (Vinen, 1994). The essentially 'ruralist' propaganda of Pétainism and the ubiquity of German troops meant that the marshal's popularity was never that strong in the occupied and predominantly industrialised north. Burrin quotes the *contrôle postal*, a process by which Vichy opened people's mail, to illustrate how, in Spring 1941, the marshal's popularity was already on the wane in the *zone occupée* (Burrin, 1995). In the south, it was the events of the war – the handshake with Hitler at Montoire, the recruitment of French labour for German factories, and the occupation of all of France in November 1942 – that led many to deconstruct the myth of Pétain. As Yves Durand has argued, a distinction should also be made between 'passive' and 'active' Pétainists (Durand, 1989). 'Active' supporters were those who openly subscribed to *maréchaliste* propaganda: a faith in leadership; a rejection of the Republican tradition, especially the Popular Front; and the creation of a new society based on the traditionalist values of family, work, order, obedience, discipline and honour. Such men and women were always the minority. Most Pétainists were 'passive' in their support, looking to the marshal as a figurehead, the man who would rescue France from chaos. In this respect, Vichy propaganda did little to rupture their illusions: few references were made to Verdun, as Pétain's task was to achieve peace not war; much was made of his physical appearance, his upright figure and striking blue eyes, signs of security amid uncertainty; and hagiographers frequently referred to his calm and forbearing, again an attempt to distinguish him from the temperamental ways of the Third Republic [*Doc. 11b*].

ONE VICHY OR SEVERAL?

Historians concur that Vichy was never a personal dictatorship. While Pétain possessed enormous constitutional powers, he was only too ready to delegate to his ministers, and rarely initiated policy himself. He was, however, prepared to dismiss members of his cabinet when it suited him. As the war dragged on and his quest for foreign policy success became more desperate, he discovered his ability to hire and fire was being undermined by others, notably Laval and the Germans. Such circumstances ensured that Vichy was a complex regime which cannot be readily labelled. It has been variously described as 'a government of expediency', a 'counter revolution', a 'fascist state' and a 'pluralistic dictatorship' (Hoffmann, 1974). Pluralism was unquestionably a feature yet, ultimately, what gave Vichy a unity was the willingness to persecute its enemies, real and imagined. Today, there is growing consensus that the regime was one of 'exclusion'.

Initial interpretations were ventured by the regime's apologists, notably Aron, who put a spin on the arguments first deployed by Jacques Isorni, the most eloquent of Pétain's defence lawyers in 1945. In their view, the government was essentially a passive one, 'holding the fort' while de Gaulle conducted resistance from overseas, and doing whatever it could to obstruct German designs. If anyone was keen to do the Germans' work for them, that man was Laval, who had few enough supporters in the *après guerre*. It is easy to scoff at claims that Vichy was merely a regime of expediency, as did many historians writing in the aftermath of Paxton (Paxton, 1972). Unquestionably, it was important to highlight the regime's repressive features yet, as Munholland has suggested, such accounts downplayed the very real restraints under which Vichy was operating (Munholland, 1994). As the richest nation in Hitler's Europe, it was inevitable that the Nazis were going to bleed France white, as the following figures and examples cited by Michel-Pierre Chélini demonstrate: during the period 1940–44 France paid 860,000,000 *francs* towards the costs of the German occupation; the exchange rate was set artificially high in favour of the *mark* (20 *francs* to a *mark*, in contrast to 12 *francs* in 1939); some 10 to 20 per cent of French agricultural produce and between 30 and 40 per cent of all industrial production was appropriated; Jewish businesses, among them the prestigious *Parfums Rubinstein* and *Galeries Lafayette*, were seized; and, in 1942–43, the Reich requisitioned more than 650,000 men for work in German factories (Cointet and Cointet, 2000: 579–80). Economic constraints were accompanied by political ones: Germany frequently disregarded Vichy legislation in the Occupied zone. In November 1942, when Germany occupied all of France, such disregard became more blatant. As Jean Tracou recalls, when in 1943 Pétain belatedly put up some half-hearted protest against German impositions, a Gauleiter Renthe-Finck was stationed to keep watch at the Hôtel du Parc, and a garrison of SS troops was based outside Vichy should the regime prove uncooperative and need disassembling in favour of a collaborationist government in Paris (Tracou, 1948). Nevertheless, to claim that Vichy was no more than a 'holding operation' is disingenuous. It downplays the very real autonomy Vichy enjoyed in the southern zone during the first two years of the Occupation, and ignores the fact that the National Revolution was very much a French invention.

Early research conducted into the nature of Vichy's domestic reforms, especially that pioneered by Rémond, revealed the presence of traditionalist right-wing values lending support to the view that Vichy amounted to a 'counter revolution', an 'emphatic rejection' of France's revolutionary heritage (Rémond, 1969). There is much in this argument. In 1941, Pétain published his *Principes de la communauté*, an elaboration of National Revolution precepts, which he hoped would supplant the revolutionary *Declaration of the Rights of Man and the Citizen* [*Doc. 12*]. Vichy legislation also looked to the past. Whereas the Republic had cherished representative government, the *Etat français* did away with elections: the 1875 Constitution was suspended (11 July 1940); municipal councils governing urban areas with a population over 2,000 were, in future, appointed (12 October 1940); known republican and left-wing sympathisers in positions of public authority were replaced by Pétainist notables; and prefectoral powers were greatly reinforced (23 December 1940) (Baruch, 1997). Whereas the Republic championed equality, Vichy endorsed hierarchy: a cult of leadership was encouraged throughout society; women's prerogatives were severely curtailed, although the Republic had not always distinguished itself in this sphere; police powers were extended; and arbitrary arrest became commonplace. Whereas the Republic valued the individual, Vichy espoused an organicist concept of the nation: the family, workplace and commune were portrayed as living organisms; trade unions were abolished and corporations put in their stead (20 October 1940); and peasants and workers were given their own Charters (2 December 1940 and 26 October 1941). Whereas the Republic had been avowedly secular, Vichy was indulgent towards the Church: religious orders were allowed to teach again and entitled to the right of association (3 September 1940 and 8 April 1942); religious instruction was briefly reintroduced into state schools (6 January 1941); state subsidies were provided to Catholic elementary schools, albeit as a temporary measure (2 November 1941); and there was talk of a new concordat to replace the separation of Church and state in 1905. Whereas the Republic had been modern in its perspective, Vichy celebrated the past: peasant folklore was exalted [*Doc. 13*]; the *Ancien Régime* was praised in new school primers; and there was talk of reorganising France along the lines of pre-1789 provinces.

Without question, traditionalist and Catholic views were prominent in the National Revolution yet, as Paxton demonstrated, this experiment was awash with all manner of projects (Paxton, 1972). Now that the rocks of parliamentary opposition had been swept away, several schemes which had been under review in the 1930s came to the surface. These drew on a variety of political traditions – modernism, Orleanism and republicanism – reinforcing Paxton's argument that Vichy marked 'continuity' rather than a 'break' in the French political tradition. As Michèle Cointet suggests, this is perhaps not surprising given the presence of prominent republicans at Vichy, for example Flandin, Laval, Marquet, Bousquet and Peyrouton, and the regime's reliance on civil servants who had cut their administrative teeth before 1940 (Cointet, 1989). So it was that several of the National Revolution's reforms looked to the future as well as to the past, mirroring those which would be discussed by the Consultative Assembly in Algiers in 1944 and later implemented under the Fourth Republic. In the social sphere, Vichy enacted a state pension and improved facilities for post-natal care. In the educational domain, greater emphasis was placed on technical subjects, vocational training and outdoor activities. In 1940 Jean Borotra, the former Wimbledon tennis champion, was appointed head of the Commissariat Général à l'Education Générale et Sportive (CGEGS). Building on the work of Léo Lagrange, the Popular Front minister in charge of sport and leisure, Borotra quickly set about improving playgrounds within schools, the building of athletic tracks and the encouragement of amateur sports. One of the few things that people remember with any fondness of their schooltime experiences during the Occupation is this greater emphasis on outdoor play. Within the economy, Pétain and his closest advisers might have espoused the values of a corporatist society, free from the class conflict of socialism and the unbridled egoism of capitalism yet, as Vinen writes, in 1941 a series of modernisers were appointed: Yves Bouthillier, minister of finance (June 1940–April 1942); Jean Bichelonne, secretary general for commerce and industry and secretary of state for industrial production (1941); Pierre Pucheu, secretary of state for industrial production (February 1941–July 1941) and minister of the interior (July 1941–May 1942); and François Lehideux, secretary of state for industrial production (July 1941–April 1942) (Vinen, 1996: 53). Although these men were never united and never constituted a semi-secret synarchy as some traditionalists rumoured, they valued economic efficiency, closed down underperforming businesses and experimented with state planning through the Délégation Générale à l'Equipement National (Dard, 1998). Yet so much that Vichy did in the economic domain was make-believe. Ultimately, it was Germany that called the shots. It is generally agreed that the only real power the regime possessed was the right to organise labour and to ensure the Reich received French riches.

This willingness to bow to Germany's whims, Vichy's autocratic nature, its brutal antisemitism, its cosy alliance with the *haute bourgeoisie*, its indulgence towards big business and its disregard for workers' rights have led to suggestions that the regime was fascist in nature. This was a charge first made by the Communists in 1940 who recalled Pétain's treatment of the mutineers in 1917 and his suppression of the 1925 Arab nationalist revolt in the Rif. It is a charge that has been repeated by left-wing historians since the war. Undoubtedly, in the months before the Liberation, Vichy followed a fascist trajectory. Within its ranks it included such extremists as Abel Bonnard, minister of education, Marcel Déat, minister of labour and national solidarity, Philippe Henriot, minister for propaganda, Joseph Darnand, minister of national security, and Charles Mercier du Paty de Clam, the final head of Vichy's Commissariat Général aux Questions Juives (CGQJ). Nonetheless, it never quite managed to complete the metamorphosis into a fascist state (Jackson, 2001). Fascist ministers were always a minority. They also had to contend with the marshal. Whereas Hitler and Mussolini liked to present themselves as dynamic, youthful leaders, Pétain adopted an avuncular image which suited his grand age. Indeed, as Vinen has commented, fascist regimes were 'youthful', yet Vichy was a 'gerontocracy', or at least a regime entering into middle-aged flabbiness: Weygand was 73 years old in 1940; General La Porte du Theil, head of the Chantiers de la Jeunesse, was 56; Jean Ybarnégaray, minister for youth and the family was 57; and Pierre Caziot, minister of agriculture, was 64. Even when Vichy introduced fresh faces in the shape of the technocrats, these men were valued more for their expertise than their youth and, adds Vinen, looked older than their years (Vinen, 1996: 42). The preponderance of grey-haired and middle-aged folk in the marshal's cabinets ensured that Vichy was not prepared to disturb social hierarchies in the manner of the Nazis. Nor, as Vinen continues, was it prepared to 'glorify' violence, although it was happy to persecute its enemies. Historians such as Denis

Peschanski have also underscored the muddle of Vichy propaganda; unlike fascist states, Vichy was in several minds as to how it should be portrayed (Peschanski, 1990). Critically, Vichy never attempted to establish a single party, a sure sign of fascist pretensions. This idea was proposed by Déat on 27 July 1940, and was revisited by Pucheu in summer 1941, who was also attracted to the notion of a *jeunesse unique*, a plan which deeply disturbed the Church which possessed its own youth movements, among them the JOC, JEC and JAC (Déat, 1989). Yet the marshal and his advisers recoiled from a *parti unique*. There was a fear that such a body might form a rival power base, especially if it fell under the spell of the Paris fascists of whom Vichy was extremely wary. Instead the regime established a series of organisations to pre-empt such a scenario: the Légion Française des Combattants, which amalgamated the many prewar veteran organisations and brought the marshal into contact with the people with whom he felt the greatest empathy; the Chantiers, which served as a type of national service, giving the young a taste of hard work; and the Compagnons de France, another youth group instigated by Henri Dhavernas, who was more influenced by Baden Powell than the Hitler Jugend. In the event, even the Paris fascists would fail to agree on a unitary movement, although Déat succeeded in creating his own organisation, the Rassemblement National Populaire (RNP).

While the marshal's government might not have fitted a fascist template, debates about the essence of the regime have proved useful in that they have underscored its ever-shifting nature. The notion of pluralism was first recognised in the 1950s by historians as diverse as Aron and Hoffmann but, as Azéma comments, it was Yves Durand who first charted the complicated path adopted by Pétain's cabinets (Durand, 1973). Crudely speaking, historians have plotted six phases in the life of the regime. The first Vichy, that of July–August 1940, was basically the remainder of Reynaud's cabinet – parliamentarians, military men and odd members of the left – and it was only natural that the marshal would want to bring in his own people. The second Vichy evolved on 6 September 1940 when Pétain dismissed former deputies, among them Adrien Marquet, minister of state, and Emile Mireux, minister of education. The most eminent former parliamentarian, Laval, remained but by the end of the year he too had outlived his usefulness, unable to bring about the foreign policy success that Vichy craved. So it was on 13 December 1940 the marshal effected a third reshuffle, dismissing Laval, and bringing in more military men and traditionalists such as Jacques Chevalier, the fervent Catholic who took over education, and Xavier Vallat who, in March 1941, became head of the CGQJ. By then, a fourth Vichy was evolving. Still anxious for a breakthrough in Franco-German relations, the marshal handed over considerable powers to Darlan, who brought with him young *dirigiste*s in the shape of

Lehideux, Pucheu and Bichelonne. It was this perennial anxiety to coax the Germans into making concessions that led Pétain, in April 1942, to recall Laval as premier. A fifth Vichy was thus born. Wary of another *coup* to oust him, Laval put his own acolytes into power, ex-deputies and syndicalists such as Max Bonnafous and Hubert Lagardelle, men united only in their dependence on the prime minister's patronage. Under mounting German pressure, in the course of 1943–44, Vichy graduated to its final stage, a semi-fascist state, watched over by the likes of Bonnard, Darnand, Henriot and Déat. Ironically, it was only in its death throes, that Vichy achieved any real semblance of ideological and ministerial unity (Rousso, 1980).

If there is a theme which unites these various stages of Vichy's development, it is the desire to stamp out subversion and rid France of 'undesirable elements', leading to a growing conviction that ultimately the regime was one of 'exclusion' (Peschanski, 1998). While the government undoubtedly required special powers to deal with an extraordinary situation and while there is a smidgen of truth in apologist claims that these powers were necessary to resist German meddling, from its inception Vichy embarked on a series of nasty and vindictive measures, persecuting minorities, most notoriously Jews. It is for these policies, rather than the progressive elements of the National Revolution, that the regime will always be remembered.

EXCLUSION AND REPRESSION

The brutal tone of Vichy was set by Pétain himself who, paradoxically, possessed a reputation as a compassionate leader. During the First World War, he had been a strict disciplinarian, but was alive to the horrors of trench warfare and regularly rotated troops in the front line, providing rest areas away from the shelling. The marshal's compassion only extended, however, to certain sectors of society. It did not include what he termed 'the anti-France' (Pétain, 1940). Although he never named those behind this conspiracy, it was clear whom he had in mind: freemasons, free-thinkers, parliamentarians (especially those of the Popular Front), Communists, foreigners and Jews. Such elements were to be closely monitored and their influence within society eliminated. The population, in turn, was actively encouraged to spy and inform on such elements, a phenomenon known as *délation*, something in which many French people participated, although it should be stressed that Vichy only approved of denunciations if this meant giving information to its own officials; denouncing other citizens to the Germans or Italians was positively frowned upon [*Doc. 19*]. As Jackson relates, to handle all the telephone calls and anonymous letters of denunciation, Vichy oversaw an expansion of police powers with several new police forces established: the Groupes Mobiles de Réserve (GMR), a paramilitary force which replaced the old Garde Mobile; the Service d'Ordre Légionnaire (SOL), created out of the Légion on 12 December 1941 and designed to defend the values of the National Revolution; the Sections d'Affaires Politiques (SAP) located in provincial cities in 1941 to monitor Communist subversion; the Police des Question Juives (PQJ), set up at the same time as SAP, to handle the sequestration of Jewish property and nationality laws; and the reconstituted Brigades Spéciales (BS2), which in 1942 were put to work tracking down Communists (Sweets, 1989; Rajsfus, 1995; Jackson, 2001). As Pierre Froment illustrates, when in 1942 René Bousquet took charge of police affairs in the Interior Ministry, he attempted to rationalise all these new bodies, albeit without much success; yet the foundations of a national police force, something which prewar France had lacked, had been more or less accomplished thanks to the reforms of 1941 (Froment, 1994). For good measure, Vichy also required all civil servants to swear an oath of loyalty to the marshal (January 1941), a requirement that was eventually extended to other groups of officials.

Not all groups who constituted the 'anti-France' had reason to fear a knock on the door in the middle of the night, in particular France's 800,000 Protestants who were largely settled in the Cévennes area of the Unoccupied zone. This tolerance was again thanks to the influence Pétain wielded over the direction of Vichy's exclusion. While a Catholic, he was only a nominal believer and valued religions, including Protestantism and Islam, in a Maurrassian, and indeed Bonapartist, sense, that is as a bulwark of stability. So it was that he enjoyed close relations with Marc Boegner, head of the Fédération Protestante, and readily included Protestants in his entourage: René Gillouin, an early speechwriter who resigned in opposition to Vichy's antisemitism (Gillouin, 1966); Paul Baudouin, minister of foreign affairs; Admiral Platon, colonial secretary; Charles Brécard, grand chancellor of the Légion d'Honneur, and Maurice Couve de Murville, a civil servant in the Ministry of Finance who defected to de Gaulle and who later served as prime minister in the Fifth Republic. Maybe Vichy regretted this indulgence towards Protestantism. Although Protestants were initially supportive of the regime, this attitude quickly cooled. As Robert Zaretsky has shown, their experience of persecution, their theological insistence on individual conscience, their awareness of the writings of the German Protestant thinker Karl Barth, a fierce critic of Nazism, and their discomfort at Vichy's clericalism, made them ever outspoken in their opposition of collaboration and antisemitism (Zaretsky, 1995; Gordon, 1998: 293–4). Small wonder that Protestants played an active part in protecting Jewish refuges, setting up the welfare group, Cimade, and becoming a powerful element in southern resistance movements.

Tolerance was not extended to freemasons who were a traditional bugbear of the French right. In 1940, past 'crimes' were readily recalled:

their involvement in the *Affaire des Fiches* of 1904 whereby the *Grand Orient* had compiled information on officers' religious beliefs; their support for democratic schooling through the so-called *école unique*, which sought to end the divisions between primary and secondary education; and their grip on the Radical Party, a bastion of anticlericalism. It has since been suggested that the subsequent assault on the Lodges was 'blunted' by the fact that freemasons were generally men of property and were thus allowed to stay in office, thanks in part to the protection of Laval, who had little time for this particular campaign; masons, it is stressed, were especially prominent in colonial administration (Vinen, 1996: 64). Darlan had several prewar masonic contacts. Nonetheless, there can be little doubting the ferocity of Vichy's attack, orchestrated by Raphaël Alibert at the Ministry of Justice. On 13 August 1940 secret societies were dissolved; freemasons were forced to declare their membership; and several civil servants and schoolteachers were ousted from office. Meanwhile, Bernard Fäy, head of Vichy's Service des Sociétés Secrètes counted how many masons had held public employment. On 12 August, the *Journal officiel* started to publish the fruits of his endeavours, naming and shaming some 18,000 masons in total. Under the direction of Jean Marquès-Rivière, head of a special anti-masonic police force, several major towns in the Occupied zone, including Paris, played host to the exhibition 'La franc-maçonnerie dévoilée'; Vichy organised a similar exhibition in Lyon, and endorsed Jean Mamy's 1943 film, *Forces occultes*, which purported to show the global influence of secret societies. Although Vichy's fear of masons was grossly exaggerated, its campaign proved effective. At the Liberation, membership of the Lodges was only a third of that in 1939 (Cointet and Cointet, 2000: 322).

Deputies and senators also endured an uncomfortable existence in the *Etat français*. While a small number found their way into government, the majority were treated as outcasts. In 1941 they lost their parliamentary immunity as more and more power was handed over to the prefects, who sported a brand new uniform fitting for their role as 'agents of national resurrection' (Marcel Peyrouton) and who pocketed an enhanced salary to reward their efforts. The most unfortunate deputies were those Popular Front ministers – Blum, Daladier, Reynaud, Mandel and La Chambre – who were put on trial at Riom, alongside Gamelin, charged with having prepared France inadequately for war. The trial was a fiasco, the defendants quickly turning the tables on their accusers. Germany was also irritated over the length of the proceedings and the failure to indict the accused with having started the war. In 1942 proceedings were suspended, while the defendants languished in French and German jails. Several other parliamentarians, as well as republican functionaries and journalists, were interned at Evaux-les-Bains, among them Auguste Champetier de Ribes, Pierre Viénot, Elie Calmon, Joseph Denais and André Blumel. Such internment was no guarantee of safety. In 1944, Mandel was killed by the *Milice,* as was Jean Zay, Blum's minister of education, probably in retaliation for the assassination of Henriot, Vichy's propaganda minister.

Communists also had reason to fear Pétain's henchmen. Historians are agreed that Vichy was profoundly marked by its renunciation of the left. The Popular Front victory had shocked the French right which was keen for revenge, despite the fact that much of the Blum legislation had been reversed by 1940. No matter. Vichy went even further in rescinding trade union rights. The regime was also fearful that the Occupation might be an occasion for a Communist-inspired rising; thus Vichy readily extended the anti-Communist measures first adopted by Daladier. Between July 1940 and June 1941, the Préfecture de Police arrested some 1,897 Communists, while prefects busily compiled lists of suspected agitators to be detained in the event of an insurrection. This campaign entered a particularly brutal phase in summer 1941 when Germany invaded the USSR and the PCF came out in favour of full-scale resistance. Henceforth, much civil disobedience was conveniently blamed on the Communists. On 14 August 1941, special courts were set up in both the Occupied and Unoccupied zones to deal specifically with Communists; penalties were severe, however minor the crimes. Meantime Pucheu, as minister of interior, willingly handed over to the Nazis Communist hostages to be shot in response to the killing of German military personnel.

Such denials of justice were matched only by Vichy's barbarous treatment of France's 330,000 Jews. Antisemitic legislation was fast and furious in the summer of 1940: categories of Jews were debarred from holding public offices; positions in medicine, law and higher education were denied; press restrictions on racism were lifted; the French citizenship of both Algerian Jews and recently naturalised Jews was revoked; Jewish businesses were appropriated; and prefects were granted the power to arrest foreign Jews. In October 1940, Vichy approved the first *Statut des juifs,* which placed even stricter controls on the kind of jobs Jews could perform. The following March the CGQJ was established under the direction of Vallat. A fervent xenophobe, his new agency set about internment, the registering of Jewish property, and the close monitoring of Jewish activities. June 1941 saw the introduction of a second *Statut des juifs.* This defined Jews in more stringent terms than the first, and placed a ban on Jews working in a bewildering array of professions, especially in the commercial sector. Further arrests, internments and seizures of Jewish property followed. As will be seen, in 1942 Vichy became a willing participant in the Final Solution, playing an active role in the round-up of Jews for deportation to the death camps in the east.

Immediately after the war, most historians preferred to ignore this legislation. If it was mentioned at all, it was conveniently blamed on the

Germans. It was Paxton who gave the lie to this argument (Paxton, 1972). In his extensive use of German papers, he found no evidence that the Reich had put any pressure on Vichy to implement an antisemitic programme; rather, Berlin had been surprised at the speed with which the French had passed their own measures. It has further been claimed that Vichy's programme was essentially a smokescreen to highlight the regime's autonomy and resist German intrusion. There is some truth in this claim, but it still does not account for the zeal with which Vichy pursued its ends. Apologists have further claimed that Vichy's antisemitism was of a cultural type, and was largely directed at recent arrivals, some 150,000 in number, who had settled in the 1920s and 1930s; much is made of the exemptions granted to Jews who had testified their 'Frenchness' by fighting in the First World War. While there is no doubt that Vichy was most agitated by recent Jewish immigrants, this is a morally bankrupt argument which does not excuse the shabby way in which foreign Jews were treated. In 1942, Laval brokered an especially sordid deal with the Germans which saw the deportation of foreign Jews ahead of French ones. It is also questionable whether Vichy's racism was solely cultural. Historians have stressed that the regime's definition of a Jew, as expressed in the two *Statuts des juifs*, was undoubtedly biological, and surpassed that of the Nuremberg Laws. By early 1942, when Darquier de Pellepoix took over the CGQJ, Vichy's racism had become interchangeable with that of the Nazis and the Paris collaborators [*Doc. 18*]. Overall, 75,721 Jews, nearly two-thirds of them foreign born, were deported from France; all but 2,567 perished (Marrus and Paxton, 1981).

Given that it was Pétain himself who set the tone for Vichy's repression, it is appropriate to conclude by questioning his involvement in the persecution of Jews. His defenders make much of the fact that he made no antisemitic remarks in his speeches, yet it is worth remembering that when members of his cabinet, notably Laval, spoke of delaying the first *Statut des juifs* it was the marshal who intervened to ensure its quick promulgation. Much, too, is made of the fact that he counted several blacks among his friends, notably Henry Lémery, minister of colonies. This evidence does not absolve him of racism, but points instead to the type of prejudice he espoused. It was an unthinking and callous brand which looked upon all foreigners as a threat to national integrity; they had to prove their loyalty by assimilating fully French traditions. This was why he was prepared to tolerate the brutal treatment of foreign Jews and, ultimately, their deportation. If French lives could be saved by the exchange of foreign ones, so be it. Although he never favoured the extermination of the Jewish race, it is significant that he failed to raise a voice of protest against the Final Solution, despite the fact that Church leaders, both Protestant and Catholic, repeatedly apprised him of what was happening in the camps. 'Pétain's crime', it is argued, was not that he instigated Jewish persecution, but that he happily facilitated the environment in which it could take place (Marrus and Paxton, 1981: 16–18, 85–6).

LIVING WITH THE ENEMY

Making sense of how the public responded to Vichy's policies, especially the exclusion of Jews and others, is not an easy task. The sources are uneven and often reflect what the authorities believed people were thinking, rather than what they actually thought: prefectoral reports, German and Allied intelligence materials, collaborationist enquiries, censored newspapers and the Armistice Commission's dossiers. This is why, in the absence of opinion polls of which the French are now so fond, historians have made increasing use of the *contrôle postal*, unpublished diaries and oral testimony. Alongside the uneven quality of the sources, there is also the problem of time. Opinion evolved in reply to the unfolding events of the war. And, then, there is the issue of geographical diversity, a diversity accentuated by the creation of separate zones. This latter difficulty explains why many historians have preferred to concentrate on particular regions instead of venturing appraisals of the country as a whole. At best, national assessments can be little more than informed generalisations.

Within the Annexed zone, principally Alsace-Lorraine, the rejection of the German presence was immediate. As Pierre Rigoulot relates, in an attempt to revive 'the true German nature' of the region, French administrators and nationals were exiled, *Gauleiters* appointed, the German language made compulsory, French street names abolished and Nazi legislation imposed wholesale, policies that alienated a majority of the local populace, not all of whom had been evacuated to southern departments at the time of the 'phoney war' (Rigoulot, 1997). The Germans did nothing for their popularity when, on 25 August 1942, conscription was introduced for all men aged between 16 and 34. Thus emerged the so-called *malgré nous* ('against our will'), although it should be noted that a smattering of pro-Nazi inhabitants readily signed up for the SS, in whose ranks they would later perpetrate atrocities elsewhere in France. Here, then, in the eastern provinces, Vichy seemed an irrelevance, and Pétain could hardly present himself as a saviour; rather Gaullism soon took a hold. A similar process can also be observed in the Nord-Pas-de-Calais which, it will be recalled, was governed by the military command in Brussels. Memories of the past German occupation in the First World War were fresh in people's minds but, as Richard Cobb has shown, this second occupation was far more intrusive and unpopular (Cobb, 1982; Taylor, 1997). There also existed, within this area, a traditional anglophilia which grew as the war progressed. Once more, Vichy seemed an abstract and faraway government and, as Burrin suggests, its traditionalist policies were hardly likely to win over an industrialised region which was strongly socialist in orientation (Burrin, 1995: 188) While there was some initial sympathy for Pétain, this quickly translated into Gaullism as it became manifest that the marshal could do little to halt the tide of Germanisation.

Within the Occupied zone, the Germans went out of their way to try to impress the local population. Burrin records how the embassy, under the supposed francophile Otto Abetz, distributed 17 million brochures, 10 million tracts and 400,000 posters of varying types (Burrin, 1995: 187). The Nazis were especially indulgent towards Paris: cultural life quickly resumed; collaborationist newspapers were subsidised; intellectuals such as Sartre were tolerated; and nightclubs, featuring such stars as Maurice Chevalier and Josephine Baker, flourished. Bertram Gordon has shown how the Germans especially valued the city as a rest area for troops, and a tourism trade quickly developed with restaurants, clubs and brothels exclusively reserved for the *Wehrmacht* (Gordon, 1996). Ordinary Parisians struggled to survive on meagre rations. As elsewhere in the Occupied zone, the German presence was quickly resented. Burrin cites a German intelligence report of September 1940 for the occupied zone: 'the population is on the whole calm, on occasion welcoming, but for the majority of time reserved, often unfriendly and to a certain degree hostile' (Burrin, 1995: 188). Vichy was likewise unpopular. The *contrôle postal* records that this dissatisfaction was widespread as early as spring 1941, and had certainly taken a hold by the middle of the year. Jean-Marie Flonneau records how Vichy ministers were greeted with derision when they visited Brittany that summer, and quotes the *sous-préfet* of Andelys in the Eure who calculated that only the presence of the occupying troops was containing an explosive situation (Flonneau, 1992: 508).

In the southern zone, it used to be believed that the population turned against Vichy sometime in 1942–43, as Paxton first suggested (Paxton, 1972). Without question, this year was pivotal. The return to power of Laval, the requisitioning of labour for German factories and the occupation of the whole of France certainly perturbed the population. W.D. Halls has shown how, at this stage, many Christians finally lost their patience with Vichy (Halls, 1995), and Kedward has underscored the way in which the labour draft gave rise to the *maquis* (Kedward, 1993). The work of Pierre Laborie and John Sweets, however, has shown that the regime probably lost its support as early as spring 1941 (Laborie, 1990; Sweets, 1986), and in August that year Pétain complained of 'an ill wind' that was sweeping through France, an allusion to growing resistance as well as to mounting public dissatisfaction [*Doc. 21*]. Even the marshal himself was losing his appeal, something borne out by the formidable evidence presented by Flonneau. He quotes the prefect of the Alpes-Maritimes who, in May 1942, reported that only 20 per cent of *Azuréens* were unreservedly behind the marshal (Flonneau, 1992: 508). In the *arrondissement* of Thiers, in the Auvergne, Laval's power base, the *sous-préfet* recorded that 60 per cent of the population was Gaullist or Anglo-Saxon in orientation, 10 per cent was Communist, and only 30 per cent 'loyal or indifferent'. Whereas de Gaulle had been an unknown quantity in 1940, his regular broadcasts to France on the BBC, and the marshal's seeming impotence to lift the burdens of the Occupation, had greatly enhanced his reputation.

It is hazardous to speculate why the southern zone should have turned against Vichy, yet four explanations present themselves. First, there appears to have been a residual sympathy for the British, despite Mers-el-Kébir, the Dakar expedition, the invasion of Syria in 1941, and early German military successes. This sentiment did not necessarily equal an anglophilia, but testified to the power of the BBC, which many turned to for more reliable news than that broadcast by Vichy, and the recognition that national salvation rested with a British victory. In early 1941, Charbonnières, a former official at the French embassy in London who was relocated to Vichy, speculated that 95 per cent of the population in the southern zone were praying for a British triumph over the Germans. As Burrin has shown, when in 1942 the USA joined the war, this hope in an Allied victory became ever stronger.

Second, it is possible to point to the ineffectual nature of Vichy propaganda. While it was not difficult to sell the marshal, given his underlying popularity, it proved far more problematic to project the regime and its values. As Dominique Rossignol has displayed, this was not for want of trying (Rossignol, 1991). Vichy devoted enormous attention to its image, its efforts neatly summarised by Jackson (Jackson, 2001). Posters were everywhere; the press was strictly controlled through a new body, the Office Français de l'Information, which replaced the independent Havas agency; the radio was exploited to the full, Pétain regularly broadcasting to his people; newsreels, controlled by the official France Actualités, portrayed a tranquil country at ease with itself; festival days such as Mother's Day and Joan of Arc Day, significantly not 14 July, were times of processions and pageantry; and, in 1941, Vichy created a team of *commissaires du pouvoir* whose job was to root out bureaucratic inefficiency, thus contrasting the effective ways of the new regime with the lethargy and supposed corruption of the old Republic. As Jackson has underscored, all this made little impact (Jackson, 2001). The splintering of France into several zones meant that Vichy propaganda was often ignored or censored in the German zones where, as we have seen, Abetz was projecting a favourable image of the occupier. The Germans soon had their own news agency, the Propaganda Abteilung, and a newsreel company, Actualités Mondiales, which got off to a shaky start as, initially, its commentators were not French. As Jackson continues, cabinet bickering also undermined Vichy's attempts to woo the public. During the early months of the regime, Laval was determined to keep the propaganda portfolio under his own wing, only to find that his opponents in government exploited other organs, in particular the Légion, to transmit a different message. In 1941, the ex-PPF man Paul Marion tried to rationalise Vichy's many propaganda departments but found the task too daunting and, ultimately, was undermined by Laval who, on his return to power in April 1942, put his own men in control. Small wonder, then, that Vichy propaganda was often badly thought out. Simon Kitson relates how posters proclaiming 'Police Nationale, Révolution Nationale', designed to project the police force, backfired as they implied that the National Revolution was another term for a police state (Kitson, 1995). Otherwise, Vichy propaganda was transparent: people could easily tell the difference between the idealised vision projected in official newsreels and the reality of their own lives.

This points to the third reason behind Vichy's unpopularity: the failure of the regime's policies which managed to alienate virtually everyone. National Revolution propaganda frequently eulogised the peasantry who benefited from Vichy's moves to improve rural housing and increase security of tenure. Yet the countryside, which had long considered itself neglected by Paris, was anxious for more concrete measures, and rapidly saw through the Corporation Paysanne which unashamedly advantaged large-scale producers. Industrial workers likewise had little time for their Charter which denied basic trade union rights and provided for the over-representation of business on the Comités d'Organisation (COs) which were supposed to implement a corporatist economy. While evidence remains impressionistic, it also appears that big business, largely located in the industrial north, felt abandoned by Vichy, although it was not averse to enlisting German assistance to enhance production and put down strikes. Students and teachers were another group of malcontents. Primary school-teachers smarted at the way in which they had been blamed for the defeat, and resented the manner in which Vichy cut their pay and curtailed their influence over what was taught in the classroom. Roger Austin has shown how, at ground level, Vichy's educational reforms were largely ineffectual; teachers largely carried on giving the same lessons, doing little to attract the attention of the authorities (Austin, 1981). Meanwhile, French youth refused to live up to Vichy's expectations. As Flonneau suggests, the student demonstration in Paris on Armistice Day, 11 November 1940, was not a one-off (Flonneau, 1992). In Clermont Ferrand, where the University of Strasbourg was in exile, students quickly rallied to de Gaulle, winning over several *lycéens* in the process. Protestant dissatisfaction with Vichy has already been commented upon; Catholics were not slow to follow suit. While a majority of the prelates, with some honourable exceptions such as

Théas and Saliège, remained loyal to the government, or at least to the marshal, rank-and-file Catholics, who had already begun to think for themselves in the 1930s, were going in a different direction. Vichy's anti-semitism, its growing authoritarianism, its limited concessions to the Church, its cosy relationship with Germany and Nazi persecution of Christians across the Rhine deeply troubled Catholic consciences. Vichy even failed to win the hearts and minds of the 1.5 million prisoners of war in Germany. Although the regime frequently praised their stoicism and discipline, which contrasted with the civil disobedience in metropolitan France, life in the *stalags* was unforgiving and, as Durand reflects, many prisoners felt forgotten by a government which seemed incapable of secur-ing their release (Durand, 1980). Ultimately, Vichy depended heavily on its core supporters: the middle-class and Pétainist *notables* who, in 1940, occupied positions of public authority. Yet even they were perturbed by the direction of the marshal's government. While Vichy's anti-Communism went down well, the general direction of the regime's foreign policy caused anxiety. Flonneau quotes the prefect of Clermont Ferrand who, in May 1941, spoke of how a majority of intellectuals and *bourgeois* were troubled by the government's deepening relationship with Germany (Flonneau, 1992).

The final factor that troubled public opinion was the shortage of food. Such scarcity was exacerbated by the disrupted harvests of 1940, the severe tariffs imposed by the Germans, the lack of manual labour, the disruption of transport, and the absence of farming equipment. Rationing, which had been introduced during the 'phoney war', became ever more stringent and, in September 1940, Vichy introduced a new system whereby food was allocated according to age and occupation. Workers in heavy industries, such as mining, received additional resources, as did pregnant women and breast-feeding mothers, although, in a further bid to promote the moral regeneration of France, women were denied tobacco coupons (Diamond, 1999: 51). Tickets were required for everything, queueing became standard practice (an opportunity for Vichy to place spies to find out what people were thinking), *ersatz* foodstuffs were commonplace, and a black market quickly flourished, sometimes actively encouraged by the Nazis [*Doc. 15*]. As the war progressed, quantities of food decreased: it is calculated that the daily consumption of bread was 430g per head in 1938; in September 1940 it was rationed to 350g; and in January 1942 it was reduced to 275g (Veillon and Flonneau, 1996). By 1944, many people in the Paris region were consuming less than 1,000 calories per day. Towns and cities quickly felt the pinch where, in a throwback to the *Ancien Régime*, food riots were frequent. Dominique Veillon cites the example of towns in the Var where, in the first five months of 1942, there were some 40 protests in front of empty shop windows (Veillon, 1995; Gordon, 1998: 368). In another throwback to the eighteenth century, townsfolk came to resent peasants who, it was believed, were deliberately hoarding produce for themselves and selling it on to the black market at hugely inflated prices. Pétain might have hoped for a return to the values of the *Ancien Régime*, yet it is doubtful that this is what he had in mind.

Without question, food shortages affected women the most. It was they who had to juggle the family budget; it was they who had to get out of bed at an extraordinarily early hour to queue for goods that had already been sold; it was they who, given the shortage of electricity and basic commodities such as fat, had to devise fresh recipes and discover new ways of cooking; it was they who had to work the black market; and it was they who, in the words of Hanna Diamond, had to devise 'strategies for survival', overcoming material hardships (Diamond, 1999: 69). Within French society, a woman's role had traditionally been that of a homemaker, and the circumstances of the Occupation only served to reinforce that position, especially given the fact that 1.5 million men were held as POWs in Germany. Vichy was likewise keen to emphasise the place of a woman as a dutiful wife and mother, and thus overturned what rights women had won under the Republic. Housecraft classes were made compulsory for girls in schools; Mother's Day was given particular prominence; a fierce campaign was led against abortion; post-natal facilities were improved; and the *Code de la Famille* was extended to encourage parents to have larger families. The Church, in turn, warmly applauded these initiatives [*Doc. 14*]. All too often, however, the humdrum of everyday existence contrasted with Vichy's idealised vision of motherhood. As Diamond relates, the regime probably made matters worse when, on 11 October 1940, it forbade married women from working in the public sector if their husbands were able to support the family, and insisted on women's retirement at the age of 50 (Diamond, 1999: 31–6). This exacerbated women's unemployment which was already severe following the closure of several munitions factories after the Armistice. In the event, women had little option but to work, and employers had little choice other than to employ them. So it was that, on 12 September 1942, Vichy suspended most of the clauses of the October 1940 legislation, although it still emphasised that a woman's place was in the home. The regime's double standards were further highlighted when it agreed that women should no longer be exempted from STO. This move was fiercely resisted by the Churches and was scuppered by the Liberation; nonetheless, some 70,000 women were employed by the Germans within France.

Women, then, constitute another element of society dissatisfied with the Pétain regime. Boasting of its grip on realities, the government had hoped to bring about a massive transformation of French society based on the values of *travail, famille, patrie*. In the event, it brought about *tracas, faim, patrouilles* ('bother, hunger, surveillance'). While for some the marshal remained a reassuring figure, his much vaunted National Revolution was an abstract and remote experiment. Wartime was never the best environment to launch such a venture, and it was the circumstances of wartime – the defeat, the Armistice, the division of France into zones, the German presence, and material shortages – that ultimately ruled people's lives. Vichy always hoped that its foreign policy would alleviate these stresses, yet negotiations with Germany resulted in little. Why this was so is the question to be addressed next.

CHAPTER FIVE

COLLABORATION

When analysing the realm of collaboration, the initial task is to scrape away the mythology carefully constructed by Vichy apologists. They usually peddle one, or both, of two arguments. First, it is claimed that the overtures for collaboration derived from Germany, not from France. While de Gaulle acted as the 'sword', carrying out resistance overseas, Pétain and his government did their best to 'shield' French men and women from the excesses of Nazi pressure, ensuring that France escaped the misfortune of 'Polandization', an allusion to the terrible fate that Hitler visited on that country. The second claim, closely related to the first, is that the marshal secretly played a double game with the Germans, maintaining regular contacts with Britain, thereby thwarting Berlin's wishes (Rougier, 1946; Girard, 1948). For such apologists, the one person at Vichy who was genuinely interested in cooperating with the Reich was Laval who, conveniently enough, had few defenders outside his immediate family in the period straight after the war (Chambrun, 1990).

The above claims have little foundation. The release of German, British, American and French archives have demonstrated that it was Vichy which courted Berlin, not the other way around. The same documents have also displayed that Pétain and his ministers had far more in common with the Paris fascists than has sometimes been appreciated, thus calling into question the contrast historians sometimes make between the *collaboration d'état* of Vichy and the ideological *collaborationisme* of Déat and his cronies (Hoffmann, 1968). While this distinction, first made by Stanley Hoffmann, is helpful, it should be noted that Vichy kept in regular contact with the Paris *collabos*. During Darlan's ministry in 1941, former PPF men Paul Marion and Pucheu found their way into government; in 1942, Laval brought in yet more creatures of the extreme right; in 1944, Vichy was brimming with fascists. Moreover, ideological links existed. The men of Vichy and the men of Paris were alike in their desire for a German victory, in their antisemitism, in their anglophobia, in their fear of social order, and in their wish to build a new France. By 1944, many of these hopes and fears would focus on the *Milice* which both collaborators and collaborationists viewed as France's salvation.

COLLABORATION D'ÉTAT

The two men initially concerned with the elaboration of Vichy foreign policy were Pétain and Laval. While the latter had extensive experience of international affairs, the marshal was not well practised in the arts of diplomacy, despite his brief tenure as ambassador to Spain in 1939. He did, however, have firm notions about what he hoped to achieve. Initially, he sought to lessen the impact of the Armistice, securing the release of the 1.5 million prisoners of war, whose fate weighed heavily on his mind. By negotiating with Berlin, he also hoped to establish time in which the National Revolution could take root and prosper. Ultimately, he believed that he would be able to secure a favourable peace settlement which would permit France to recover its former prestige. In this respect, his mind was as much on his own posterity as on French interests. As Kedward has shown, by facilitating the moral restoration of France, together with the restitution of its international standing, the marshal would have again saved his country, much as he had done in the First World War (Kedward, 1985a: 32). It could not be a military triumph such as that he executed in 1916; instead, in Louis-Dominique Girard's famous phrase, it would be a 'Verdun diplomatique' (Girard, 1948).

To bring about these ends, Pétain was reluctant to involve himself in active diplomacy, just as he was disinclined to partake personally in politicking. He considered only a personal meeting with Hitler would suffice, and trusted a series of envoys – Colonel Fonck, a former flying ace, Georges Scapini, a veterans' leader, and Laval – with the task of bringing about this top-level conference (Griffiths, 1970). Laval, of course, had been chosen precisely because of his ability as a wheeler-dealer, a skill notable in his destruction of the Republic. Historians usually make play of the differences between the marshal and his *dauphin*: Pétain the soldier, Laval the shifty politician; Pétain the well-turned-out head of state, Laval seemingly scruffy in a white cravat which emphasised his swarthiness; Pétain the abstemious smoker who limited himself to five cigarettes a day, Laval the *fumeur par excellence* who was always photographed with *Gitanes* dangling out of his mouth. There were also differences in their perception of collaboration. Geoffrey Warner has shown how Laval, through his appreciation of history and distaste for battle, considered it essential that Germany and France should arrive at some mutual understanding in order to avoid repeated conflicts (Warner, 1968). To achieve that end, Laval had despaired of the parliamentary democracy which had served him so well in the past, and believed only an authoritarian republic could bring about the necessary *rapprochement*. In this sense, he had no plans for a National Revolution as did Pétain, yet in many other regards they were at one in their foreign policy objectives. Both believed that a German victory would have several benefits for France. It would halt the tide of Bolshevism, it would end the influence of Britain in Europe, and it would guarantee social stability at home. No wonder the marshal put up with his leading minister for so long.

Whereas Pétain trusted in discreet approaches to Berlin, Laval was more direct, and was confident that he could deploy France's assets, notably its navy and empire, to bring about a favourable deal (Thomas, 1998). He built up especially close relations with Otto Abetz, who was appointed 'ambassador' to France and who was charged with conducting political relations with Vichy. As I have remarked before, while Laval and Pétain made an odd couple, it was not hard to understand why Laval and Abetz got on so well: both came from modest backgrounds; both had been teachers, Laval albeit briefly before taking up law; both had flirted with socialism before drifting to the right; both had expressed a desire for Franco–German friendship; both disliked war as an instrument of policy; both were great talkers; both had hugely inflated notions of their own importance; both could be bullies; and both exercised little real power (Atkin, 2000). Berlin retained a suspicion of Abetz, thanks to his professed Francophilia and French wife. Hitler need not have worried. While Abetz had perhaps once been genuine in his wish for Franco-German friendship, in the 1930s he had fallen under the spell of Nazism, was a fervent disciple of the Führer and believed in the supremacy of German culture. Before the war, through his many contacts in France, especially in the cultural body Comité France-Allemagne, he had deployed diplomatic means to persuade the French of the merits of the Nazi system. In July 1940, his true colours shone through as he prepared the 'Strasbourg memorandum' in which he made clear that everything should be done to ensure the internal division of the country he supposedly loved. He was thus happy to fulfil his allotted task of 'divide and rule', making extravagant promises to Laval and lavishly entertaining the *collabos* while disseminating disunity among them.

Typical of the topsy-turvy world of Hitler's empire, Abetz was not the sole German agency dealing with France. There was also the Armistice Commission at Wiesbaden and the Military Command in Brussels. All, however, were instructed to make no real concessions to the French, a race Hitler despised. At the close of the war, he had no intention of permitting the recovery of France as a nation, but instead looked towards the break-up of the country into smaller parts, a policy already apparent in the creation of several zones. This helps explain why the Germans actively encouraged separatists such as the fascist journalist Yann Fouéré in Brittany. If Hitler was ever to do business with Vichy, then it was going to be very much on his terms.

That moment came in October 1940. Already planning ahead for his invasion of the Soviet Union and anxious to prosecute the war against Britain in the Mediterranean, Hitler toyed with the idea of a loose alliance of Latin European states – comprising Spain, Italy and France, very much the junior partner – in an attempt to protect Germany's back. To explore the idea, he spoke first with Mussolini, and then travelled for discussions with Franco at Hendaye. As the Führer's special train snaked its way through France on its way to Spain, on 22 October the German leader met with Laval at the little town of Montoire-sur-Loir. Expecting an interview with Ribbentrop, Laval arranged a second encounter for two days later when Hitler was making his return to Germany. It was at this meeting that Pétain realised his dream of a top-level conference with the Nazi leader. Typically, at the first interview, Laval had been forthright and enthusiastic, pressing for concessions and making vague promises in return. The second meeting, again unscripted although faithfully transcribed, was a rambling affair, Pétain agreeing to the principle of collaboration, and both sides anxious to emphasise their respect for each other [*Doc. 16*]. The archives of the Reich Foreign Ministry have since revealed that the Germans had, in preparation for Montoire, prepared documents which would have brought France into the war alongside the Axis powers, albeit as a junior power, to be rewarded by British colonies at the end of the fighting. It is Warner who has explained why these papers were never handed over (Warner, 1968: 238–9). Hitler retained deep misgivings about France; he disliked Laval, although he admired Pétain; he had been disheartened by the lukewarm response of Mussolini and the downright obstinacy of Franco; and he rightly calculated that he could get what he wanted without giving anything away to Vichy which seemed keen enough to defend its colonies against the British, thus raising the possibility of an Anglo-French war.

For their part, the French delegates were disappointed that the meetings did not result in any major revision of the Armistice. A few POWs were released, France was given greater rights of protection over prisoners held in Germany, but that was it. There was no relaxation of the Demarcation Line, no let up in the financial demands of the Armistice Commission, and no further high-level interviews with German heads of state, although one was apparently promised with Ribbentrop for December, something which was scuppered by Laval's dismissal on the 13th of that month. The postwar claims made by the Vichy apologist Girard that Montoire equalled a 'Verdun diplomatique', rescuing France from further German pressure and deterring Hitler from pressing his claims in French North Africa, should be treated with a pinch of salt. Historians now agree that the real significance of Montoire was symbolic. On 30 October, the marshal took to the radio and announced that he had sat face to face with Hitler. 'A collaboration has been envisaged between our two countries', he announced, 'I have accepted the principle of it. This collaboration must be sincere.' While some of his audience believed that this must be part of his double-game strategy, others were disturbed that such a patriot should have agreed to the proposition of collaboration. Photographs displaying the two leaders shaking hands, photographs which Richard Carswell has shown appeared freely in the press of the Occupied zone and in a select number of Vichy papers, were hardly reassuring (Carswell, 1999). Nor was the reaction of the *collabos*. Although some bemoaned the fact that the marshal had been too lukewarm in his support for collaboration, others saw this as a sign that Vichy was now going to march firmly in step with Germany.

The disappointment of Montoire also had repercussions within Vichy itself, strengthening Pétain's dislike of Laval. In this regard, apologists claim the marshal eventually acted against his deputy because he was a liability to the secret negotiations that were being conducted with the British through two envoys, Professor Rougier and the Canadian Jean Dupuy. As R.T. Thomas and Robert Frank have shown, while Vichy certainly did talk to London, this was never part of a double-game diplomacy (Thomas, 1979; Frank, 1992). The meetings only revealed the enormous chasm that now existed between the former allies. Rather, Pétain had other motives in getting rid of his *dauphin*. Laval had been brought into government because of his ability to get things done; he no longer seemed able to do this. Meanwhile, his arrogance knew no bounds. He was openly dismissive of the National Revolution and displayed little respect to the marshal when in his presence, often surrounding the old man in plumes of cigarette smoke. To Pétain, Laval also seemed increasingly a loose cannon. In November, it was learned that the Belgian gold reserves and Bor copper mines, entrusted to France for safekeeping, had been handed over to Berlin without Laval uttering a murmur of protest. The time he spent in the Occupied zone, mixing with Abetz and Déat, raised further paranoia. What was he doing there? What was he agreeing to? What was he plotting? Was he planning an alternative French collaborationist administration in Paris under his leadership? Notions that Laval was insatiable for power, rumours almost certainly fanned by British agents at Vichy, were shared by members of the marshal's entourage. Griffiths has shown how Baudouin disliked the way in which Laval had usurped his post as foreign minister and excluded him from Montoire; Bouthillier, at finance, was smarting at the Belgian gold and Bor copper incidents; Peyrouton, in his post as interior minister, was certain that Laval was after his job (Griffiths, 1970). They thus agreed to press Pétain to sack his deputy. The opportunity came in December when, in a spontaneous act typical of his personality, Hitler returned to France the ashes of the Duc de Reichstadt, Napoleon's son. A reinterment ceremony was planned in Paris and the marshal was invited 'to attend'. Mistakenly fearing this was a ruse to ensnare him and force him to take collaborationists into a new government headed by Laval, Pétain refused to go, prompting Laval to drive down to Vichy on 13 December. This is when the plotters struck, persuading the marshal that the time was ripe to rid himself of his troublesome *dauphin*. That evening, in the manner of the Third Republic, Pétain asked each one of his ministers to resign, only accepting the signatures of Laval and Ripert, the education minister who wanted to go anyway to make room for Chevalier, a traditionalist more in keeping with the type of man with whom the marshal now wished to surround himself.

Paradoxically, Pétain replaced one parliamentarian with another in the shape of Pierre-Etienne Flandin, former leader of the Alliance Démo-cratique and a *munichois*, who took over Laval's job as foreign minister. Later sentenced to a symbolic 12 hours of national degradation by the High Court of Justice, Flandin's tenure at Vichy was almost as short, marked by its inability to arouse any German excitement in collaboration and by a complete failure to get on with Abetz who was sulking that his great friend had been forced out of office. So it was that, in February 1941, the marshal called on Darlan to take over at foreign affairs, as well as anointing him *dauphin* and nominally charging him with several other ministries. Once viewed as the unprincipled opportunist, who sided first with Vichy and later with the Americans, Darlan has been more sympathetically treated in recent years. Hervé Coutau-Bégarie and Claude Huan have persuasively argued that the admiral possessed a strategic vision similar in scope to de Gaulle's (Coutau-Bégarie and Huan, 1989). At the end of a protracted war, Darlan foresaw the emergence of two camps: while the European and African continents would be dominated by Germany, the USA would prevail elsewhere, supported by a weakened Britain, shorn of its colonies. The authors further suggest that Darlan attempted to adopt a middle, and neutral, course between these two blocs. The evidence is not convincing. An ugly antisemite (it was during his period of office that the CGQJ was set up), determinedly anti-Bolshevik (it was under him that Communists were summarily handed over as hostages to be shot by the Germans), a believer in an authoritarian republic (during his tenure of office technocrats were appointed in number), and a decided anglophobe, Darlan always leant towards the Nazis. As Paxton has shown, the admiral believed he could carve out an imperial and naval role for France in the new world order, his so-called 'Grand Design' (Paxton, 1972). It was only under intense US pressure, when trapped in Algiers in November 1942, that he gracelessly went over to the Allies, only to arouse a storm of indignation among American and British public opinion which was shocked that their leaders could consort with such a man. His assassination on Christmas Eve that year was a relief to everyone.

As well as sharing with Laval in his like of smoking – a vast collection of pipes was found in his tent after his death – Darlan was similar in that he had little clue how to interest the Germans in collaboration. The difference lay in that Laval was far more restrained in what he was prepared to give away. In the words of Jean-Baptiste Duroselle, Darlan conceived a policy of 'donnant donnant' ('give and take'), yet all too often he seemed to be giving instead of receiving anything back (Duroselle, 1981). The flaws in his policy were displayed in May 1941 when, once again, wider developments in the war led the Germans to limited negotiations with the French. Rommel's advance in North Africa and the eruption of an anti-British revolt in Iraq opened Berlin's eyes to the usefulness of French air bases at Aleppo and Palmyra in Syria, as well as the Tunisian port of Bizerte. Vichy agreed to the restricted use of these depots, but sought something more. On 28 May 1941, Darlan signed the so-called Paris Protocols, the first three of which provided for greater German access to these strategic centres, French naval protection of German Mediterranean convoys and the creation of a U-Boat base at Dakar. There was a fourth complementary protocol, authored by Benoist-Méchin and only signed by Abetz, who of course carried little authority, that foresaw the release of French First World War veterans held as POWs, a relaxation of the Demarcation Line and reduced occupation costs. For Darlan, this was the first stage to the definitive peace settlement that Laval had failed to secure. It was nothing of the sort. British success against the Iraqi rebels, and the start of the German campaign in the USSR, led Berlin to disregard the Protocols which, ultimately, were worth little.

This whole episode exposed Darlan's poor judgement, argues Paxton. If the agreements had gone ahead, it is likely that France would have suffered heavy British reprisals and might have re-entered the war alongside the Axis, something which Pétain wanted to avoid and something which would have antagonised public opinion. Darlan was only marginally more popular than Laval; when a lone voice amid a crowd shouting 'Vive Pétain' cried out 'Vive Darlan', the marshal turned round to the admiral and quipped, 'I did not know you were a ventriloquist'. Undeterred, Darlan pressed ahead with yet further meetings with senior Nazi personnel, conducting an interview with Göring at Saint-Florentin on 1 September 1941, where the marshal apparently ended up by stuffing a series of French demands into the obstinate German's pockets. Unable to break the foreign policy impasse, at the end of 1941 Darlan was spending much of his time guarding his back against ministerial intrigues. In November he was instrumental in securing the dismissal of Weygand as High Commissioner in French North Africa, who earlier in June had vigorously argued against the Paris Protocols. Contrary to what is sometimes thought, Weygand was not in the process of rallying the French colonial army to fight alongside either the Gaullists or the British but, as a true Germanophobe, he was seriously concerned about Vichy's pro-Axis foreign policy, and still had influence over the marshal, hence Darlan's preemptive strike.

In April 1942, in order to kick-start Franco-German negotiations, Pétain reluctantly conceded that he had little choice other than to recall Laval, who was reinstated as deputy prime minister and *dauphin*. It was a very different international situation from that of summer 1940. Then France had possessed its navy and colonies, important bargaining tools; by 1942 much of the empire had gone over to de Gaulle. In 1940, Britain had stood alone against the Axis; by 1942, the USA and USSR had entered the war, although Germany was still enjoying a series of military victories. In 1940, the German economy was brimming with the spoils of victory; by 1942, it was suffering from 'total war'. This led Fritz Sauckel, the Reich's plenipotentiary for labour and a fervent Francophobe, to demand 250,000 men from Vichy. Laval's response was to haggle and procrastinate, and the resulting compromise of 16 June 1942 was a characteristic piece of his diplomacy. This was the *Relève* scheme by which one French prisoner of war would be returned for every three French skilled workers who volunteered to work in German factories. On 22 June, when he took to the airwaves to broadcast his deal, Laval uttered a sentence which, historians agree, is better remembered than any one of Pétain's broadcasts: 'I desire the victory of Germany for without it Bolshevism will install itself everywhere' [*Doc. 23*]. As Kedward says, it was this phrase which guaranteed the Auvergnat's place in front of a firing post in 1945 (Kedward, 1985a). In truth, Laval was not expressing any new sentiment; he had always been steadfastly anti-Communist and, as Jean-Paul Cointet relates, he had used the same speech some ten days earlier at a convention of the Légion (J.P. Cointet, 1993). At his own trial, Pétain tried to dissociate himself from the broadcast yet, as Warner and Griffiths have shown, he had in fact personally approved an earlier draft which contained the offending words (Warner, 1968; Griffiths, 1970).

Inevitably the *Relève* never enticed sufficient workers to voyage to Germany (maybe 49,000 in total) thus ensuring further pressure which, in September 1942, led Laval to take the first steps towards the compulsory recruitment of labour. This plan coincided with the massive deportations of Jews from France to the east. By that stage, the Holocaust was well under way and, in summer 1942, Vichy was faced with demands to hand over significant numbers of Jews. In response, Laval negotiated the arrangement whereby foreign Jews would be handed over in preference to French-born ones. This sordid deal done, René Bousquet, Vichy's head of police, and Darquier de Pellepoix, the new head of the CGQJ, readily provided French help in the round-ups, a task made easier by the recent requirement in the Occupied zone that Jews should wear the Yellow Star of David on an outer garment. On 16 July 1942, some 13,152 Jews, mainly of foreign origin, among them 4,115 children, were herded together in atrocious conditions in the Vél d'Hiv, an indoor sports arena in Paris, near the Eiffel tower, before being transferred to a half-built housing estate at Drancy in the suburbs, and thence to Auschwitz. Some 50 years later Mitterrand would declare 16 July a 'national day of mourning', although he was at pains to stress that the French state was not at fault for this terrible incident but Vichy itself, which he conveniently labelled an 'illegitimate regime'.

These round-ups shook public opinion, which had not been unduly concerned about antisemitism in the past, and revealed the extent to which Vichy was pandering to German wishes. The questionable degree of Vichy's autonomy was highlighted further on 11 November 1942 when, in response to the Allied landings in Morocco and Algeria three days earlier as part of Operation Torch, German troops occupied the whole of France. While Laval attempted to rescue something out of the situation, seeking German reassurances, the marshal considered whether this was the point that he should quit France for North Africa where Darlan was already talking to the Allies. Several of his close entourage suggested such a solution, yet he feebly replied that his heart was not up to the flight across the Mediterranean. It has since been rumoured that he was embarrassed by his incontinence which would have been exposed on the plane. It is more likely that his reasons for staying were the same as in June 1940. He still considered it dishonourable to leave his country in its hour of need. He still retained a compassion for the French people, although the selective nature of that humanity had been vividly exposed. He was still set on the National Revolution, even though it had been mocked by Darlan and Laval. Astonishingly, he still believed that something could be retrieved from the situation and that the Germans would make concessions, despite the fact that an Allied victory was now all the more certain. And, of course, he still thought about his reputation. By standing alongside his people, by engineering a revival of traditional values, by securing a definitive peace, he would be heralded as the greatest saviour in his country's history.

If the marshal had left, the Americans would undoubtedly have made him head of the French Resistance, although it is also likely that de Gaulle would still have outfoxed his former mentor. Even so, Pétain would probably today be recalled as a hero, misguided perhaps in his earlier actions, but a man strong enough to acknowledge his mistakes, instead of being remembered as a supine leader who presided over an enfeebled and immoral regime which did many of the Germans' squalid misdeeds for them. Indeed, the final months of the Occupation witnessed the evaporation of Vichy's remaining autonomy and the growth of unprecedented civil unrest, much of it precipitated by the formal introduction of STO in February 1943 which obliged men between the ages of 18 and 50, and ultimately women, to work on behalf of the Reich. Meanwhile, Laval haggled over further deportations of Jews, and did at least refuse to deprive further quotas of French Jews of their citizenship. For his part, Pétain resented being reduced to a figurehead and tried to reassert his authority by attempting another *coup* against his deputy in autumn 1943, this time unsuccessfully. That November, irritated by Berlin's endless demands, the old man went 'on strike', refusing to sign any legislation put before him and drawing up a broadcast, stymied by the Germans, announcing his displeasure. For some historians, this is one of his moments of bravery, albeit belated bravery, when he at last stood up to the occupier. For others, it is the action of a vain and obstinate leader who had failed to take earlier action. Whatever the case, his *grève* was shortlived and precipitated further German controls. In came the fascist ministers he had previously resisted; in came a German *Gauleiter* Renthe-Finck, assisted by SS guards, to watch over matters; and with them, came yet further demands for Jews, workers and the crushing of internal resistance. One aspect of Vichy's collaboration had always been to forestall social and civil unrest, yet successive foreign policy failures resulted in exactly that. As Paxton has shown, the balance sheet of Vichy's foreign policy was not impressive: 120,000 POWs released; the retention of control of important military bases in Morocco and Dakar; the occasional reduction of occupation costs; and the requirement for Jews not to wear the Yellow Star in the southern zone. In return, concludes Paxton, the Germans secured the neutrality of the French state and obtained a tremendous contribution to their war effort, all without spending a 'single mark' (Azéma and Bédarida, 1993; Paxton, 1993: 361).

COLLABORATIONISME

If, in the final months of the Occupation, Pétain and his ministers lived in a surreal, looking-glass world in which they deluded themselves that they actually exercised some sway over the Germans, the same was true of those French collaborationists in Paris who were ideologically attracted to Nazism. Making sense of these fascists is no easy task. Journalists, intellectuals, writers, artists, *liguers*, various n'er-do-wells, criminals and black-market racketeers, they constituted a heterogeneous group which was characterised by internal squabbles, rivalries and competing overtures for German favour. One of the best oversights into this twilight world is provided by Philippe Burrin, who identifies three tendencies: the first, an eclectic mix of former socialists, congregating around Déat; the second, a cultural body gravitating towards Châteaubriant; and third, a 'hard right' which centred on Doriot (Burrin, 1995).

The muddled world of the collaborationists is immediately revealed by a glance at the career and political associates of Marcel Déat. A former schoolteacher and decorated First World War veteran, Déat's quarrels with Blum led him to leave the Socialist Party in 1933 to found the Parti Socialiste de France (PSF) and edit *L'Œuvre*, a *munichois* and anti-

Communist newspaper which, in 1939, printed the infamous headline 'Must one die for Danzig?', an allusion to the conflict over the Polish corridor. In July 1940, he travelled to Vichy with ambitious plans for a *parti unique*, a scheme that was rejected by Pétain and Laval, who both feared that such an instrument might end up in the wrong hands. Disillusioned, Déat returned to Paris where he resumed his journalistic activities – he was always a frustrated 'man of letters' – attacking Vichy for its timidity, traditionalism and clericalism. Such attacks ensured his arrest on 13 December 1940, the day on which Laval was sacked by the marshal. Freed shortly afterwards by Abetz, Déat threw himself more completely into the world of collaboration and, in February 1941, established the Rassemblement National Populaire (RNP), which historians agree was the first political body of note to have been set up since the defeat. Hoping that this would become the dominant collaborationist organisation, he cultivated several links, bringing in Georges Albertini, another ex-teacher and socialist, who had been busying himself with his own Parti National Populaire (PNP) in his home department of the Aube. Elaborating an anti-Communist position, favouring a totalitarian republic and advocating a radical programme of wealth redistribution, the RNP also built up ties with the extreme rightist, Eugène Deloncle. Another distinguished First World War veteran, Deloncle had parted company with the AF, which he saw as too traditional, and, in 1936, founded the Comité Secret d'Action Révolutionnaire (CSAR), better known as the Cagoule, a terrorist body which developed links in the army and which specialised in bombing synagogues and political murders, notably Carlo and Nello Rosselli, two Italian critics of Mussolini (Gordon, 1998: 102). In 1940, Deloncle set up the Mouvement Social Révolutionnaire (MSR), a pro-Pétainist association which emulated the Cagoule by blowing up Jewish properties and partaking in further political killings, possibly that of Marx Dornoy, the former interior minister who had ordered Deloncle's arrest in 1937. It was also rumoured that Deloncle was behind the failed assassination attempt on Déat and Laval in August 1941. Whatever the case, he never hit it off with the RNP leader and they split in 1942. Given his barbarous past, it was perhaps appropriate that Deloncle should have come to a violent end in a rain of gun fire in 1944, shot by either the Resistance, MSR agents or the *Gestapo*, who were troubled that he had flirted with the British and Darlan in North Africa.

It will be recalled that a second loose grouping of collaborationists emanated from literary and artistic circles. They included Robert Brasillach, editor of *Je Suis Partout* and a fanatical anti-Communist; Louis Ferdinand Céline, a novelist whose first book, *Voyage au bout de la nuit* (1932), had been applauded for its revolutionary style, only for the author to become an obsessive antisemite; Pierre Drieu la Rochelle, novelist, editor of the Nouvelle Revue Française (NRF) and former PPF member; Jean Giono, another innovative writer and vehement pacifist (he was a veteran of Verdun); and Henry de Montherlant, a prewar anti-fascist and supporter of the Popular Front who, in 1940, decided to use his considerable literary talents in support of collaborationism. Many of these intellectuals wrote for *La Gerbe*, the newspaper of Alphonse de Châteaubriant, which revelled in antisemitism and advocacy of the New Order [*Doc. 17*]. In 1940, Châteaubriant established Groupe Collaboration, a rather up-market body which attracted prominent intellectuals such as Georges Claude, Abel Bonnard and Abel Hermant. As Kay Chadwick has shown, Châteaubriant arrived at his collaboration through his Catholicism (Chadwick, 1994). A keen admirer of Hitler, he saw the Führer as the reincarnation of Charlemagne, who would bring about the reunification of Catholic Europe. As Chadwick has further demonstrated, the Catholic Church was fortunate that it included few true collaborators, otherwise its postwar record would have been even more in tatters: Mgr Dutoit, the bishop of Arras; Mgr Mayol de Lupé, chaplain of the LVF; and Cardinal Baudrillart, the octogenarian rector of the Institut Catholique in Paris, already senile and whose pro-German views were so outrageous that Cardinal Suhard, archbishop of Paris, frequently felt obliged to apologise for him (Chadwick, 1998). Unlike Déat and his cronies, who preferred to live in Paris, Catholic collaborationists gravitated to Bordeaux where they were tolerated by the bishop, Mgr Feltin, later archbishop of Paris in 1949, and where they could use the local clerical presses to print such poisonous publications as the *Soutanes de France*.

The remaining group of collaborationists, identified by Burrin, constituted a hard right, although its advocates had often started life as Communists. This 'droite musclée' comprised: the Parti Ouvrier et Paysan Français (POPF), a Paris-based body established by the ex-Communist Marcel Gitton; the Centre Syndicaliste de Propagande (CSP), which was behind the newspaper *L'Atelier*; and the group France–Europe (Socialisme et Nation), headed by the ex-Socialists Francis Desphelippon and Paul Rives, which published the journal *La France socialiste* (Burrin, 1993). Together, these newspapers were scathing of Vichy's reactionary nature, denouncing the regime as a front for the *bourgeoisie* and *patronat*. Their efforts were eclipsed by the former Communist, Jacques Doriot. Another distinguished veteran of the First World War, a former secretary of the Internationale Communiste des Jeunes, and mayor of the Parisian working-class suburb of Saint-Denis, it will be recalled that Doriot had split from the PCF for advocating a 'union of the left' against fascism before Moscow had given its approval for such an alliance. In 1936, he had founded the PPF, taking with him some 300,000 supporters who warmed to his new anti-Communist message. In 1940 Doriot, like Déat, made his way to Vichy, only for his services to be similarly rejected. He subsequently became one of the most prominent *collabos*, but retained an admiration for the marshal which he frequently advertised in his paper, *Le Cri du Peuple* (Burrin, 1986).

Doriot discovered his true vocation in June 1941 when Germany invaded the Soviet Union. Two months later, alongside Déat, Deloncle and Marcel Bucard, he unveiled a new organisation, the Légion des Volontaires Français contre le Bolchevisme (LVF), whose headquarters in Paris were the old premises of Aeroflot. By the close of the year, the LVF had raised a regiment of French volunteers to fight on the eastern front and received a letter of encouragement from Pétain, although it was later claimed that this message had been forged by de Brinon. Whatever the case, in 1942 Vichy gave its official sanction to a new body, the Légion Tricolore which, under the control of General Jaly and Colonel Puaud, had authorisation to recruit men from the French army to fight alongside the *Wehrmacht* both in Russia and on other fronts. It is calculated that anywhere between 40,000 and 50,000 Frenchmen donned German uniform, many of them killed by the Soviets. In 1944–45, those still alive helped form the *Charlemagne* division of the SS, whose final task, as Jean-Paul Cointet wryly observes, was to defend Hitler's bunker in Berlin (Cointet and Cointet, 2000). Doriot, who had spent most of the war in Russia, was killed in 1944 following an attack by two unidentified aeroplanes.

The collaborationists never achieved much popularity. In his seminal 1978 study, Bertram Gordon calculated their membership to be around 150,000 (Gordon, 1978). Burrin has recently raised that figure to 250,000, although that sum includes the *Milice* and covers the whole of the Occupation period (Burrin, 1995). It is generally agreed that the biggest movement was Groupe Collaboration which boasted 100,000 members, closely followed by Francisme (50,000), the PPF (30,000) and the RNP (20,000), but all fascist organisations were prone to exaggeration. Occasionally, they calculated their membership according to sales of their newspapers which, as Pascal Ory has shown, were impressive: between 1940 and January 1943, *La Gerbe* sold 140,000 copies; *Je Suis Partout*, 125,000; *L'Œuvre*, 131,000; and *Le Cri du Peuple*, 58,000 (Ory, 1976). Yet, as Parisians joked, people bought the collaborationist press because German subsidies ensured it was printed on better quality paper than other journals; it was thus better for lining drawers and starting fires in the hearth. What is clear is that collaborationists predominated in the Occupied zone, largely because Vichy made it difficult for them to operate in the south. Support was also centred in Paris and other urban areas. Ory quotes the examples of the departments of the Côte d'Or and Mayenne, where membership was concentrated in towns such as Dijon. It is said that the Nazis could afford more protection to their supporters in the cities as collaborationists were always vulnerable to Resistance attacks. In terms of their social composition, they tended to originate from the middle classes,

Plate 1 The right-wing protests of 6 February 1934 were so well supported that they gave rise to the fear of a possible *coup d'état*. This photograph illustrates the fighting in the Place de la Concorde, opposite the Chamber of Deputies.
© Collection Roger-Viollet

Plate 2 In expectation of the Popular Front electoral victory of June 1936, thousands of workers improvised strikes and demonstrations, which often took on a celebratory atmosphere. This photograph depicts a Communist march at Boulogne-Billancourt, Paris. © Collection Roger-Viollet

Plate 3 The meeting between Hitler and Pétain on 24 October 1940 at Montoire was of symbolic status rather than diplomatic importance. This photograph of the two men shaking hands, released in sections of the French press, caused astonishment. © Collection Roger-Viollet

Plate 4 Part of Marshal Pétain's enormous popularity during the Occupation stemmed from the fact that he was a hero people could see and hear, conducting extensive tours of the Unoccupied zone. This photograph is of a crowd of people listening to him speak at Thiers, 1 May 1942.   © Collection Roger-Viollet

Plate 5 Because of German requisitioning and material shortages, queueing became a regular part of life during the Occupation. As this photograph of a Parisian bakers of August 1944 displays, it was a chore that fell primarily to women.
© Collection Roger-Viollet

Plate 6 The first major round-up of Jews in the Occupied zone took place on 16 July 1942 when some 14,000, among them 4,000 children, were herded into the Parisian sports stadium, the Vél d'Hiv. From there they were escorted to the half-built housing estate of Drancy, pictured here, which has been called the 'antechamber of Auschwitz'.
© Collection Roger-Viollet

Plate 7 Initially wary of enlisting French volunteers into German uniform, later in the war, the Germans consented to this to fight both Communism abroad and resistance within France: 'SIDE BY SIDE AGAINST THE COMMON ENEMY!'.
© Collection Roger-Viollet

Plate 8   Although the unofficial purges of 1944 were not as severe as some later claimed, there were often disparities in the meting-out of justice. As this picture shows, women suspected of collaboration had their heads shaved and swastikas daubed on their chests.
© Collection Roger-Viollet

especially the liberal professions. Drawing on figures compiled by the CHDGM in the 1970s, Burrin has illustrated how both the peasantry and working class were under represented (Burrin, 1993). Collaborationists were also young and, with the exception of the PPF and Francisme, do not appear to have been members of political parties before 1940, suggesting that the peculiar circumstances of the Occupation somehow radicalised elements of the population. Women were not prominent. By summer 1941, only 57 women had signed up to collaborationist movements in the Mayenne, principally the RNP; groupings in the Côte d'Or claimed a similar total of 58. Overall, it has been calculated that women constituted a mere 15 per cent of all collaborationist movements, although the recent research of Hanna Diamond has suggested that this figure might be an underestimate (Diamond, 1999). Belonging to a collaborationist movement, she writes, could bring prestige, money (especially if working for the Germans), excitement, responsibility, and escape from the drudgery of everyday life. It is generally acknowledged, however, that if women did collaborate, they did so in 'individualistic, opportunistic and unorganized forms' such as 'denunciation' and sleeping with German soldiers, *la collaboration horizontale* (Diamond, 1999: 97).

The reasons collaborationist movements remained unpopular are not hard to perceive. To join was a brave decision in much the same way as joining the Resistance was a brave decision. Nor did the collaborationists put on a united front. Personal jealousies were fierce. Déat and Doriot could not stand each other, thus scuppering the idea of a single party. Ideological differences, especially from the prewar years, also persisted. Deloncle could not tolerate Doriot's earlier Communism, while Déat banished Deloncle from the RNP because of his rightist sympathies; Deloncle himself was expelled from the MSR by his former supporters. The attacks on Pétain might also have backfired on the collaborationists. Certainly Vichy itself was eager to restrain the *collabos*. Laval might have shared their company when in Paris, but knew full well the dangers of a united party, and did his bit to foment division. So too did the occupier. Initially, the German military authorities took no notice of these Nazi 'wannabes', yet Abetz did. It was his job to 'divide and rule', handing out money, exacerbating jealousies, spreading gossip and exploiting the *collabos* for his own ends. Burrin has shown how he used Déat's *L'Œuvre* as a vehicle to criticise the traditionalism of Vichy; he deployed Doriot's PPF as a means of scaring Vichy about the possibility of a single party; and he exploited Châteaubriant's Groupe Collaboration to put across a favourable image of Germany (Burrin, 1993). It was his misfortune that the time he spent in Paris led to suspicions in Berlin that he had gone 'native', when all the while he was fulfilling Hitler's orders, preventing the emergence of a militant French nationalism among fascist circles.

While playing this game of 'divide and rule', the Germans increasingly saw the benefits that collaborationists could provide in the maintenance of law and order, especially after the total occupation of the country and the growth of internal resistance. Here attention focused on Joseph Darnand, a haulier from Nice, who had fought with bravery in both world wars and who was an active right-wing sympathiser, having moved from the AF to the Croix de Feu and Cagoule. An early supporter of both the Légion and the marshal, in December 1941 he set up the Service d'Ordre Légionnaire (SOL), a paramilitary group in the Alpes Maritimes which dedicated itself to a 21-point programme which was rabidly anti-semitic and anti-democratic. Whereas the Légion was largely a conservative force, comprising mostly veterans of the 1914–18 campaign and drawing its support from the countryside, the SOL was militant and was often opposed by local *Légionnaires*. Never numbering more than 20,000 members, the Germans banned Darnand's creation from operating in the northern zone, but in late 1942 it seemed an ideal solution to the problems of disorder. So it was, on 30 January 1943, that Vichy and Berlin consented to the transformation of the SOL into the *Milice Française*, which was charged with a dual function: the suppression of dissent in all its guises and the advocacy of National Revolution values, jobs for which its leaders were trained at the leadership school at Uriage [*Doc. 24*]. Warming to its task, the *Milice* was closely identified with the German cause despite the fact that it was of Vichy inspiration and functioned principally in the old southern zone. In mid-1943, Darnand had the honour of becoming an SS *Obersturmführer*, and a handful of his 30,000 *miliciens* joined the SS. Among its most infamous members was Paul Touvier, a prominent Catholic and right-wing sympathiser from Chambéry, who was involved in the murder of Victor Basch, the civil rights lawyer and supporter of Dreyfus, as well as in the shooting of seven Jews at Rillieux-la-Pape. Protected after the war by fundamentalist Catholics, Touvier was brought to trial in 1973 but was pardoned by Pompidou, only to be convicted of 'crimes against humanity' in 1994 [*Doc. 28*]. Darnand, meanwhile, had been executed in 1945.

The growth of the *Milice* illustrated the way in which the distinctions between *collaboration d'état* and *collaborationisme* had become blurred by 1944. Laval had welcomed the *Milice* in part as a counterweight against the RNP and other Paris-based groupings, yet it was Pétain who was its great champion. Although Darnand was unlike the many high-ranking soldiers to be found at Vichy, he was a personal friend of the marshal, who had known him during the First World War. His courage, his political views and his loyalty to the head of state made him exactly the right sort of man to campaign against the tide of indiscipline that was overtaking the country. It is significant that on 5 June 1944, the day before the Allies landed at Normandy, the marshal broadcast a speech in which he described *miliciens* as the most loyal of his servants. What Pétain failed to appreciate was that the *Milice* had in itself done much to provoke civil unrest. This was the tragedy of the collaboration/ism practised by both the men of Vichy and of Paris. By undertaking the Nazis' sordid work for them, they were in danger of doing exactly what they wanted to avoid, that is transforming France into another Poland, a downtrodden and brutalised state.

CHAPTER SIX

RESISTANCE

While the public rapidly became disenchanted with Vichy, this dissatisfaction did not automatically translate into resistance. Paxton provocatively suggested that maybe only 400,000 people, in other words one in ten of the population, actively took a part in defying the Germans (Paxton, 1972). New investigations, however, especially those conducted into gender and resistance by Paula Schwarz and Hanna Diamond, have suggested that the numbers might be much higher (Schwarz, 1989; Diamond, 1999). Women were often discounted in the *après-guerre* because they had generally not fulfilled a military role. Whatever the case, the obstacles to joining the Resistance were formidable. In his interviews with resisters, Kedward discovered that the cult of Pétain was a major hurdle (Kedward, 1984). Many people believed that, in signing the Armistice, the marshal had taken the only sensible position; to defy that decision was to defy realism. The divisions of France also created difficulties. Thanks to the vast German presence, it was hard for resisters to operate in the forbidden, military and Occupied zones. This is why, in the early stages of the war, resistance tended to be more conspicuous in Vichy France. Resisters also had to develop networks – no easy task. This explains the prominence of the Communists. Given their traditionally secretive behaviour, they already possessed a nationwide network of cells and underground links which they reactivated following the Nazi invasion of the Soviet Union in June 1941. A further problem was the need to articulate an alternative ideology to that peddled by Vichy. As Kedward, again, has shown, this search for a philosophy of disobedience accounts for why many resisters scrutinised French history for instruction and why resistance often emerged in areas such as the Cévennes with long traditions of protest (Kedward, 1978). It is telling that the titles of Resistance newspapers frequently recalled past struggles against repression: *Valmy*, *Père Dûchène*, *L'Insurgé*.

LA RÉSISTANCE À LONDRES

The honour of being the first resister in France is contested by historians, yet the credit is often given to Edmond Michelet, a former Action Française sympathiser who, in the 1930s, had converted to the cause of Christian Democracy. On 17 June 1940, he sat down at his typewriter and battered out a protest against the Armistice which he subsequently distributed in the streets of his home town, Brive-la-Gaillarde. It is, however, de Gaulle's appeal of 18 June that most people now remember, although few listened to it at the time; even the BBC considered it insignificant, and no recording was made until the speech was rebroadcast the following day. Forty-nine years of age, the author of some little understood books on modern warfare, the commander of a tank division which enjoyed a notable success over the Germans at Abbeville in May 1940, and under-secretary of state for war in Reynaud's last cabinet, de Gaulle was a virtual unknown both in France and in Britain (de Gaulle, 1934). On 17 June, no longer able to act on behalf of the new Pétain government, he stepped into an aeroplane bound for London. As he later recorded in his memoirs: 'I seemed to myself, alone as I was and deprived of everything, like a man on the shore of an ocean, proposing to swim across.' The next day, his famous broadcast betrayed none of these self-doubts, urging Frenchmen to join him in London to continue the fight.

There has been much discussion as to why de Gaulle made this stand. His detractors among the exiled French community in London accused him of being a Bonaparte or a Boulanger, an ambitious general waiting to make his political mark and all too willing to circumvent constitutional procedures. That de Gaulle was arrogant, right-wing in his politics, and extremely rude to his *aides* and British hosts cannot be disputed. Yet personal ambition was not uppermost in his mind. Perhaps the most penetrating analysis of his psychology in June 1940 is that given by the writer Crémieux-Brilhac who was with the general in London at the time (Crémieux-Brilhac, 1997). To be great, calculated de Gaulle, it was necessary to make brave decisions, even if this meant defying authority, something which he had been doing for much of his life, notably when he broke from his mentor Pétain in the early 1930s. As Crémieux-Brilhac continues, the general also possessed an extraordinary grasp of geo-politics. Contemptuous of Pétain's faintheartedness and convinced of Churchill's resolve, he foresaw how the war would become a drawn-out affair in which the USA and USSR would almost certainly be embroiled. In such circumstances, German victory was an impossibility. And, of course, de Gaulle was driven by his patriotism, a belief that French honour had to be salvaged, just as it had been in 1870 when Paris defied the Prussians. In this respect, the choice to leave his homeland for Britain was not an easy one.

Jean-Paul and Michèle Cointet have suggested that it was made easier by the fact that, in 1907–8, he had attended school in Antoing, Belgium, following the expulsion of the teaching orders from France (Cointet and Cointet, 1987). Yet, as Crémieux-Brilhac again suggests, the flight to Britain sprang from his patriotism and his conviction that in resisting the defeat and the Germans he had become the embodiment of France. This is why the general and many of his supporters made a virtue of their Frenchness, and refused to view themselves as *émigrés*. 'Rome', writes Crémieux-Brilhac, 'was no longer in Rome'; it was in London instead (Crémieux-Brilhac, 1997: 47).

As another historian has commented, in June 1940 there was 'an almost absurd disproportion between de Gaulle's ambitions and his means' (Shennan, 1993: 13) [*Doc. 10*]. Certainly, the odds were stacked against him. First, his status compared poorly with that of Pétain. Whereas the marshal was the most famous of France's First World War soldiers, de Gaulle was a little-known two-star general. Whereas Pétain was politically experienced, the head of an internationally recognised government, de Gaulle appeared a disloyal citizen whose claim to represent France rested on dubious criteria. Second, de Gaulle lacked resources, maybe 7,000 men in total by the end of July, a handful of ships, and a cramped headquarters at Carlton Gardens behind Downing Street. Few made the perilous journey across the Channel to join him, and even the sizeable French community in Britain – convalescing troops, refugees, intellectual exiles and a significant London-based colony – kept their distance, often opting for repatriation. Third, de Gaulle was heavily reliant on British help, something which, in the aftermath of Mers-el-Kébir, counted against him in France. Even British support was not as solid as he had hoped for. On 28 June, Churchill recognised de Gaulle merely as leader of the Free French, not as the head of state of an exiled government, as the general had wished; and while the British prime minister admired his courage, there was always a hope – especially within the Foreign Office which despaired at de Gaulle's arrogance – that a more senior French figure would travel to London.

In these circumstances, 'de Gaulle fought a political war' (Vinen, 1996: 73). Playing a minimal role in the ongoing campaigns against the Germans, the general built up his support in London, surrounding himself with men of undisputed ability. In his pithy yet penetrating 1990 biography of de Gaulle, Jackson cites the most important of these disciples, who would remain loyal to their leader until his death, thus establishing Gaullism as a formidable political force in postwar France. Jackson lists the following: General Catroux, a former colonial governor and accomplished diplomat; René Cassin, a lawyer who gave invaluable advice on legal matters; Maurice Schumann, a journalist who became a captivating broadcaster; Gaston Palewiski, a former aide to Reynaud who advised on political questions; and Captain Dewavrin ('Passy'), who formed the Bureau Central de Renseignement et d'Action (BCRA), the Free French intelligence service (Jackson, 1990: 11–12).

Next, de Gaulle concentrated on building up support in the colonies. Recognising that the empire would play an invaluable role in the bargaining with Germany, Vichy had insisted upon complete obedience on the part of its imperial possessions and, among the overseas governors, only Catroux in Indochina initially sided with the Free French. This need to keep the empire intact explains why the Pétain regime resisted the Gaullist attack on Dakar in September 1940 with such vigour, and why Admiral Georges Robert quickly crushed any signs of disobedience among the indigenous people of the French West Indies. Much effort was also expended on the promotion of National Revolution values abroad, ideals which went down well among French settlers in Algeria. Nonetheless, there was a growing feeling within the colonies that they had been badly let down by metropolitan government. So it was that a steady drip of territories began to go over to de Gaulle: the New Hebrides, Chad, Cameroon, the French Congo and Tahiti had all rallied by the end of November 1940. The following June, Syria and the Lebanon followed suit after a joint British–Gaullist expedition there, although suspicions remained, on the part of both Vichy and the Free French, that London ultimately sought to take over the French empire. De Gaulle was dismayed that the Syrian campaign resulted in an armistice from which the Free French were excluded, and which permitted Pétainist troops under General Dentz to return to France. Further quarrels ensued in May 1942 when British troops landed in Madagascar without any prior consultation with Carlton Gardens. When, in December 1941, de Gaulle had taken unilateral action himself, claiming the islands of St Pierre and Miquelon, just off the Canadian coast, he had merely provoked American fury (Gordon, 1998: 120–3).

De Gaulle's position was still very precarious, and the USA's entry into the war only worsened the situation as Roosevelt had little time for the recalcitrant and autocratic general. The State Department's policy, 'our Vichy gamble' as the diplomat Walter Langer remarked, was to court the Pétain government in the hope that the marshal would ultimately change sides. That de Gaulle was able to retain his standing may be credited, in part, to his own political ability to fend off British and American designs, as well as his popularity among the British public which, in the dark days of 1940–41, had been desperate to cling on to any sign of resistance to German power. De Gaulle further benefited from the backing of the USSR which, like him, was keen to reduce Anglo-Saxon influence. Most importantly, as Vinen comments, he drew strength from the fact that many resisters inside metropolitan France now looked on him as their leader (Vinen, 1996: 75).

METROPOLITAN MOVEMENTS

In their analysis of resistance within France, historians have drawn three broad conclusions. First, it is clear that the different nature of the two zones had a profound effect on the emergence of protest. Because of the German presence, those organisations that emerged in Occupied France tended to be smaller and more fragile than their counterparts in the south. Second, historians have established that it was difficult for resistance to operate across both zones. The only grouping to achieve this with any great success was the Communist-dominated Front National, which boasted another unique characteristic in that it was the sole movement to be linked specifically to a political party. This has led to a third observation. While most partisan groups were not ostensibly linked to political parties, they did recruit among existing networks of friends and work colleagues.

These points are evident in the groupings that first appeared in the Occupied zone. As Jean-François Muracciole observes, these included Musée de l'Homme, the brainchild of the Parisian academics Anatole Lewitsky, Yvonne Oddon and Boris Vildé; Avocats Socialistes, the work of the lawyers André Weil-Curiel, Léon-Maurice Nordmann and Jubineau; La Quatrième République, the inspiration of Socialists in Roubaix; and the conservative-orientated Défense de la France, founded in the cellars of the Sorbonne by the students Philippe Viannay and Robert Salmon (Muracciole, 1996) [*Doc. 22*]. Such precarious groupings came to be eclipsed by the four principal movements in the north: Ceux de la Résistance (CDLR), Ceux de la Libération (CDLL), Organisation Civile et Militaire (OCM) and Libération Nord. Established in 1942 by the civil servant Jacques Lecompte-Boinet, the CDLR included members of the Paris-based *haute bourgeoisie*, notably the industrialist, Jean de Vogüé, yet the majority stemmed from outside the capital and were of varied political outlooks (Gordon, 1998: 59–60). This was not true of the CDLL, created in August 1940 by Maurice Ripoche, a First World War flying ace and prominent engineer. Several of its members originated from the extreme rightist PSF and the movement soon found itself in difficulties because of its early antisemitism, a stance it quickly repudiated. Occasionally, the virulence of such views among the Resistance raises eyebrows, but it should be stressed that Vichy did not have a monopoly over prejudice, and it was not uncommon to find right and left alongside one another in underground organisations. Antisemitism was also an initial characteristic of the OCM, established in 1940 by Colonel Heurtaux, a former intelligence officer, who grouped around him several middle-ranking military personnel. The movement quickly dropped its racism, but remained conservative in its general orientation. By contrast Libération Nord, the biggest of the northern-based groupings, founded in November 1941 by Christian Pineau, drew together non-Communist trade union representatives from both the CGT and the Christian Democrat CFTC, and adopted a decidedly syndicalist platform (Sadoun, 1982).

Many resistance organisations also emerged in the south. Among the smaller of these, Muracciole cites the following: *L'Insurgé*, a newspaper created by Lyon Socialists; Libérer et Fédérer, founded in Toulouse by Silvio Trentin, an Italian Socialist who had taken refuge in France; *Le Coq enchaîné*, a Republican-orientated journal; *Temps nouveau*, a Christian-Democrat publication established by the Jesuit Father Chaillet; and *Les Cahiers du Témoignage chrétien*, an influential Catholic periodical which chastised members of the Church hierarchy for their antisemitism and spine-lessness in standing up to Vichy (Muracciole, 1996). Yet the three largest southern movements, much bigger than their northern counterparts, were Combat, Libération Sud and Franc-Tireur. Combat resulted from the union in 1941 of two existing groupings: Henri Frenay's Mouvement de Libération Nationale (MLN) and François de Menthon's Liberté. Active throughout much of the southern zone, Combat boasted its own newspaper, leadership schools, welfare services and military training centres. Libération Sud originated in Clermont Ferrand, the brainchild of the journalist Emmanuel d'Astier de la Vigerie and Lucie Aubrac, a schoolteacher and one of the few women to head an underground grouping. Left-wing in orientation, it has occasionally been suggested that PCF members infiltrated Libération Sud in order to influence the non-Communist Mouvements Unis de Résistance (MUR), an umbrella movement which brought together the principal southern movements in 1943, yet there is little evidence to substantiate this charge (Douzou, 1995). The remaining southern-based movement, Franc-Tireur, emerged in December 1941, the inspiration of the prominent Lyonnais politicians, Auguste Pinton and Noël Clavier, and Jean-Pierre Lévy, a weaver of Jewish-Alsatian origin. Garnering support from the intellectual *bourgeoisie*, Franc-Tireur was left in its orientation, drawing sustenance from the ideals of 1789 and devising a radical political programme which called for the nationalisation of key industries (Gordon, 1998: 144–5).

The one movement linked closely to a political party and able to move across both zones was, of course, the Communist-influenced Front National. This is the subject of lively controversy. The organisation's detractors frequently highlight the fact that, thanks to the Molotov–Ribbentrop Pact of August 1939, the PCF did not place its muscle behind resistance until the German invasion of the Soviet Union in June 1941. It is also recalled that, shortly after the defeat, the PCF leader in France, Jacques Duclos – Maurice Thorez was in exile in Moscow – approached the Germans with an un-successful request to start republishing the party's newspaper *L'Humanité*, which had been dissolved by Daladier. It is further suggested that, while individual Communists were influential in forming partisan groups such the Organisation Secrète (OS) well before June 1941, these bodies were essentially instruments to eliminate party dissenters. Nonetheless, Communist resistance credentials are substantial. First, it should be remembered that prior to the Nazi–Soviet Pact the PCF had the best anti-fascist record of any French political party, although it could be countered that it had the best anti-democratic record as well. Second, there is an element of truth in the Communist argument that the period August 1939–May 1941 was one of unbroken struggle against the forces of reaction: the Daladier government, Vichy and the Germans. In November 1940, a clandestine version of *L'Humanité* appeared which did not mince its words in its attacks on both Vichy and the Germans. Third, there is ample evidence of individual Communists taking resistance action before Moscow gave the nod: Charles Tillon in Bordeaux and Charles Debarge in the Nord. It was also in the Nord that Communists assisted the courageous miners' strikes of May–June 1941. Nonetheless, it was undoubtedly Operation Barbarossa which gave the PCF its cue to enter full-scale resistance [*Doc. 20*]. Under the umbrella of the Front National, the party marshalled various movements in an armed struggle against the Germans. Alongside the OS, it set up the Bataillons de la Jeunesse, a youth group; the Main d'Œuvre Immigré (MOI), an organisation of foreign workers; and, most importantly, the Francs-Tireurs et Partisans Français (FTP) which had its own paper *France d'abord* and which recruited among the working-class districts of the Occupied zone.

DIVERSITY

Communist involvement unquestionably divided the many underground movements that existed throughout France in 1941, yet it is apparent that diversity was always a characteristic of the Resistance. This has already been observed in the social composition of resisters who emanated from all walks of life: industrialists and workers; *bourgeois* and intellectuals; journalists and military personnel; right and left. Diversity was also apparent in resistance activities, the geography of resistance and the ideological conflicts that became ever fiercer as liberation approached.

Forms of resistance action were varied. The publication of clandestine journals was extremely important. Kedward has emphasised how, prior to 1939, France possessed one of the most extensive political presses in the world (Kedward, 1984). All this came to an end in June 1940 when censorship became the norm in both the Occupied and Unoccupied zones; the empty white columns that featured in such prominent newspapers as *Le Temps* were a constant reminder of censors-at-work. It was vital, therefore, to put across an alternative message to that articulated by Vichy and the Germans. It is significant that all the major resistance networks had their own journals which sought to put across information otherwise inaccessible to the French people. Pineau of Libération Nord regularly published news obtained from listening to the BBC. Resistance papers also became more sophisticated than that first typed by Michelet in June 1940. Paul Simon recalls how the journal *Valmy* was initially put together using a child's printing set, before he and his friends could attempt something more ambitious (Simon, 1942). In January 1944, 300,000 issues of *Combat* were distributed; the figure in 1943 had been a mere 40,000. At the time of the Liberation, 450,000 copies of *Défense de la France* circulated, a far cry from the paltry 5,000 when the journal was initially founded in July 1941 (Wiewiorka, 1995). Most impressive was the distribution of *L'Humanité*: 5,000,000 copies for the whole of the Occupation period.

No less impressive were the extensive resistance networks which were set up to aid resisters, pass information and enable Allied airmen, who had bailed out over France, to return to Britain. It has been calculated that, at the end of the war, some 266 such *réseaux* existed, criss-crossing the whole of the country. Many of these, perhaps one-fifth in total, were set up by the Special Operations Executive (SOE), part of the British secret service which dropped some 393 agents into France. Not to be outdone, the Gaullist BCRA and the American Office of Strategic Services (OSS) established their own information chains which were critical in the garnering of intelligence for D-Day. Inevitably, the Resistance will always be linked with military action, the Communists being especially active in the underground war against the Germans. The first German to be assassinated on French soil in August 1941 was the victim of the FTP militant, Pierre Georges, otherwise known as Colonel Fabien, who was later prominent in the battle for Paris in August 1944. The military contribution that the Resistance made to the Liberation will be discussed later, but it should be stressed that not all resistance activity was so dramatic. Listening to the BBC, refusing to serve German soldiers, scrawling 'V' signs on the walls were all forms of 'passive' resistance, forms of disobedience which the Nazis took extremely seriously. As Hanna Diamond has shown, women were especially active in this type of protest. While women were rare among the leadership of clandestine movements – Marie-Louise Disart, head of the Françoise network, Marie-Madeleine Fourcade, chief of Alliance, and Lucie Aubrac of Libération Sud were the exceptions to the rule – their position within society often enabled them to thwart both the German and Vichy authorities. Within offices, women employed as secretaries frequently had access to privileged information and could steal identity documents (Diamond, 1999: 104). Within their homes, women could store arms, hide Jews and *réfractaires* from STO and, as Kedward writes, open the door to the inquisitive authorities, thus allowing any fugitives to escape through the back. And in fulfilling their traditional role as wife and mother, the role allocated by Vichy, women could often pass through the streets unnoticed, pushing a pram which might contain underground publications or a machine gun as well as a baby.

Such ambiguous behaviour was always an overriding characteristic of resistance activity, affecting both men and women. Although Paxton might have underestimated the number of resisters, it is undeniable that only a small minority could ever be classified as 'professional' resisters in the sense that they were constantly engaged in a struggle against Vichy and the Germans. Most carried on their jobs, carrying out occasional acts of defiance whenever possible. In so doing, they often aided the German war effort as much as they disrupted it. By 1942–43, the total occupation of France and economic necessity meant that overwhelming numbers were working directly or indirectly for the Germans, however much they disliked the policy of collaboration that Vichy was pursuing with Berlin. This inevitably forced them into ambivalent actions. While railway workers, often praised for their resistance credentials, held up supplies for the *Wehrmacht*, it was the same railwaymen who were helping transport Jews and fellow workers to the Reich. Likewise, as Simon Kitson has shown, the police and civil servants often did much to shield resisters, yet the very nature of their jobs meant that they were also at the forefront of repression (Kitson, 1995).

Geography further contributed to the diverse nature of resistance. The effect of the two zones has already been mentioned, yet so too should the influence of town and countryside. Kedward has demonstrated how, in its initial stages, resistance was centred in urban areas (Kedward, 1984). There were several reasons for this. It was the towns that suffered the brunt of material hardships. Towns also housed the cumbersome printing presses which made so much clatter that they would have been immediately uncovered if situated in a rural farmhouse. Towns were also where intellectuals, journalists and politicians tended to reside. Most critically, towns provided the best hiding places. Kedward cites the medieval quarters of Lyon, Montpellier and Perpignan where it was possible to enter a house on one level and later emerge in an entirely different place (Kedward, 1985a). Christine Levisse-Touzé has shown how Paris apartment blocks, with their double entrances and many balconies, offered several escape routes (Levisse-Touzé, 1995). The capital's *métro* system offered another quick exit, while the city's telephone exchange was sufficiently large for conversations to go unrecorded.

Gradually resisters began to gravitate to the countryside where they formed *maquis* bands in the scrubland [*Doc. 25*]. Four factors contributed to the rise of the *maquis*. First, it is possible to cite the Communist armed struggle against the Germans. Whereas much of the farmed French countryside was unsuited to military operations, the rugged hill and mountainsides offered excellent cover. Second, it is possible that the *maquis* offered an 'alternative lifestyle' that might well have appealed to the young. Descriptions of life in the bush, albeit often romanticised, show how class boundaries disappeared and how a community of spirit developed, all very different from the mawkish morality that was to be found in the Chantiers and other of Vichy's youth groups which, by 1942, were often engaged in pointless physical tasks and banal exhortations of the National Revolution. Third, the intensification of Vichy and German measures against civil disobedience in 1942 forced many to flee to rural safety. Finally, and most importantly, it was STO that swelled the ranks of the *maquis*. Just how many men and women sought shelter in rural hideaways is unknown, but one estimate suggests 10,000 in the Occupied zone and 30,000 in southern France. For a long time, their existence went untouched by historians, and it is due to the pioneering research of Kedward that we now know a good deal about what he calls their 'outlaw culture' (Kedward, 1985b). Generally speaking, *maquisards* were youthful, urban and not always well disciplined. To survive, they depended on foodstuffs they appropriated from Vichy organisations such as the Secours National, the supply of arms from Algeria and London, and the assistance of local communities. This support was not always forthcoming, especially in traditionally conservative departments such as the Haute Savoie (Abrahams, 1991). Even so, Kedward has shown how the Pétain government's authority was so ragged and the *maquisards* so entrenched that, in 1944, we should speak of 'Resistance France' rather than 'Vichy France' as the critical determinant in the daily life of rural areas (Kedward, 1993).

The ill discipline of certain *maquisards*, their unwillingness to hand over their weapons at the Liberation and their eagerness to seek revenge on collaborators, real and imagined, created tensions within the ranks of the Resistance which, by 1944, was suffering from severe fragmentation. Personal jealousies were a constant problem, especially as certain resisters created their own little 'empires'. There was also resentment at those who had decided to join up late in the day, and there was always a worry about potential infiltrators. The maintenance of secrecy was paramount. The CDLL had seven leaders in total, all of whom were caught, apart from the final one, André Mutter, later to become a minister in the Fourth Republic. Gender differences were a further concern. Despite their critical role, in 1944 only six women were awarded the honour of the Compagnon de la Libération; 1,057 medals were distributed altogether (Muracciole, 1996: 97). In the event, such male chauvinism did not create too much resentment, possibly because women remained reluctant to step beyond the traditional female values of modesty and discretion.

It was, of course, political divisions that did most to split the Resistance. Arguments raged between movements in the separate zones: arguments about the future of France; arguments about spheres of influence; arguments about what to do with Vichy and its accomplices; arguments about what position to adopt towards de Gaulle; and, crucially, arguments between Communists and non-Communists. It was not merely de Gaulle, but a wide range of resisters who were worried that the Front National would monopolise protest against the Germans, using its considerable networks to eliminate its opponents and execute a revolution. What is astonishing is that, amid this division, the Resistance ultimately achieved an impressive measure of unity.

UNITY

The factors that facilitated the coming together of the Resistance have been aptly summarised by Vinen (1996: 78). First, he stresses the role of Moscow, which dissolved the Comintern in 1943. In future, the role of Communist parties throughout Europe was less to foment revolution than to build partnerships with other groupings in an effort to combat Nazism. This change in approach thus made it easier for the Front National to consider moving into some kind of relationship with fellow resistance movements. Vinen further stresses the involvement of former prominent republican politicians, and cites examples as varied as Joseph Laniel, Louis Marin, Henri Queuille, Pierre Brossolette and Pierre Cot. Although the arrival of these newcomers was resented by some 'resisters of the first hour', especially as some such as Laniel had voted in favour of granting Pétain full powers, they gave resistance a cloak of legitimacy and helped curb the more militant tendencies of young partisans.

In the attempts to build unity, all historians underscore the importance of Gaullist envoys, in particular Jean Moulin. Forty-one years of age at the time of the defeat, Moulin had made his mark as the youngest prefect in France, and had ably assisted Pierre Cot in the Popular Front government. Believing it dishonourable to desert his post, he remained as prefect of the Eure-et-Loir in June 1940, only for Vichy to dismiss him five months later. Making contact with various southern resistance movements, in 1941 he travelled to London where he met de Gaulle. Impressed by the courage of this supreme organiser, the general made Moulin his personal envoy and asked him to liaise further between resistance leaders. Often working under the name of 'Rex', just one of many aliases, his task was made easier by a further factor that promoted unity among the partisans: the total occupation of France in November 1942. Against this background, in March 1943 Moulin created the Mouvement Unis de la Résistance (MUR), which drew together Libération Sud, Combat and Franc-Tireur. In May, he assembled delegates from eight resistance movements, including the Communists, at the first meeting of the Conseil National de la Résistance (CNR). This body subsequently became the voice of the internal resistance, and agreed to recognise de Gaulle as the sole representative of French interests, an invaluable bargaining tool for the general in his ongoing negotiations with the Anglo-Saxons. The CNR also drew up a Charter on 15 March 1944, laying out radical plans for the restructuring of France, plans which did not necessarily meet with the general's approval. Moulin did not live to see their fulfilment. In June 1943, he was betrayed to the Germans and died at the hands of the infamous SS torturer, Klaus Barbie. Although in 1964 his body was transferred to the Panthéon, the resting place for national heroes, his legacy would not go uncontested. In the 1980s, various figures for varied reasons – Frenay, leader of Combat, Barbie on trial at Lyon for 'crimes against humanity', and Thierry Wolton, an intelligence expert – alleged that he had been a Communist spy, charges that were denied by Daniel Cordier, Moulin's first secretary, who countered by claiming his former boss had been an early sympathiser of Pétain, as well as being antisemitic (Cordier, 1989–93). Such allegations shocked the public, shattered the image of an heroic resistance, and shrouded the Occupation with yet more claims and counter-claims. The archival truth is that Moulin was steadfastly anti-fascist, a committed republican, and a loyal servant of de Gaulle.

Although Moulin was a valuable asset, de Gaulle still had to win his battle with the Anglo-Saxons. This entered a new phase in November 1942 when American forces landed in Morocco and Algeria. Keen to exclude the general, Roosevelt was prepared to do business with existing Vichy representatives, and was happy that Darlan, who by coincidence happened to be in Algiers at the time visiting his sick son, should become High Commissioner in North Africa. This policy backfired. As well as drawing Gaullist disapproval, Darlan's appointment unsettled British and American public opinion which recalled his role in the persecution of Jews and other minorities. It was, then, with some relief that the USA greeted news of Darlan's assassination on Christmas Eve 1942. Still desperate to exclude de Gaulle, Roosevelt turned to the man whom he had initially ear-marked for taking over as leader in North Africa: General Giraud. Taken prisoner in 1940 by the Germans, Giraud made a courageous escape in 1942 and initially offered his services to Pétain, before rallying to the Americans. This highlighted his lack of political nous, the very quality that the Americans cherished. Essentially, they wanted an apolitical general who would do as he was told and who carried greater authority than de Gaulle. They had not bargained on de Gaulle's determination. He rightly calculated that, if Giraud were to take charge, the very interests of a liberated French state would be subordinate to those of the Allies. While, in January 1943, the two French generals were persuaded to shake hands at a meeting in Casablanca and although, in May 1943, they agreed to the creation of a Comité Français de Libération Nationale (CFLN) in which they shared equal power, it was only a matter of time before de Gaulle's superior political acumen won through. In October 1943, de Gaulle took over as president, and Giraud faded into the background.

Once in position, de Gaulle took steps to assert his authority and pre-empt any plans the USA might have for France, important as an Allied invasion of the Continent was understood to be only months away. As Shennan has demonstrated, this 'preemptive action' took 'four forms' (Shennan, 1993: 32–4). First, de Gaulle was keen to highlight the legitimacy of the CFLN over Vichy. To this end, he referred to this body as 'the government of France', extended its membership to include respectable republican figures (and two Communists), and assented to the establishment of a Consultative Assembly in Algiers. In June 1944, the CFLN significantly retitled itself the Gouvernement Provisoire de la République Française (GPRF). In his separate work on postwar plans for renewal, Shennan has shown how this government-in-waiting quickly debated plans for the nationalisation of industry, the democratisation of education and the constitutional restructuring of the French state, plans that had been discussed in the 1930s and which, paradoxically, also figured in Vichy's National Revolution (Shennan, 1985). This programme for renewal formed a second step in de Gaulle's plans for legitimacy. The CFLN schemes neatly dovetailed with the CNR Charter, illustrating that the general was committed to the restoration of liberal democracy after the Liberation and had long-term political goals. Such intentions had also been illustrated in late January/early February 1944 when colonial governors gathered at Brazzaville, under de Gaulle's stewardship, to discuss the revitalisation of the French empire, schemes which involved the devolution of power from Paris to the peripheries. Third, writes Shennan, de Gaulle tried to undermine US plans for the administration of liberated French territory through the Allied Military Government of Occupied Territories (AMGOT). Instead, he hand-picked 18 *Commissaires de la République*, sometimes described as 'super prefects', who would oversee the smooth transition of authority in France. Finally, concludes Shennan, de Gaulle built up French military forces, easier in that he had inherited Vichy's North African army, some 400,000 men in number who, under General Juin, had already played an active part in the 1944 Italian campaign. Within France, the Resistance responded by setting up the Forces Françaises de l'Intérieur (FFI) which had its own High Command to coordinate military operations come the Liberation.

The Resistance played a small part in assisting the D-Day landings, although SOE did drop in agents to form *Jedburghs*, small teams which engaged in sabotage work. The reasons why partisans were given such a role are not hard to fathom. Given the magnitude of the operation, secrecy was all important. The Resistance was hardly 'leak proof'; the betrayal of Moulin, most likely by Combat member René Hardy, was an uncomfortable reminder of the power of informers. Nor did the Allies have any accurate idea of the numbers of resisters and the strength of their equipment. While the *maquis* undoubtedly aided Allied forces, constantly hindering the Germans and delaying reinforcements to the Normandy front, they were no match for the *Wehrmacht* in open battle. At Glières in March 1944, at Mont Mouchet and on the Vercors during the Liberation, the *maquisards* were hopelessly outnumbered and outfought. Ultimately, D-Day depended on conventional weaponry: tanks, aircraft, infantry power and canon fire. That said, Allied planners were aware of the contribution of Resistance units and, as Arthur Funk has shown, American troops landing in southern France in August 1944, as part of Operation Dragoon, worked closely with the FFI and irregular *maquis* units (Funk, 1992).

LIBERATION

At the Liberation, de Gaulle's worst nightmare – and Pétain's for that matter – was a civil war in France that might lead to a Communist uprising. Certainly, the extreme left's role in June–July 1944 was formidable. As Gildea has shown, Communists were prominent in the FFI, which fell under the overall control of the Communist-dominated Comité d'Action Militaire (COMAC), the military arm of the CNR (Gildea, 1995: 30–1). They were also conspicuous in the Comités de Libération (CDL) which were set up at both communal and departmental levels to take over the running of civil administration. In the event, both civil war and revolution were easily avoided. Why?

Part of the answer lies in the fact that there was little public support for Vichy in 1944, and that the *Milice* was almost entirely dependent on the Germans for everything. Once the Allies had secured a firm foothold in France, only out-and-out collaborators dared take on the Resistance. Credit must also be extended to the *Commissaires de la République* that de Gaulle had initiated, a scheme that outwitted the American plans for AMGOT. As the Vichy regime disappeared, whisked off to Sigmaringen by a German guard, the administrators fulfilled their task with aplomb and took care not to upset the CDL which eventually gave way to new elected bodies in April–May 1945. While Kedward has shown that several *maquisards* were reluctant to relinquish their 'outlaw status', most FFI members gave up their arms or agreed to be assimilated into the regular army, as did the *milices patriotiques*, small bands of citizens whom the FFI mobilised to take part in the Liberation (Kedward, 1993). Historians have further shown that the majority of the PCF did not favour revolution in 1944. Given the prominent role of the Front National, Communists knew they could not be denied posts in the new provisional government; and, in the elections of the new Fourth Republic, their credentials as the most 'patriotic' of resistance movements, the party of the '75,000 martyrs', ensured that they won more seats than at any other time in their history. In any case, as Gildea reminds us, a revolution in France did not correspond with Stalin's plans (Gildea, 1995: 32). He was keener on establishing his foothold in Eastern Europe and saw the value of a Gaullist regime in the West which would be a thorn in the side of the Americans. Whether the USA would have permitted a Communist revolution is another matter. While AMGOT never got off the ground, it was the Allies who ultimately freed most of France; de Gaulle himself was merely granted the symbolic liberation of Paris, bypassed by Allied tanks. The formidable American military presence would surely have crushed Communist insurgents as easily as the Germans had held off the *maquis*.

A further reason why France avoided a revolutionary situation in 1944 lay in the relative moderation of the purges. This restraint could have backfired in that it could have encouraged yet more summary justice yet, as we shall see, such indiscipline was restrained and, on balance, the rule of law prevailed. The *épuration* had, in fact, begun in 1943 at Algiers where the CFLN had announced its intention of trying all those who had served the Pétain regime. The most prominent victim was Pucheu, who had volunteered to assist Giraud. Unlike some other Vichyites who were welcomed with open arms, the former minister of the interior was tainted by his role in the hostage crisis of 1941 and, after a brief trial, was put in front of a firing squad. At the Liberation itself, the purges operated on several levels. A special High Court of Justice was set up to try some 108 Vichy personnel, including Pétain and Laval. The former's double-game argument cut little ice with a jury consisting of Resistance veterans, and he was sentenced to death, a verdict that was commuted to life imprisonment on the intervention of de Gaulle, who did not want the indignity of an 89-year-old man being hauled before an execution squad. That was the fate of Laval, dragged squirming from his cell after a botched suicide attempt and a spirited defence in which he recalled his old powers as an advocate. Other leading Vichyites, at least those who had not found exile in Franco's Spain such as Bonnard, generally received prison terms. Only seven key figures of the regime were shot, and a tiny number were acquitted thanks to their later acts of complicity with the Resistance. A further series of trials was conducted by *cours de justice* of the Provisional Government and Fourth Republic. These resulted in 2,853 death sentences, of which 1,502 were carried out; 3,910 death sentences for persons *in absentia*; 38,266 terms of imprisonment; and 46,145 sentences of 'national degradation', which involved losing property and civil status. Subsequent amnesty laws of 1947, 1951 and 1953 commuted several of these punishments. Meanwhile, in 1945, the purge of civil administrators was much milder than that perpetrated by Vichy; only 22,000 or so civil servants of varying importance lost their jobs. Historians have since pointed to the anomalies of post-Liberation justice, emphasising the way in which pro-collaborationist cultural and intellectual figures, such as Robert Brasillach, were far more likely to receive harsh treatment than industrialists whose contribution to the Nazi war effort had probably been much greater. Historians have also given the lie to Vichyite claims that some 100,000 people were summarily killed at the end of the war. Aron, it will be recalled, plumped for the figure of 30,000 [*Doc. 26*]. In truth, vigilante justice claimed the lives of around 9,000, fewer than in Belgium or Holland where the purges were far fiercer. What was shameful was the treatment of women suspected of 'horizontal collaboration'. Many of these women had their heads shaved (*femmes tondues*) and were sometimes paraded naked through the streets, often with swastikas daubed on their backs and breasts. Several of those treated in this barbaric fashion were innocent of any real crime. For gender historians, the shaving of heads was not merely a traditional act of purification, which had been meted out in the past to adulterous women, but a way of attacking a woman's 'sexual being' and reasserting male dominance (Diamond, 1999: 139).

Whatever the case, the Liberation did mark one step towards women's rights in that they were at last given the vote which they first exercised in the referendum of October 1945 where they overwhelmingly rejected a return to the Third Republic. The green light had thus been given to the drawing up of a new constitution, something in which the key political parties – the Communists, Socialists and the newly formed Christian Democrats (MRP) – eagerly participated. Agreeing on a new political format, however, proved trickier than they had imagined. All they agreed upon was the need to combat de Gaulle who had assumed extensive personal powers during this transitional period and who they mistakenly believed was set on a dictatorship. Ultimately, the new constitution they drafted was eerily akin to that of the Third, providing for a bicameral chamber and strong parties, the very solution de Gaulle had feared. Forced into the political wilderness, in 1958 he had no hesitation in denouncing the weaknesses of the Fourth Republic, just as the Third Republic had been denounced in 1940. Yet the record of the Fourth was not all bad. In its early stages, indeed during the transitional phase in which de Gaulle himself had been in charge, it inaugurated an impressive series of reforms, some drawn from the CNR Charter, which historians have compared favourably with the 'New Jerusalem' built in 1945 by the Labour government in Britain (Larkin, 1988: 128). The welfare state was overhauled, economic planning fostered modernisation, nationalisation was extended to key industries, and French education, traditionally elitist, was made more accessible. The reasons for the eventual collapse of the Fourth Republic remain outside this study, but derive partially from the failure of successive governments to sustain and build on this progressive legacy.

CHAPTER SEVEN

AN UNCONQUERABLE PAST?

The period 1934 to 1944 was a decidedly unhappy one for many French men and women. During the Occupation, they were confronted by a series of agonising decisions which were never easy to reconcile. Nor had the pre-war years bred optimism and contentment. The self-confidence that emerged out of the victory of 1918 proved brittle, and was unable to withstand the impact of a Depression, which stubbornly refused to go away. As the gloom settled, unease spread through all walks of life. Politically, the Republic appeared incapable of sustaining firm government. Economically, France seemed at a standstill, especially in the countryside, and where there was technological innovation in industry, it exacerbated social divisions, swelling a working class which already felt isolated from the rest of the nation. Demographically, the population stagnated despite strict controls on abortion and contraception, the encouragement of immigration and an official pro-natalist campaign that sometimes bordered on the licentious. Religiously, whole areas of northern industrial France seemed lost to Catholicism. And, culturally, France was thought vulnerable to the harmful currents of Americanization that swept across the Atlantic.

For many commentators, especially on the right, France was in the grip of a moral malaise, a 'decadence' that went to the very heart of the nation. Several 'solutions' were proffered; yet, as Jackson relates, few solved the underlying problems (Jackson, 1999). In 1934–35 the centrist right, in the shape of the Doumergue and Laval governments, offered orthodox economics – deflationary policies which exacerbated financial difficulties. The extreme right, most obviously in the form of the Croix de Feu, developed a programme which to all intents and purposes equated a form of fascism, if only because it mirrored the ambiguities and contradictions that were characteristic of fascist movements elsewhere. The French people, however, were unimpressed by smart blue uniforms, brawling in the streets and violent rhetoric. In 1936 it was the turn of the left to provide its own solution. The Popular Front delivered an imaginative and bold agenda which sought to include a section of society that had been overlooked by previous governments. It was a programme which proved too daring for a society that remained traditionally cautious. However honourable Blum's mission to combat fascism at home and abroad, his government contributed to the radicalisation of French politics both on the left and the right. While the Communists soon became disillusioned, the extreme right gained ground. If there had been elections in 1940, the PSF would probably have won some 100 seats, but at least its anti-liberal tendencies would have been kept in check within the republican framework. Paradoxically, as Jackson argues, it was the Radicals under Daladier, a party synonymous with the failings of the Republic, that elaborated the most effective solution, even if it meant shifting the centre ground to the right. The irony is that the Republic in 1939 was in a leaner, fitter state than it had been for several years: rearmed and ready to stand up to Hitler. While the Vichyites might have blamed defeat on moral deficiencies, let it not be forgotten that it was military failings, principally those of strategy, that brought about collapse in 1940.

Vichy, in a sense, was another answer to the crisis of the 1930s, and it is significant that many historians have interpreted it as a reaction to the Popular Front. To be fair, the marshal's National Revolution, an extremely eclectic and muddled affair, did contain some forward-thinking ideas, especially in its use of experts and the promotion of efficiency, even though these ideas often sat uneasily alongside the reactionary rhetoric of traditionalist ministers. It has occasionally been suggested that, despite its contradictions, the National Revolution would have worked had it not been for the unpropitious environment of the Occupation. Yet, as historians have pointed out, the National Revolution owed its very existence to the defeat, Armistice and destruction of the Third Republic (Kedward, 1985a). Moreover, as Paxton first suggested, the ministers at Vichy committed a folly of frightening proportions (Paxton, 1972). Enemy occupation was not the ideal moment, or indeed the right moment morally, to conduct such an ambitious experiment in political and social engineering. When the deputies had voted full powers to Pétain, several had believed these were a temporary expedient until the recall of parliament. De Gaulle might have been wrong in accusing the marshal of seizing power illegally, but there is no doubt that Vichy never possessed a mandate to progress with its plans for renewal.

Much of the blame for Vichy's mistakes must rest with Pétain. Given his reputation in the First World War and given the horror of the *exode*, it is understandable why men and women looked to him as a saviour. Few knew the real man behind the avuncular image. He was no selfless patriot with merely his country's interests at heart, but an extremely self-important and ambitious individual who had long craved power, and who possessed an extremely otiose vision of a France which simply did not correspond to social and economic realities. Despite his talk of pragmatism, his answers to France's problems were hopelessly unrealistic.

This failure to grasp reality was also conspicuous in Vichy's policies towards Germany. These were breathtaking in their naivety. They were also striking in their consistency. While it is true that the three men involved in the elaboration of foreign policy – Pétain, Darlan and Laval – had different priorities, the similarities in their overall objectives outweighed the particulars of how they conducted their business. All desired a German victory; all wanted to see the demise of Communism; all wanted to free France of its ties with Britain; all believed an authoritarian regime was necessary for the effective conduct of foreign policy; and all considered collaboration a desirable option. In these regards, this unlikely triumvirate was not so different from the collaborationists at Paris who berated Vichy for its failure to back wholeheartedly the German war effort. To be fair, Pétain and Laval, if not Darlan, were aware of the pitfalls in giving the Germans whatever they wanted, but both collaborators and collaborationists failed to comprehend what Berlin truly sought. Behind Abetz's pleasantries and falsehoods lay Hitler's uncompromising position which foresaw the immediate exploitation of France for resources and, ultimately, its geographical dissection. At least if Hitler had won the war the French would have been cured of their self-doubts as there would no longer have been a France.

The cowardice of Vichy, the ineffectiveness of the National Revolution and the outrageousness of collaboration quickly alienated public opinion. Although different parts of France responded at different times, it is clear that within the southern zone disenchantment with Vichy, if not with Pétain, set in as early as January 1941. Such disillusionment, however, did not suddenly give rise to widespread resistance. This was a long time coming and, as noted, 'professional' resisters were a minority. For the vast majority of resisters, an ambiguity would always surround their actions. However much they despised Vichy and the Germans, however honourable their patriotism, however brave their actions, by 1943 France was so utterly tied into the German war effort that it was difficult not to assist the occupier in one way or another.

It is testimony to the power of the 'resistancialist' myth, carefully elaborated by de Gaulle and others, that it is only comparatively recently that such ambiguity, together with knowledge of the internal dissent which bedevilled resisters, is coming to the fore. Nonetheless, the achievements of the Resistance were remarkable. Resisters may not have played a significant military role in the Liberation and their indiscipline certainly led to unnecessary deaths through summary executions. Yet it was the Resistance, especially under de Gaulle, which contributed to the restrained nature of the *épuration*. It was also the Resistance, in its many guises, that drafted plans for the renewal of France, schemes which proved both popular and workable. And, of course, it was the Resistance that salvaged national honour, permitting France to play a part in the final defeat of Germany. As Kedward says, this achievement was all the more remarkable given the fact that most resisters were not Jean Moulins but 'ordinary men and women' (Kedward, 1984).

While the 'resistancialist' myth might have been shattered, France can still take pride in its defiance of Germany, and this has gone some way in curing what Rousso labelled the Vichy *syndrome* (Rousso, 1989). There are signs that France is finally coming to terms with this most painful of episodes. Those who lived through the Occupation are now few on the ground; the opening of state archives has left few skeletons in the cupboard; and the extensive research into the war years has revealed the true horrors of Vichy's complicity in the murder of Jews and other minorities. That public attention is also shifting to the Algerian war, another painful memory in the French national consciousness, is perhaps further evidence that the *syndrome* is becoming less painful.

Nonetheless, there must remain doubts whether the French state or the French public will ever truly be at ease with the Occupation, in particular the persecution of Jews. It is highly significant that when in 1992 Mitterrand officially declared 16 July a day of remembrance for the Vél d'Hiv round-ups, he refused to accept blame for the persecutions on behalf of the French state, deploying the Gaullist argument that Vichy had been an illegal regime, an aberration in French history, when of course it had been nothing of the sort. It is also significant that those who have been put on trial in recent years for 'crimes against humanity' have only been the small fry. After 1944–46, the bigger fish largely evaded justice. The existence of Le Pen's Front National is evidence that the extreme right-wing has not disappeared, and as Europe moves unsteadily towards greater integration it is certain that nationalist and xenophobic voices will become louder. Just as German schoolchildren are still required to visit the extermination camps, maybe there is a need that the French should revisit wartime persecution and should not attempt a cure for the *syndrome*. Such a statement may seem patronising, especially coming from a British author. Yet it is to be wondered whether the British would have behaved any differently had the Germans crossed the Channel. The experience of the Channel Islands under Occupation, recently chronicled by Madeleine Bunting, suggests not (Bunting, 1995). It is Britain's good fortune that this question can never be properly answered.

Ambiguity surrounds whether the Croix de Feu was truly fascist and intent on a coup d'état. *In the 1935 parliamentary enquiry into the events of 6 February 1934, left-wing deputies pressed Colonel de La Rocque on these very issues.*

La Rocque: I return to article 2 which relates to the aims of our group, and I reiterate these words: 'in general, the moral and material recovery of France.'

I make this distinction which one has always affirmed in the association. When someone asks me – 'Do you make or do you not make politics?' – I reply – and here we are in agreement and have always been in agreement – 'To make politics, this is to affiliate to a certain party, it is to adopt a programme, a political position.' Looked at in this manner, which is perhaps a vulgar conception of the question, we do not make politics. But article 2 of our statutes and, in particular, the last six words – those which I have just reread – give us the right to work for the maintenance of that for which we have struggled.

M. Petrus Faure: I conclude from that, that in your opinion, you do not make politics.

La Rocque: We are simply concerned with the public interest.

M. Petrus Faure: Do you not consider that the influence of socialism plays a part in the public good?

La Rocque: In a rather crude way, but who will interpret our thought clearly? Here is what I can say to you – we serve the tricolour alone, and we are ready to serve it alongside all those who honour it. But when we see a flag of another colour, we are not in support.

The declaration is sufficiently vague, and the Radical-Socialist deputy Catalan tries to force the colonel to make clear his ideological position.

Catalan: You have written, 'Our frontiers are, on the right, monarchism; on the left, the red flag.' My question is this. Have you made public declarations in the same vein, by tracts, posters, newspaper articles before the 6th of February?

La Rocque: Yes, at the general assembly of the Croix de Feu of March 1931, if I'm not mistaken, the question asked of me by the Croix de Feu – 'Are you a republican, or aren't you?' – at the general assembly, I declared that the Croix de Feu were republicans and that I was one myself.

Proceedings of the Commission of Enquiry into 6 February 1934 contained in Serge Berstein, *Le 6 février 1934* (Paris, Gallimard, 1975), pp. 63–4.

DOCUMENT 2   THE POPULAR FRONT

In anticipation of the Popular Front victory in June 1936, several spontaneous strikes erupted in factories, protests which were brought to an end by the Matignon Agreements. The concessions granted sent shockwaves through the French right and, although many were rescinded in 1938, the Matignon Agreements help explain the virulence with which Vichy assaulted the left.

1. The employers' delegation allows the immediate establishment of collective labour contracts.

2. These contracts will include the following provisions (articles 3 to 5).

3. Since all citizens are required to observe the law, the employers recognise their employers' freedom of opinion, and the right of the workers freely to join a trade union constituted under the terms of the labour code.

The employers agree to take no account of the fact that a worker might belong to a union when taking decisions relating to the hiring of labour, the allocation of jobs, the imposition of disciplinary action or the dismissal of employees.

If one of the contracting parties claims that the dismissal of a worker had occurred in violation of the trade union rights mentioned above, the two parties agree to establish the facts and reach an equitable solution to the question at issue.

This, however, does not prevent the parties from attempting to obtain legal redress for any injury caused.

The exercise of trade union rights must not result in actions contrary to the law.

4. From the day on which work resumes, all real wages, as they stood on 25 May 1936, shall be increased on a sliding scale ranging from 15 per cent for the lowest wages to 7 per cent for the highest. In no factory shall the total increase in wages exceed 12 per cent.

Any increases in wages granted since the above mentioned date shall be included in the readjustments in wages mentioned in the previous paragraph. But to the extent that these increases exceed the aforementioned readjustments they will be paid.

In the negotiations which will commence immediately to establish collective contracts prescribing a minimum wage by region and by category, special attention must be paid to the necessary readjustments of abnormally low wages.

The representatives of the employers agree to carry out the adjustments necessary to maintain a normal relationship between wages and white-collar salaries.

5. Except in special cases already covered by the law, every factory

employing more than 10 workers will create two or several (depending on the size of the factory) workers' delegates after agreement between the union organisations or, if there is no union, between the interested parties. These delegates will present to the management individual claims which have not been satisfied, relating to the application of laws, decrees and regulations contained in the labour code, to wage levels and to measures concerning hygiene and safety.

The delegates will be elected by all workers, male and female, over eighteen, providing that they have worked in the factory at least three months and have not been deprived of their civic rights.

Workers over 25, of French nationality, who have worked in the factory without interruption for a year (or less if this provision reduces the number of eligible candidates to less than five) are eligible for election as delegates.

Workers holding a retail business of whatever kind, either themselves or through their spouses are not eligible for election.

6. The employers' delegation undertakes not to take any reprisals against the strikers.

7. The CGT delegates request the workers on strike to resume work as soon as the management of their factory has accepted this general agreement, and as soon as conversations concerning its application have begun between workers and management.

> The Matignon Agreements, reproduced and translated by Julian Jackson, *The Popular Front.*
> *Defending Democracy, 1934–1938* (Cambridge, Cambridge University Press, 1988),
> pp. 305–6.

DOCUMENT 3 MUNICH

In this extract, the British journalist and experienced French commentator Alexander Werth observes the Chamber of Deputies' reaction to the Munich Agreements, which marked the high point of appeasement in France.

Parliament was called for a brief 'exceptional' session on 4 October. The whole debate on Munich lasted barely six hours; and technically it was only a discussion on the motion of adjournment approved by the Government.

Although it was on the *grandes journées* of parliament, and the Chamber was crowded, everybody felt that the calling of Parliament was, to the Government, little more than an unpleasant formality. The whole crisis had occurred without Parliament having been consulted at any moment – in spite of numerous requests that Parliament be called. These requests, incidentally, came chiefly from the 'pacifists' who were convinced that the majority of the Chamber and Senate was 'pacifist' like themselves. M. Flandin was especially firm on this point; and one of the principal arguments used against a 'firm' policy was that the Chamber would in no circumstances consent to declare war on Germany even if Czechoslovakia were invaded. The argument certainly reflected to some extent the state of mind in French Parliamentary quarters at the end of September, that is, before the guns had gone off; what Parliament would have done once the war had actually started can only be a matter of speculation. Even an ardent 'pacifist' like M. Pierre Dominique was not certain that Parliament would not have been swept off its feet by the reaction of public opinion to an actual outbreak of war. But one thing is certain: and that is the desperate fear of the majority of French deputies of being suspected of *bellicisme*; a charge of 'warmongering' might prove fatal in the next election. And it is significant that, although opinion was greatly divided in every party on the merits of Munich, the motion of adjournment (which, in effect, implied the approval of Munich) was voted unanimously with the exception of the Communists, and of M. de Kérillis. There were one or two abstentions. Unlike the Labour Party, the French Socialists, though profoundly divided, all voted 'for Munich'.

Alexander Werth, *The Twilight of France* (London, Hamish Hamilton, 1942), pp. 283–4.

DOCUMENT 4   FRENCH STRATEGY

A prewar advocate of a professional army equipped with mobile armour, although not necessarily attack aircraft, here General de Gaulle provides a critique of the shortcomings of French strategy in 1940, without acknowledging the changes effected by General Gamelin.

The military, who received from the state no more than spasmodic and contradictory impulses, fell back within their deference to doctrine. The Army became stuck in a set of ideas which had had their hey-day before the end of the previous war. It was all the more inclined that way because its leaders were growing old at their posts, wedded to errors that had once constituted their glory.

Hence, the concept of the fixed and continuous front dominated the strategy envisaged for a future action. Organisation, doctrine, training and armament derived from it directly. It was understood that, in case of war, France would mobilise the mass of her reserves and would build up the largest possible number of divisions, designed not for manoeuvring, attacking and exploiting, but for holding sectors. They would be placed in position all along the French and Belgian frontiers – Belgium being, then, explicitly our ally – and would there await the enemy's offensive.

As for the means: tanks, aircraft, mobile and revolving guns, which the last battles of the First World War had already shown to be capable of effecting surprise and the breakthrough, and whose power had since been growing continuously, were to be used only for reinforcing the line and, at need, restoring it by local counter-attacks. The types of weapon were established with this in mind: heavy tanks, armed with light, short pieces and intended for escorting infantry, not for rapid, independent action; interceptor aircraft designed for defending areas of sky, beside which the Air Force could muster few bombers and no dive bombers; artillery designed to fire from fixed positions with a narrow horizontal field of action, not to push ahead through all sorts of country and fire at all angles. Besides, the front was traced in advance by the works of the Maginot Line, prolonged by the Belgian fortifications. Thus the nation-in-arms would hold a barrier, behind which it would wait – so it was thought – for the equipment.

Charles de Gaulle, *The Call to Honour, 1940–1942* (London, Collins, 1958), pp. 13–14, translated by Jonathan Griffin.

DOCUMENT 5   **THE PHONEY WAR**

The Paris correspondent of New Yorker *magazine, A.J. Liebling, observes how tension visibly increased in the French capital as the 'phoney war' came to a close and the German offensive in the west began in earnest.*

There was a hot heavy pause the next few days (after 18 May 1940). I took long walks on the boulevards and up and down dull, deserted business streets. The wartime population of Paris had slowly increased from late November until April, as evacuated families returned from the provinces, but since the beginning of the offensive the population had again decreased. All the people who had remained in town seemed to concentrate on the boulevards. It gave them comfort to look at one another. They were not consciously afraid, however. There were long queues in front of the movie houses, especially those that showed double features. You could get a table at a sidewalk café only with difficulty, and the ones that had girl orchestras did particularly well. One girl orchestra, at the Grande Maxeville, was called the Joyous Wings, and its bandstand and instruments had been decorated with blue aeroplanes. There were no young soldiers in the streets, because no furloughs were being issued.

It is simple now to say, 'The war on the Continent was lost on 15 May.' But as the days in May passed, people in Paris only gradually came to suspect how disastrous that day had been. There was a time lag between every blow and the effect on public morale. I can't remember exactly when I first became frightened, or when I first began to notice that the shapes of people's faces were changing. There was plenty of food in Paris. People got thin worrying. I think I noticed first the thinning faces of the sporting girls in the cafés every night, it was easy to keep track. Then I became aware that the cheekbones, the noses, and the jaws of all Paris were becoming more prominent.

A.J. Liebling, *The Road Back to Paris* (New York, Tesoro Books, 1944), p. 74.

DOCUMENT 6   THE *EXODE*

A soldier of Franco-British citizenship and later a member of the Free French, Vila gives a first-hand account of the confusion that was part of the exode. This flight of millions of people helps explain why Pétain and the declaration of the Armistice were greeted with such acclamation.

Once in Montreuil, we very soon realised the tragic panic situation and the full extent of the upheaval which the war had brought to France. Normal life was completely upset and as we moved along the road leading out of the town we were shocked at the transformation which the deteriorating position had caused. Everywhere crowds of refugees were on the move in cars, lorries, on bicycles and most on foot taking with them only whatever they were able to transport in clothing and bedding. Most people were watching from their houses uncertain whether they should join the exodus or remain and hope for the best when the Germans arrived. There was no further doubt that nothing could be done to stop the progress of the invaders since the army was moving south with the civilians. It was a difficult decision to make for the people watching on their door steps, but those who remained at home were in the end more fortunate than the millions who took to the road, abandoning their possessions to bands of looters who followed the crowds.

Unpublished diary of Monsieur Vila, 13 June 1940, Imperial War Museum, 97/7/1.

DOCUMENT 7   PÉTAIN

On 17 June 1940, Pétain took to the radio to announce the Armistice and, at the same time, betrayed both his naivety and enormous self-belief.

My fellow French,
At the call of the president of the Republic, I assume from today the direction of the government of France. Certain of the affection of our admirable army, which fights with a heroism worthy of its long military traditions against an enemy superior in numbers and weapons, certain that by its magnificent resistance, it has fulfilled our duties in regard to our allies, confident of the support of the veterans that I was proud to

command, certain of the confidence of the whole population, I give to France the gift of my person to attenuate for its suffering.

In these unhappy hours, I think of the unfortunate refugees who, in extreme distress, line our roads. I express to them my compassion and my concern. It is with a broken heart that I say to you today that it is necessary to cease the fighting.

This evening I have addressed our adversary to ask if he is ready to search with me, as fellow soldiers, after struggle and in honour, the means of putting an end to the hostilities.

All Frenchmen should rally round the government over which I preside during these testing days and suppress their anguish so as to obey only their faith in the destiny of their country.

Speech of Pétain 17 June 1940, reproduced in Jean-Claude Barbas, *Philippe Pétain. Discours aux Français, 17 juin 1940–20 août 1944* (Paris, Albin Michel, 1989), pp. 57–8.

DOCUMENT 8   **THE ARMISTICE**

Comprising 24 articles, the Franco-German Armistice was a relatively brief document, betraying the speed with which it had been drawn up. In many ways, the most important clauses were the following.

Article 1. The French Government will order the cessation of hostilities against the German Reich on French soil as well as in its possessions, colonies and protectorates, and at sea. It will order those French troops that are already surrounded to lay down their arms immediately.

Article 2. With a view to safeguarding the interests of the Reich the following French territory will be occupied by German troops, that is to say, to the north and west of a line shown on the map from the region of Geneva, Dôle, Châlon-sur-Saône, Paray-le-Monial, Moulins, Bourges, Vierzon, then in the direction of Tours up to twenty kilometres east of Tours, this boundary to run parallel with the railway Angoulême–Bordeaux down to Mont-de-Marsan and Saint Jean-Pied-de-Port. In so far as the territory to be occupied is not yet under the control of the German troops it will be occupied by them immediately after the conclusion of the present convention.

Article 3. In the occupied area the German Reich has all the rights of the occupying power (to the exclusion of the administration of the country without interference in the regime). The French government pledges itself to facilitate in every way the regulations relating to the exercise of these rights and to their execution with the cooperation of the French administration.

The German government intends to reduce to the bare minimum the occupation of the west coast after the cessation of hostilities with England.

The French government is free to choose its capital in unoccupied territory or, should it so desire, to transfer the seat of government to Paris. In the latter event the German government undertakes to give all the necessary facilities to the French government and to its central administrative services so that they may be in a position to administer from Paris both the occupied and unoccupied territory.

Article 4. The French armed forces on land, sea, and air are to be demobilized and disarmed within a period still to be fixed, but the troops necessary to maintain order within the country are excepted. Their strength and their armaments respectively will be fixed by Germany and Italy. The French armed forces stationed in the districts occupied by Germany are to be withdrawn into the unoccupied zone and demobilized.

Before being withdrawn into the unoccupied zone these troops will leave their arms and equipment in the places where they were at the conclusion of the armistice. They will be responsible for the due delivery of the equipment and arms to the German troops. ...

Article 10. The French Government pledges itself not to undertake any hostile action against the German Reich with any part of the armed forces remaining in its service, or in any other manner.

In the same way the French Government will prevent the members of the French armed forces from leaving French territory, and will see that no arms, equipment, no ships, no aeroplanes, etc., are transported to England or abroad. The French Government will forbid French subjects to fight against Germany in the service of the States with which Germany is at war. French subjects who do not conform to this regulation will be treated as *francs-tireurs* by the German troops.

Article 19. All German prisoners of war and civilians, including those awaiting trial and sentenced, who have been arrested and condemned for acts committed in favour of the German Reich are to be handed over without delay to the German troops. The French Government must hand over on demand all German subjects, designated by the Government of the Reich, who are in France, in French colonial possessions, protectorates or mandated territories. The French Government promises to prevent the transfer of prisoners of war, or of German civilian prisoners, from France to the French possessions or abroad.

As for prisoners already moved out of France, including sick and wounded, accurate lists must be presented giving the name of the place where they are.

The German High Command will look after the sick and wounded German prisoners of war.

The Franco-German Armistice terms, 23 June 1940, reproduced from Paul Baudouin,
The Private Diaries of Paul Baudouin (London, Eyre & Spottiswoode, 1948)
translated by Sir Charles Petrie, pp. 301–4.

DOCUMENT 9   A CATHOLIC RESPONSE TO THE DEFEAT

In the aftermath of the defeat, few commentators mentioned military unpreparedness, but laid stress instead on moral decadence. Prominent among such critics were churchmen who hoped to profit from the defeat by reversing the institutionalised secularism which had been a part of the Republic.

Before the war, what had our country done to merit heaven's protection? Is it necessary to recall the national apostasy in which our governments gloried: the war conducted for sixty years against the Church, the religious congregations, the private education system, in essence the only spiritual forces capable of safeguarding the soul of France, in conserving France for the faith? Everything was put into place to chase God from our courts, from our hospitals, from the army, from the school, so as to secularise the French people.

Declaration of Mgr Durieux, Bishop of Chambéry, July 1940, contained in

Renée Bédarida, *Les Armes de l'Esprit. Témoignage Chrétien, 1941–1944*

(Paris, Editions Ouvrières, 1977), p.15.

DOCUMENT 10   THE BEGINNING OF THE FREE FRENCH

On 17 June 1940, General de Gaulle, disgruntled at the Armistice, boarded a plane for England from where he broadcast the next day. Here, he puts forward his own explanation as to why he initially won few recruits for his fledgling Free French movement.

Meanwhile isolated volunteers were reaching England daily. They came mostly from France, brought by the last ships to have left there normally, or escaping in small boats which they had managed to seize, or, again, having with great difficulty got across Spain, evading its police which shut up in the camp of Miranda those it caught. Some airmen saved their machines from the control of Vichy and contrived to get away from North Africa and reach Gibralter. Some merchant seamen, placed outside French ports by the chances of navigation, or, sometimes, by the escape of a ship – as, for example, the Capo Olmo (Commandant Vuillemin) – asked to be enrolled as combatants. Some Frenchmen resident abroad came and demanded to serve. Having called a meeting at the White City of two thousand men who had been wounded at Dunkirk and were convalescing in British hospitals, I got two hundred enlistments. A Colonial battalion, which happened to be in Cyprus, detached from the *Armée du Levant*, rallied spontaneously under its leader, Commandant Lorette. In the last days of June a flotilla of fishing boats reached Cornwall, bringing over to General de Gaulle all the able-bodied men from the island of Sein. Day after day the enrolment of these lads so splendid in their keeness, many of whom had performed exploits to get to us, strengthened our determination. Messages from all parts of the world piled up on my table, bringing me, from individuals or from small groups, moving requests for enlistment. My office and those of the Spears mission expended prodigies of ingenuity and obstinacy to arrange their transport.

Suddenly a lamentable event occurred to stop the stream. On July 4th the radio and the newspapers announced that on the previous day the British Mediterranean Fleet had attacked the French Squadron at anchor at Mers-el-Kébir. At the same time we were informed that the British had occupied by surprise the French warships which had taken refuge in British ports and had taken ashore and interned – not without some bloodshed – their officers and crews. Finally, on the 10th, the news was made public of the torpedoing, by British aircraft, of the battleship Richelieu, at anchor in Dakar Roads. In London the official *communiqués* and the newspapers tended to represent this series of aggressions as a sort of naval victory.

Charles de Gaulle, *The Call to Honour, 1940–1942* (London, Collins, 1958), pp. 95–6, translated by Jonathan Griffin.

DOCUMENT 11   THE CULT OF THE MARSHAL

These documents reveal different dimensions of the cult of marshalship. The first is an unsolicited letter from a child; the second a glowing portrait from a leading hagiographer, René Benjamin; and the third, a cynical adolescent perspective, crafted by the novelist Alphonse Boudard.

(a) Happy Christmas, *Monsieur le Maréchal*. Not having been able to offer you flowers on your visit to Marseilles, I send you, on this paper, this little basket that I drew for your attention. I will make my Christmas communion for you, *Monsieur le Maréchal*, and for France. I know that you have sorrow, but I know that God aids you and he will always help us. I will always be obedient to the laws that you will make. I give you my heart as you have given yours to France.

Letter of a child to Pétain, Christmas 1940, in *La Croix*, 30 December 1940.

(b) He walks with a clear step. His moustache has the impeccable whiteness of virtue. The face is clear; nothing has dimmed it; it remains smooth. All the wrinkles are around the eyes, because the eye crinkles when it observes, when he speaks to a man who is not of his nature – when he seeks how to understand him, or merely how not to be duped by him

René Benjamin, *Le Maréchal et son peuple* (Paris, Plon, 1941), p.6.

(c) The time that I recount to you is badly known, poorly recalled by those who make history for us. There was everywhere ... *nous voilà* ... our Marshal! At the town hall, at the Church, in all the shops, at the school, in the bistros, in the brothels, the portrait of the Marshal ... the immortal phrases of the Marshal! The white moustache of the Marshal, his blue gaze which fixes on eternal France! He is a good child, the Marshal. He promises us, if we are wise, the flowers in the garden ... a beautiful harvest for the day after tomorrow. He is of the fields and is pastoral. He embraces little girls ... let them come to me! He lifts them with his cane. He distributes good marks to good pupils. He goes from town to town in the southern zone, and everywhere he is waited with fervour. One offers him the most beautiful grapes from our vines ... the most beautiful mutton from the flock. He is on gold medals, on the calendars of the Post Office, in images in place of Marianne.

Alphonse Boudard, *Les Combattants du petit bonheur* (Paris, La Table Ronde, 1977), p. 72.

DOCUMENT 12   THE NATIONAL REVOLUTION

Composed in 1941, this document was intended as a definitive exposition of the values of the National Revolution and was designed to replace the revolutionary charter of 1789. It was even sent to Pope Pius XII who was uneasy that it did not accord sufficient liberties to the individual.

1. Man's fundamental rights derive from nature. But they are only guaranteed to him by the communities that surround him: the family which raises him, the job which nourishes him, the nation which protects him.

2. To recognise rights for man without imposing duties on him is to corrupt him. To impose duties on him without recognising his rights is to debase him.

3. Liberty and justice are conquests. They are only maintained by the virtues that they have engendered: work and courage, discipline and obedience to the law.

4. Citizens must work always to improve society. They should not complain that it is not always perfect.

5. A demanding spirit sets back the progress that the spirit of collaboration can bring about.

6. Every citizen who seeks his own welfare outside the common interest goes counter to reason and counter to his very own interest.

7. Citizens owe to the country their labour, their resources and even their lives. No political conviction, no doctrinal preference frees them from these obligations.

8. Every community requires a leader. Every leader, carrying responsibility, must be honoured and served. A leader is no longer worthy of being a leader when he becomes an oppressor.

9. The state has, as its objectives, the happiness and the prosperity of the nation. It owes imprisonment to the criminal, protection to the innocent, and to everyone the sovereignty of the laws. These great duties define its mission. The state can only accomplish this mission in exercising its authority in justice.

10. The state must be dependent and strong. No group can be tolerated which places citizens against one another, and threatens to ruin the authority of the state. The unity of the state is put in peril by sectional interests. The state has a duty to destroy these.

11. The state demands from its citizens the equality of their sacrifices: it guarantees them, in return, the equality of opportunity.

12. The school is the extension of the family. It must make the child understand the benefits of the human order which surrounds him and supports him. It must render him sensitive to the beauty, the grandeur and the continuity of the country. It must teach him the respect for moral and religious beliefs, in particular those that France has professed since the origins of her national existence.

13. Neither birth nor wealth confer the right of command. The true hierarchy is that of talent and of merit.

14. The economy of a country is healthy only insofar as the prosperity of private enterprises supports the general good of the community.

15. Wealth has not only rights; it also has duties proportionate to the powers it confers.

16. The state delegates to its officials a part of its authority and trusts them to exercise this in its name; but for this same reason, it punishes their weaknesses with an exemplary severity.

Principles of the Community, 1941, contained in Jean-Claude Barbas, *Philippe Pétain. Discours aux Français, 17 juin 1940–20 août 1944* (Paris, Albin Michel, 1989), pp. 363–5.

DOCUMENT 13   VICHY PROPAGANDA

Posters were commonplace under Vichy, testifying to the regime's awareness of the power of visual images. The example extols the virtues of the new France, built on the foundations of 'work, family, country' which has replaced 'France and Company' which rested on 'laziness, demagogy, internationalism'.

© Collection VIOLLET

Vichy intended women to play a traditional role in society, as dutiful wives and mothers, positions which tallied with the Catholic Church's perspective on the family. At the same time, this document betrays the Church's enthusiasm for the National Revolution project.

WHO WILL GIVE US HOUSEWIVES?

The proverb says, 'Every cloud has a silver lining.' We have hardly begun to discover some of the moral benefits that the tragic ordeal of this unfortunate war will bring us, so that something of our desolate spirit, resigned to defeat, reshapes itself under a hand which strikes only to rebuild.

Would we have thought, a few months ago, that in so little time so many problems we held important would be resolved? The return to the land; the return of women to the home; education rediscovering its purest national traditions; and, above all, the numerical growth and moral enrichment of the family.

But this young girl, that woman, who must in future renounce the factory, the office and the workplace, to rediscover, inside the home, the true mission to which Providence destined them: are they ready to fulfil the new tasks that await them?

How many times, in these last years, have we heard husbands and fathers groan: 'My wife, my daughter do not know how to do their housework! They are incapable of darning a sock, even of cooking two eggs on the stove.'

All the money which was earned above, and often much more than that, was swallowed up in fees for the washerwoman, for the dressmaker, for the milliner, for the housekeeper, in restaurant bills which frequently took the place of meals which had not been prepared.

A true waste of money! Incalculable moral dangers! It would take too long to list them all: one no longer lived in one's house; the home had lost its attraction and intimacy. And who paid the price for this disorder? The beauteous and harmonious fraternity of hearts.

La Croix, 18 December 1940.

One of the founder members of the Paris-based Resistance movement Valmy, which attracted several academics, in 1941 Paul Simon fled to Britain where he produced a book about living conditions in France.

Unquestionably a piece of propaganda designed for a British audience, it was also a perceptive piece of writing.

An entire book would be needed for a really complete account of living conditions in France. In any case, I have been unable to give more than an incomplete outline because prices are changing all the time. Nevertheless, something would be sadly lacking if I did not say anything about the queueing which has to be done for everything, particularly for vegetables, meat, fish, chocolate, and milk.

The queues have their own experts. One queues for cooked food, another for fish. By queueing one may do a good turn for relatives or friends. For some workless and old people it has become a paying proposition.

Holders of the special cards issued to the disabled and to large families have priority in the queues, a privilege which causes many disputes. It has been admitted that these priority cards are held by one person in three.

Not long ago, queueing began hours in advance. A police regulation has since been issued forbidding the formation of queues more than half an hour before shops open. Those who have to queue have found a way round this regulation. They walk up and down outside the shop. The *concierges* of some buildings near to shops make a charge for the use of corridors so that those whose legs do not permit them to run fast enough still have a chance to be first in the queue when it is at last formed.

One waits one's turn patiently, either standing or on a folding stool, under the vigilant eye of a policeman or municipal guard. Acquaintances are made, one learns news of the district, the days for distribution of this or that foodstuff, and which numbered cards are available on such and such a day at the butcher's or tobacconist's.

The queue is an outdoor public meeting, no matter what the weather. There is talk of events, of the men in power, and of 'collaborators'. I am convinced that the queues have already formed their verdict on the Riom trials.

The Germans have noted the excellent scope for propaganda which the queues offer. They have sent women Gestapo agents to them. These praise Hitler and Pétain. They talk loudly, having nothing to fear, and they denounce suspects.

The people are not duped; they keep quiet when one of these gossips is spotted, knowing very well that candid queuers have paid with their freedom for too sharp a retort.

Paul Simon, *One Enemy Only. The Invader* (London, Hodder & Stoughton, 1942), pp. 119–20.

DOCUMENT 16   MONTOIRE

On 24 October, Pétain realised his long-held dream of a meeting with Hitler, yet as the official German records recount, it is clear that he had not properly thought through what he was going to ask of the Nazi dictator. The meeting took on greater symbolic than diplomatic importance.

The Marshal replied that he was gratified by the Führer's welcome, despite the painful atmosphere pervading the whole situation. He was especially impressed by the Führer's understanding for the difficult position in which he (the Marshal) found himself. His position was truly a tragic one. He had at all times been an opponent of the war with Germany. In consequence, past French Governments had sent him as Ambassador to Spain. When the crisis approached in 1939, he had twice requested to be allowed to return to France and to resume his functions in the War Council. He did so because the information reaching him indicated that France was on the point of plunging into a disastrous adventure. This was a very painful time for him and when he finally learned that France had declared war on Germany, he was barely able to restrain his grief. This declaration of war he considered an act of great folly. He, who had been throughout against this war, was now called upon to atone for the errors of past Governments.

  M. Laval had reported to him the conversation he had with the Führer the day before yesterday. He understood that the subject of that conversation was the question of cooperation between the two countries. He was sorry that such cooperation had not begun before, in the years before this war. But there was perhaps still time to regain what had been lost. The English were affording the best opportunity for that. As France's allies their conduct towards that country had been exceedingly bad since the Armistice. France would not forget the events of Oran and the attack on Dakar. The latter action, upon England's instigation, had been headed by a bad Frenchman, a French general, who had denied his country. Today's France no longer tolerated things of this kind and this officer accordingly was promptly condemned to death, to the confiscation of his property, and perpetual banishment from France. Justice had thus taken its course against him.

  The English, however, were continuing their attacks on France, principally against her colonial empire and especially in Africa. France had effectively resisted at Dakar. He (Pétain) had sent an officer to the African colonies with the mission of restoring the disaffected to the cause of France. In this respect, and since the Führer had done the honour of speaking of cooperation, a field might be found where its realisation between the two countries was a practical possibility. He did not wish to go into details, but he could give assurances for his own person that as far as matters depended on him everything would be done in order to secure these colonial territories for France.

Memorandum by an official of the Foreign Minister's Secretariat on the meeting between Hitler and Pétain, Montoire, 24 October 1940, *Documents on German Foreign Policy*, Series D, vol. 11, pp. 385–6.

DOCUMENT 17   COLLABORATIONISM

In this interview, Hermann Eich recalls his time in Paris where he worked in the Press section of the Propaganda Abteilung *overseeing collaborationist publications.*

Editors in chief were by no means servile in their conduct. Jeantet, for instance, with his pretentious manner, made an impression on the younger members of the *Presse Gruppe*. I was once invited by him, and felt flattered. Sordet I knew as a *bonhomme*, and nothing but. I met Hibbelen once in 1944; he was a man between frontiers. Suarez, who had *Aujourd'hui*, was Abetz's man. He asked me once if I knew that before the war he had written articles in which Hitler was depicted as criminal and mad. I had read his four stout volumes on Briand and been impressed by them, but in fact I answered that what he had written before the war would not interest anyone. Lesca I saw from time to time. Châteaubriant, with his limp and his beard and the venerable madame Castelot in tow, was the incarnation all in one of goodwill, naivety and optimism. Because he could not bring himself to believe that his idol could commit crimes, he kept his eyes closed right to the end. Luchaire liked the good life, money and women. Already before the war he had been propagating Franco-German *rapprochement*, and in that respect he was remaining consistent. ... I used to receive anonymous letters about how Luchaire's corruption was ruining the German image – but then every day we also received letters accusing French journalists of being Jewish, and sometimes accusing us too, in thoroughly antisemitic depictions, always unsigned. George Prade, Luchaire's colleague on *Les Nouveaux Temps* was also a friend – he was a magistrate in Paris, I believe. A score of journalists were helped by Luchaire to leave Paris at the end of the Occupation, though some, like Jeantet, stayed. Had Brasillach been arrested a year later, I believe he would have been judged less severely. With Henri Jeanson, whom I knew, I always had the impression of a man who was a constant cabaret turn; he took nothing seriously, as though we were running an assembly of lunatics who by some misfortune had settled themselves in Paris. I can say that I know of no case of money going from our department to a paper or to a journalist. No editor or director or journalist came into my office to ask for a subsidy. My personal salary as a lieutenant was, I think, two hundred marks a month.

Interview, no date, in David Pryce-Jones, *Paris in the Third Reich. A History of the German Occupation, 1940–1944* (London, Collins, 1981), pp. 246–7.

DOCUMENT 18   ANTISEMITISM

With Vichy's abrogation of the Daladier–Marchandeau law of 1938, the way was open for a particularly vicious type of antisemitism, especially in the collaborationist press, which betrayed the biological roots of French antisemitism, which was not merely cultural as is sometimes claimed. The following pretends to be an extract from a newspaper in the future, the year 2142.

14 July 2142. Marvellous news runs through the streets of Paris. The bulletins of the national Radiotelevision have informed us of the news.

The last Jew has just died.

So, this is the end of this despicable race, whose last representative lived, since his birth, at the former zoo in the Bois de Vincennes, in a cage specially reserved for his use, and where our children were able to see him frolic, not for the pleasure of their eyes, but for their moral edification.

He is dead. In essence, this is for the best. Personally, I always feared that he would escape, and God knows all the evil that a Jew can do at liberty. He remained alone since the death of his companion ten years ago, who thankfully was sterile, but with this race one never knows. I must go to the zoo to reassure myself that the news is true.

15 July 2142. I went to see the skin of the Jew. It is clearly him who is dead. This was not a rumour. Ouf! I can breathe again ... That morning, several hundred of us had come for news. That's all for the good. As to myself, I disapproved of the indulgence the public powers displayed towards the Jew.

What need had one of guarding so zealously an example, moreover an awful example, of a race which has thankfully disappeared?

God, he was ugly! The crimped hair, never combed, the bleary eyes, surrounded by fat, the banana nose, the thick lips shaped like the rim of a chamber pot: he looked more like a monkey (Sorry! Monkeys ...) than a human being.

When I think that this vile race was on the point of conquering the world and imposing, through its domination, its own notions of beauty. I shudder retrospectively at the thought.

18 July 2142. From where did the initial idea, the mighty idea, the saving idea, spring from? Was it Drumont, Gobineau or the genial Céline,

who had the genius to put forward this wonderful idea? A single means of getting rid of the Jews, without massacres, without pogroms: sterilise them. Yes, all of them: men and women. First to lock them up in vast camps, to take them one at a time, and snip, the incision; a timely little reminder of circumcision.

But where did the miracle come from – when was the thing done? After the Second World War in 1939–45, there was throughout the world a general consensus on the Jewish problem and its solution. This evil race had done too much harm, it had let loose too many cataclysms. The cup overflowed and it was to offend God to leave the Jews without punishment. This punishment was the extinction of the Jewish race cited above. STERILISATION! What a wonderful thing this was. Today, the earth nourishes twice as many men as in 1930. There are no longer any Jews to starve them.

20 July 2142. There was a fine brouhaha in the camps of Jews when the STERILISATION DECREE appeared. The Weeping Wall was almost submerged by the flood of the tears of the chosen people.

The Decree, dated 25 June 1950, was framed as such:

Article 1. All Jews, whatever sex, faith or whatever nationality, will be sterilised.

Article 2. The sterilisation operations must be finished no later than 25 June 1953.

Article 3. For the edification of future generations, three Jewish couples, chosen among the healthiest, will be kept.

L'Appel, 16 July 1942, reproduced in Ganier Raymond, *Une certaine France*.
L'Antisémitisme 40–44 (Paris, Balland, 1975), pp. 177–80.

DOCUMENT 19   DENUNCIATIONS

To rid France of so-called 'undesirable' elements, both the Vichy regime and various of its organisations encouraged the population to spy on itself, reporting friends, work colleagues and neighbours for their behaviour, a process known as 'délation', although it should be stressed that informing for the Germans was actively discouraged. This resulted in some 5 million letters which were often no more than petty resentments, although some were more serious in their intentions.

Monsieur ... there exists at Chazelles-sur-Lyon, a little industrial town on the Loire, 60 kilometres from Lyon, a candle-moulding factory. This factory ought to work for German armaments. It is led by a Jew. The latter has declared, perhaps too late in the day, that the central management was at London and that, when he wanted to speak with it, he went to Vichy where he made contact within quarter of an hour. It is my belief we should keep a much closer eye over this. Evidently, this matter does not concern me, but we have too many interests in a German victory not to help our former adversaries by all means. I assure you that, if I was a boy, I would not take long to respond to the appeal of the anti-Bolshevik legion.

> Letter of 20 September 1941 to a collaborationist organisation, in André Lefébure, *Les Conversations secrètes des Français sous l'occupation* (Paris, Plon, 1993), p. 264.

DOCUMENT 20   THE COMMUNISTS

The period between the Nazi–Soviet Pact of August 1939 and the German invasion of the USSR in June 1941 was a deeply unsettling one for French Communists. The launch of Operation Barbarossa at last freed the party as a whole to engage fully in resistance, mobilising its massive networks in an extremely violent struggle against the occupier.

Frenchmen and Frenchwomen.
The liberation of France depends on the victory of the USSR. Our duty is thus to aid, by all means, the land of socialism in its struggle against the fascism of Hitler and his oriole Mussolini, the man who stabbed France in the back in June 1940.

When a munitions train *en route* to Germany mistakes its route or gets lost in the sidings, this is a step in our struggle for the liberation of France.

When the production of coal and the engines of war decreases, this is a step in our struggle for the liberation of France.

When foodstuffs destined for France's invader become scarce, this is a bonus for French consumers and is a step in the struggle for the liberation of France.

Not a man, not a *sou*, not any productive effort for the criminal war Hitler conducts against the USSR.

> *L'Humanité clandestine*, 14 July 1941, reproduced in Dominique Veillon, *La Collaboration.*
> *Textes et débats* (Paris, Livre de Poche, 1984), pp.266–7.

DOCUMENT 21   THE GROWTH OF POPULAR PROTEST

In August 1941, Vichy was alarmed at the growth of civil disobedience and passed a wide series of laws extending police powers. To accompany these, Pétain broadcast the longest of all his radio speeches in which he reiterated the values of the National Revolution.

My fellow French,
I have some serious things to say to you.

From many regions of France, I sense that for several weeks an ill wind has begun to blow.

Anxiety wins over spirits of many. Doubt takes possession of souls. The authority of my government is questioned. Orders are often badly executed.

In an atmosphere of rumours and intrigues, the forces of recovery are inhibited. Others attempt to employ substitutes for themselves who have neither their nobility nor their impartiality. My patronage is too often invoked, even against the government, in order to justify false enterprises of salvation which are, in fact, merely calls to indiscipline. A real malaise affects the French people.

Speech of Marshal Pétain, 12 August 1940, contained in Jean-Claude Barbas, *Philippe Pétain. Discours aux Français, 17 juin 1940–20 août 1944* (Paris, Albin Michel, 1989), p.164.

DOCUMENT 22   THE RIGHT-WING RESISTANCE

Some of the 'false enterprises of salvation', to which Pétain referred above, stemmed from the right-wing resistance which retained a degree of admiration for the marshal, but was disheartened by the actions of his government.

Marshal Pétain. You want to unify France. For that, you ask us for our trust. You tell us to follow you.

This trust, monsieur Marshal, we will not refuse you. You must simply allow us not to have a childlike confidence, not to revere you in a cult of idolatry. This trust will not prevent us from criticising that which must be criticised, of resisting when this is necessary. You are too fond of plain speaking not to wish that we speak frankly with you.

You want to create unity. You tell us to unite behind you.

Sir, we will make unity much better, the chain will be much more solid, if we know why we are uniting ourselves. Unity in France can only be truly made around an idea, and not behind a man, even if he were a superhuman; we are not Germans, we are human beings. If you want to create union, it is necessary that you have the agreement of the country.

We have given our genuine support to your foreign policy since you proved to us that you were resisting. We understand full well that many obscurities remain and that you are not able to say everything. Foreign policy is too shrewd a game to be played out in public. We can wait.

But we know not to subscribe to your domestic policy.

There are men from whom you must disassociate yourself. M. von Brinon has nothing to do at Paris. Benoist-Méchin, the smug admirer of the Reich, is not made to govern France.

The French people will never accept the laws of exception against certain citizens. That the problem of foreigners is a terrible problem, that France must defend itself against the invasion of Israel or any other invasion, we do not doubt. The fifth column is proof of this. It is necessary that the title of French citizen should be an honour to which only a few foreigners can aspire. They must be integrated only after they have proven themselves. But let's not go back to the Flood to determine who is French! In any case, a question of religion should never be brought into play. Turning baptism into an exhibit is to dishonour its meaning. There ought to be a French way of treating these problems, not a German way.

Finally, sir, it is necessary that those who believed it their duty to continue the struggle through war, those who proved their love of France by fighting in de Gaulle's army, should not be accused of treason by your government. In their own way, they are heroes.

Défense de la France, no. 9, 25 January 1942, reproduced in Dominique Veillon, *La Collaboration. Textes et débats* (Paris, Livre de Poche, 1984), pp. 128–9.

DOCUMENT 23   THE *RELÈVE*

It was in this speech, introducing the voluntary work service in Germany, that Laval uttered the infamous words, 'I desire the victory of Germany'. With the drafting of French labour for German factories, many young people abandoned any remaining faith in the Vichy regime and several opted for resistance, particularly in the maquis.

In France, we lack essential materials, our factories work at a snail's pace, unemployment grows worse. Numerous workers are without jobs when Germany has urgent need of manual labour.

In this situation, a new hope emerges for our prisoners. I know that it is never in vain that one makes an appeal to the reason and generosity of the workers of France. It is towards them that I now turn, for it is on them, for the most part, that the fate of our prisoners is going to depend henceforward.

It is necessary that the workers of France respond to my appeal. I have serious reasons to demand it of them, and they must understand that it is a question of something more than our daily existence. France cannot remain passive and indifferent in the face of the enormous sacrifices that Germany consents to in order to build a Europe in which we must take our place.

Workers of France, it is for the liberation of prisoners that you are going to work in Germany. It is for your country that you will go in large numbers. It is in order to allow France to find its place in the new Europe that you will respond to my appeal.

Speech of Laval, 22 June 1942, reproduced in Dominique Veillon, *La Collaboration. Textes et débats* (Paris, Livre de Poche, 1984), p. 353.

THE *MILICE*

Founded to root out resisters and deserters from the STO, the Milice *under Joseph Darnand was a loyal servant of Marshal Pétain and, as this document reveals, invoked several* National Revolution *values. The Twenty-One Points of the Milice were not that far removed from Vichy's Principles of the Community (see Doc. 12).*

Against the Ancien Régime.	For the new order
Against bourgeois egoism.	For French solidarity.
Against apathy.	For enthusiasm.
Against scepticism.	For the faith.
Against routine.	For the spirit of initiative.
Against influence.	For merit.
Against seniority.	For merit.
Against individualism.	For the community spirit.
Against vain liberty.	For true freedoms.
Against egalitarianism.	For hierarchy.
Against democracy.	For authority.
Against demagogy.	For the truth.
Against anarchy.	For discipline.
Against the tutelage of money.	For the supremacy of labour.
Against the trust.	For craftsmanship.
Against international capitalism.	For French corporatism.
Against the proletarian condition.	For social justice.
Against bolshevism.	For nationalism.
Against Gaullist dissidence.	For French unity.
Against the Jewish leper.	For French purity.
Against pagan freemasonry.	For Christian civilisation.
Against the oversight of crimes.	For the imprisonment of those responsible.

The Twenty-One Points of the Milice, 1943, reproduced from François Bédarida, ed., *Touvier. Le Dossier de l'accusation* (Paris, Seuil, 1996), p. 285.

THE *MAQUIS*

In recreating the world of the maquis, *historians have had to be ever inventive, as resistance left behind few written documents. This explains why oral evidence has been so highly valued, and it was the British historian H.R. Kedward who was the first to conduct extensive interviews with* maquisards.

Monsieur: A large proportion of the department of the Aude is covered in forests, but a *maquis* needed water as well. Piccaussel was almost a model *maquis* area, and excellent for parachute drops, being well above the local German headquarters. The population was favourable for three reasons. The leaders were known to them: both I and my *adjoint* were local *instituteurs*. Our contacts with London carried status. And thirdly, the ancient Cathar mentality was still alive – an old tradition of liberty and resistance just as strong as in the struggles against Simon Montfort. ...

The Aude is a monocultural region, but in the farms higher up there was a little bit of everything. When peasants were on our side we arrived as if they were hostile. A little bit of theatre was staged to make it look as if they had no choice. But if peasants were really against us then we cut out the play acting, making our raids at night. On the whole these were a rarity. It was barbaric really, the darkest point of the Resistance. They were grave mistakes. It allowed all abuse to be imputed to the Resistance. Of course there was abuse. We were not saints. But the vast majority of crimes of the period were not committed by the *maquis*. We were not bandits.

Madame: I was an *institutrice*. When my husband was hunted by the Gestapo he left his job as a teacher and signed up in the Beaux Arts in Toulouse as cover. While he was away there was a parachute drop. I made up the code on the spur of the moment and sent him the message. The role of women was equal to that of men. ...

> Interview between H.R. Kedward and Lucien and Françoise Maury, 24 June 1982, in H.R. Kedward, *In Search of the Maquis* (Oxford, Oxford University Press, 1994), pp. 270–1.

DOCUMENT 26   THE PURGES

The purges of 1944 remain one of the most sensitive aspects of the Occupation period. The historian Robert Aron, who was the first to write in 1954 a history of the Vichy regime, was well aware of the delicacy of the matter and, in his later history of the Liberation, attempted to steer a middle course between the claims of Pétainists and Republican officials.

We now come to some of the most painful episodes of the period. These summary executions, by which many French died, were not carried out by the Gestapo or the Militia, but by men who seemed to their victims to be among their liberators. Excesses such as these were doubtless inevitable in the dramatic circumstances that accompanied the departure of the Germans. They were often reprisals for the treatment suffered by the Resistance during the Occupation. But this could not alter the fact that they aroused passionate resentments which in some cases still exist and distort the truth. Consciences were troubled and still continue to be so. Any account of them must therefore be objective. ...

Approximately one Frenchman in a thousand was the victim to the excesses committed at the Liberation – a figure sufficiently high to create a psychosis that will remain forever in the memories of the survivors. It would be vain to try to appease their despair and their rancour: all one can suggest – and this would be confirmed by a more extensive study of the post-Liberation period – is that without the action, however insufficient, taken by the authorities, the disorder would have been still greater and the victims still more numerous. The presence of the Gaullist administration ensured that the extreme figure of 105,000 executions was not surpassed, nor indeed even attained.

Robert Aron, *De Gaulle Triumphant. The Liberation of France August 1944–1945* (London, Putnam, 1964), translated by Humphrey Hare from the French edition, *Histoire de la Libération de la France* (Paris, 1959), pp. 269 and 285.

DOCUMENT 27 OPHULS' *THE SORROW AND THE PITY*

Marcel Ophuls' film of 1969 was a landmark in the remembrance of the Vichy regime and did much to destroy the mythology with which Aron and de Gaulle had shrouded the Occupation years.

In the courtyard of the Lycée Pascal in Clermont.

André Harris: Were there any Jewish teachers at your school?

M. Dionnet, librarian at the Lycée Pascal in Clermont: Yes, one. He was dismissed.

M. Danton, teacher at the Lycée Pascal in Clermont: He came ...

M. Dionnet: Always the same – no one said a word.

M. Danton: Well, if I may add a word, take the case of Never. I think we tried to find him some private tutoring The same went for another colleague who had been dismissed. But as you say, it wasn't much; but I still think there was some sympathy. Yes, there was.

A.H.: When you say – 'What could we do?' – what do you mean? Ultimately, you could have offered a collective resignation from the lycée couldn't you?

M. Dionnet: Well, that was out of the question. You don't have any understanding of teachers ... collective resignation, come on!

Marcel Ophuls, *The Sorrow and the Pity* (London, Paladin, 1971), pp. 74–5, translated by Mireille Johnston.

DOCUMENT 28   TOUVIER

A milicien in the Lyon area, Touvier escaped justice in 1945 by hiding in monasteries run by fundamentalist Catholics. In 1971 he was pardoned by President Pompidou, but shortly afterwards was indicted with 'crimes against humanity', a charge which bears no statute of limitations. After many more years on the run, he was eventually arrested and brought to trial in 1994, when he was sentenced to life imprisonment. Here Henry Rousso contemplates the historical significance of the trial.

Did the historian learn anything from the Touvier trial? Factually, very little. However, the scholarly inquiries into the activities of the French *Milice* are few, and one would hope that such an assembling of witnesses and documents might add to what we know about it.

The first surprise was the fact that very few documents were uncovered that came directly from the *Milice* or from the *Sipo-SD* that were contemporaneous with the deeds themselves. Most of the items in the case came from postwar trials, from later witnesses, or from the statements of the accused. The trial, when it wasn't confusing the issues, only confirmed what was already known.

On the other hand, less was known about the three-year investigation into the links between Touvier and the Catholic Church carried out by the Rémond Commission from June 1989 to January 1992, which furnished a description of the mental world of a collaborator. But this supplementary information told us more about the contemporary church and about certain dysfunctions of our republican government than about the Occupation itself.

The trial, however, thanks to the witnesses, provides an inexhaustible source for reflection on the respective roles of the judiciary and the historian in the establishment of truth. This is less because of the actual material than because testimony in a courtroom differs greatly from a historical account, which must always depend on written records. In a criminal court, the spoken debate counts more than the written evidence, the jury decides after hearing oral arguments.

Henry Rousso, *Libération*, 20 April 1994, reproduced and translated by Richard J. Golsan, *Memory, the Holocaust and French Justice. The Bousquet and Touvier Affairs* (Hanover, NH, University Press of New England, 1996), pp. 163–4.

GLOSSARY

TERMS

Ancien Régime   The 'old regime', the term used to describe pre-revolutionary France (pre-1789), a period from which Pétain and his traditionalist ministers borrowed several values. Under the Occupation, the Third Republic was also labelled, in a pejorative sense, as the *Ancien Régime*.

années noires   The 'dark years', a popular phrase to describe the Nazi occupation of France (1940–44).

après-guerre   The period (1944–46) immediately after the Liberation of France.

attentisme   A 'waiting on events', a neutral position adopted by many French men and women after the defeat of June 1940. This stance avoided the choices of siding with either the collaborationists or the Resistance; occasionally some *attentistes* had chosen sides but were still waiting on events before they took any action. This was a criticism levelled, in particular, against the Armée Secrète of the Resistance. Many people in the Unoccupied zone retained an *attentiste* position until the terrible events of 1942–44 forced them to adopt other postures.

collabos   A popular word used to denote the collaborationists who congregated in Paris.

dirigistes   A term used to describe the technocratic ministers who belonged to Darlan's cabinet in 1941. The Third Republic had inaugurated the process of appointing experts to ministerial positions during the 1930s, but their influence was never as profound as under Vichy.

école unique   A project for the breaking down of the strong class and institutional divisions which existed in French education during the Third Republic. Primary and secondary schooling were parallel systems; and, as secondary education charged fees, it was largely the preserve of the wealthy. The *école unique* was popular with schoolteachers who had fought together in the First World War and who wished to preserve the camaraderie of the trenches through a more democratic educational system.

Elysée   The official residence of the French president.

épuration   The expression used for the purges, both official and unofficial, in postwar France (1944–46). Although Vichyites claimed that the unofficial purges cost the lives of over 100,000 people, a more accurate figure would be around 10,000. The official purge was very moderate, especially when compared with what happened in Belgium and Holland, and when placed alongside Vichy's own purge of republican officials in 1940–41.

Etat français   The term favoured by the Vichy regime, emphasising the break with the Third Republic.

exode   The 'exodus' of refugees from Belgium and northern France, fleeing the advance of the German army in the summer of 1940. Anywhere between 6 to 8 million took to the roads. Although elaborate plans had been put into place for the orderly evacuation of civilians, these were undermined by the speed of the German advance. The chaos that accompanied the *exode* helps explain why many people looked to Pétain as a saviour.

liguers   Members of the extreme right-wing Leagues of interwar France.

maquisards   Members of the Resistance who, in 1943, took refuge in the scrubland (*maquis*), usually to avoid labour service in Germany. Numbering some 10,000 in the Occupied zone and perhaps 30,000 in the Unoccupied zone, *maquisards* lived off the land and engaged in a variety of activities, eventually confronting the Germans in a series of pitched battles in the course of 1944. Although outnumbered and outfought by the SS and *Wehrmacht*, it is agreed that the *maquis* held greater authority in the countryside than did Vichy by the time of the Liberation.

Munichois   Supporters of the Munich Agreements concluded between Germany, Italy, France and Britain in September 1938. Support for Munich cut across party loyalties. *Munichois* were to be found in the Socialist Party, among centrists in parliament and, notably, among the far right.

notables   The prominent Pétainist officials who took charge of local government and many of Vichy's organisations, and who were often drawn from the ranks of the middle classes. Such people are often described as 'active' Pétainists, denoting their ideological commitment to the National Revolution, thus distinguishing them from 'passive' Pétainists, the majority, who expressed a loyalty to the marshal, but not necessarily to his government and its policies.

parti unique   The notion of a 'single party' was favoured by collaborationists such as Déat in summer 1940, but was rejected by Vichy which feared that such an instrument might end up in the wrong hands. Vichy preferred to rely on a wide range of movements, notably the Légion Française des Combattants. In 1941, Déat was successful in creating the Rassemblement National Populaire but this did not win universal approval among collaborators and was prohibited from operating in the Unoccupied zone. The failure to launch a *parti unique* is one of the reasons why historians are reluctant to describe Vichy as 'fascist'.

pays de mission   A 'missionary country', a term used by Catholics to describe France in the 1930s and 1940s, a state believed to be in need of rechristianisation.

Relève   The scheme introduced by Laval in June 1942 by which one French prisoner-of-war would be released for every three skilled volunteers who offered to work in German factories. Introduced in June 1942, it proved ineffectual and led to the compulsory call-up of labour later that year in the Service du Travail Obligatoire (STO). The introduction of STO ended many people's illusions about Vichy and contributed to the growth of widespread resistance, especially in the *maquis*. Nonetheless, some 650,000 workers left for Germany; only Poland contributed more.

Vél d'Hiv   The popular name for the Vélodrome d'Hiver, an indoor cycle track, close to the Eiffel Tower in Paris which, on 16 July 1942, housed some 14,000 Jews, of whom 4,000 were children, in readiness for their deportation, first to

Drancy, a half-built housing estate on the suburbs of the city, and from there to Auschwitz. The site of the first massive deportations from France, the Vél d'Hiv symbolised the sordid nature of the deal which Laval struck with the Germans in May 1942, promising to hand over foreign Jews ahead of French ones. In 1992, Mitterrand declared 16 July a day of national mourning, but refused to accept responsibility for the round-ups on behalf of the French state, something President Chirac recognised in 1995.

GROUPS AND ORGANISATIONS

Action Française (AF) A neo-royalist and ultra nationalist movement, the Action Française was founded in 1898–99 by Charles Maurras and was at the forefront of extreme right-wing politics in the aftermath of the Dreyfus Affair, attracting the support of several intellectuals. It underwent a reverse during the interwar years as it was condemned by Pope Pius XI in 1926 and many of its younger members gravitated to the right-wing leagues such as the Croix de Feu. Nonetheless, its ideological influence lingered and several Maurrassian values were prominent in Vichy's National Revolution, although it was doubted whether Pétain had ever read more than 'twenty pages of Maurras'. The movement folded with the collapse of Vichy.

Cagoule Literally the 'Hood', the Cagoule was the popular name used to describe the Comité Secret d'Action Révolutionnaire (CSAR), a terrorist organisation set up in 1935 by the former naval engineer, Eugène Deloncle, who later founded the Mouvement Social Révolutionnaire (MSR) in 1940. Violently anti-Communist, the Cagoule was particularly active after the election of the Popular Front in 1936, planting several bombs in Paris. It was suppressed in 1937.

Ceux de la Libération (CDLL) Created in 1940 by Maurice Ripoche, a First World War air ace, the CDLL was a key resistance organisation of the Occupied zone. Initially right-wing in its political leanings, it recruited among officers from the services. With an intelligence wing, and actively involved in military actions, it also founded networks to assist Allied airmen shot down over France. One of the founder members of the Conseil National de la Résistance, the CDLL also forged close links with de Gaulle's Free/Fighting French.

Ceux de la Résistance (CDLR) Established in 1942 by the civil servant Jacques Lecompte-Boinet, the CDLR was another of the principal resistance movements in the Occupied zone, with both a military and civil wing. Drawing support from a wide variety of social groups, and avowedly non-Communist, the CDLR was a founder member of the Conseil National de la Résistance (CNR).

Combat One of the principal resistance movements in the Unoccupied zone, and later to operate in the Occupied zone, Combat founded its own newspaper in Lyon, an influential journal which continued to appear two years after the war. Garnering considerable support, especially in Catholic circles, in 1943 Combat became a part of Mouvements Unis de la Résistance. It boasted an impressive internal framework and was involved in multiple actions: intelligence gathering; military action; and welfare assistance.

Comité Français de la Libération Nationale (CFLN)   In the wake of the Allied invasion of North Africa, the USA appointed Darlan, and then Giraud, as head of French forces there, hoping to dislodge de Gaulle in the process. Arriving in Algiers in May 1943, de Gaulle agreed to become co-president of the CFLN, alongside Giraud. Within weeks, the politically inexperienced Giraud had been pushed aside, and was eventually dropped altogether. The CFLN oversaw the establishment of the Consultative Assembly in Algiers and effectively became the French government-in-waiting.

Commissariat Général aux Questions Juives (CGQJ)   Established in March 1941 under the direction of Xavier Vallat, a Catholic nationalist and former Vichy minister for veterans' affairs, the task of the CGQJ was to oversee the prosecution of anti-Jewish measures, notably the two *Statuts des Juifs*. A trenchant Germanophobe, Vallat hoped that the French themselves would become solely responsible for Jewish affairs, but the Nazis had other plans and had Vallat removed in March 1942. His replacement was Louis Darquier de Pellepoix, an unashamed bigot, who greatly enhanced the CGQJ's policing powers, cooperating willingly in the round-up of Jews in summer 1942. Darquier, in turn, was ousted by Charles Mercier du Paty de Clam, a narrow-minded bureaucrat, who ensured that the CGQJ became more or less an instrument of Nazi policy.

Conseil National de la Résistance (CNR)   In May 1943, de Gaulle's representative Jean Moulin drew together delegates of both resistance movements and political parties at a meeting in Paris. There they agreed to acknowledge the general as head of the Resistance and he, in turn, vowed to restore democracy to France. Active in planning for the Liberation, in March 1944 the CNR published its own Charter which contained wide-sweeping social and economic reforms. These were too radical for de Gaulle, but nonetheless influenced the Constituent Assembly of 1945 which responded by a widescale nationalisation programme. Some allege that the failure to implement the CNR Charter in full was the cause of later problems for the Fourth Republic.

Croix de Feu (CF)   Originally a First World War veterans' organisation, founded in 1927 by Maurice d'Hartoy and open to holders of the Croix de Feu medal, in 1931 the Croix de Feu was transformed into a political movement by its new leader, Colonel de La Rocque, a nationalist army officer. Prominent in the 6 February 1934 demonstrations, debate rages as to whether the CF was truly fascist. In 1936, the Popular Front's outlawing of the leagues forced La Rocque to transform the CF into a political party, the Parti Social Français (PSF) which performed handsomely in by-elections and would no doubt have won several seats had there been an election in 1940. The advent of Vichy led La Rocque to change the PSF into the Progrès Social Français (PSF) which was ardently Pétainist, campaigning for National Revolution values. La Rocque, meanwhile, detested the Germans and became involved in resistance activities before being arrested by the *Gestapo* in 1943.

Forces Françaises de l'Intérieur (FFI)   Officially established on 1 June 1944, the task of the FFI was to draw together and coordinate the many military activities of resistance movements during the Liberation. Under the control of the Comité Français de la Libération Nationale, the numbers of the FFI grew from 100,000 to 500,000 in the course of 1944–45; many *maquisards* enrolled. Performing sabotage work, and assisting the allies with invaluable intelligence, the FFI made a significant contribution to the defeat of the occupier. In 1945, the FFI was disbanded and members were given the option of joining the regular army.

Franc-Tireur Another of the key resistance movements in the Unoccupied zone, Franc-Tireur originated in Lyon, before operating in much of southern France. Solidly republican and left-wing in its orientation, Franc-Tireur supported de Gaulle and acknowledged him as undisputed leader of the Resistance. The movement was a part of the Mouvements Unis de la Résistance (MUR) as well as the Conseil National de la Résistance (CNR).

Francs-Tireurs et Partisans Français (FTPF) When in May 1941, the French Communists came out openly in favour of armed struggle against the occupier, they founded the Front National which, in early 1942, organised various Communist resistance movements into the Franc-Tireurs et Partisans Français. This eventually became the military branch of the Front National, operating in both zones, although its support was always stronger in the more industrialised north. By 1943, the FTPF was involved in extensive military actions with the Germans, but was mistrusted by both the British and the Gaullists who feared they might be the vanguard for a revolution at the Liberation. In the event, most FTPF members were either demobilised or incorporated into the regular army.

Free French The Free French, later known as the Fighting French, was founded on 18 June 1940 when General de Gaulle issued his famous broadcast from London inviting Frenchmen to join him in continuing the struggle. Dependent on British support, which was not always forthcoming, the Free French initially comprised some 6,000 men, largely opportunists, recalcitrant officers and colonial officials who felt let down by the metropolitan government. It was in the colonies that the Free French developed support; de Gaulle was especially fearful that the British, and later the Americans, were attempting to undermine French imperial influence. Relations with the USA reached a nadir at the time of the Allied invasion of North Africa in November 1942 when Roosevelt appointed first Darlan and then Giraud to govern French forces there. Through his political skill, de Gaulle ensured that he became co-president, with Giraud, of the newly formed Comité Français de la Libération Nationale. He soon outmanoeuvred Giraud and became undisputed head of the Resistance both at home and abroad. In this capacity, he oversaw the creation of the Consultative Assembly in Algiers and ensured that Free French officials manned the Provisional Government in 1944, thus offsetting any American plans for Allied control in France.

Front National The loose coalition of Communist resistance organisations formed in 1941, not to be mistaken for the extreme right-wing Front National founded in the Fifth Republic by Jean-Marie Le Pen. In 1943, the Front National agreed to join the Conseil National de la Résistance, yet always retained its independent spirit, and was influential in organising local resistance activities at the Liberation, although it never aspired to use this moment as an opportunity for revolution.

Gouvernement Provisoire de la République Française (GPRF) In June 1944, the Comité Français de la Libération Nationale gave way to the Provisional Government which smoothed the way for a restoration of democracy in France, keeping Anglo-Saxon influence at bay and containing any threat posed by the Communists and Vichyites. While de Gaulle presided over the Provisional Government, its members busied themselves in the organisation of the purges, the repatriation of POWs and the broader issues of economic and social reconstruction, implementing some of the plans of the CNR Charter. Additionally, the Provisional Government oversaw constitutional arrangements resulting in the creation of the Fourth Republic, a regime which, to de Gaulle's annoyance, bore an uncanny resemblance to the Third.

Groupe Collaboration   Founded in September 1940 by the prominent Catholic writer, Alphonse de Châteaubriant, Groupe Collaboration was a loose grouping of intellectuals, including Abel Bonnard and Cardinal Alfred Baudrillart, who were committed to Franco-German collaboration. Financed by German money, the organisation developed considerable support, but this fell away after 1942 when the tide of the war began to turn.

Légion Française des Combattants (LFC)   In August 1940, the many veteran organisations of the Third Republic were grouped together under the Légion Française des Combattants, which pledged its support for Pétain and which was active in the propagation of National Revolution values. Vichy, in turn, valued the movement, dominated by conservative and rural elements, as a bulwark against any plans for a *parti unique*. In 1941, more youthful members, under the leadership of Joseph Darnand, founded the Service d'Ordre Légionnaire which, in 1943, was transformed into the *Milice*.

Légion des Volontaires Français contre le Bolchevisme (LVF) Following Hitler's invasion of the USSR in June 1941, leading Parisian collaborators, notably Doriot, Déat and Deloncle, worked to create a regiment to fight alongside German troops on the Eastern Front. Given the go-ahead by the Nazis in October 1941, the LVF was formed, although it was never very popular and performed poorly in action. It did, however, engage in several propaganda activities and received the approbation of Pétain.

Libération Nord   Drawing support from non-Communist trade unionists, this resistance movement was one of the biggest in the Unoccupied zone. Created in November 1941, it published its own newspaper and went on to engage in military action. It later became a part of the Conseil National de la Résistance.

Libération Sud   The brainchild of the writer Emmanuel d'Astier de la Vigerie, Libération Sud began life in Clermont-Ferrand in autumn 1940 and became one of the key resistance movements in the Unoccupied zone, winning support from left-wing quarters. In 1943 it became part of the Mouvements Unis de la Résistance and widened its activities to include military action.

Milice   The paramilitary organisation created by Vichy in 1943 to crush internal dissent. Created out of the Service d'Ordre Légionnaire (SOL) and headed by Joseph Darnand, a distinguished First World War veteran, there were around 30,000 *miliciens* by June 1943. Always suspect in the eyes of the Germans, members were nonetheless allowed to join the SS, and cooperated willingly with the occupier in the rounding up of Jews, resisters and deserters from STO. In 1944, the *Milice* was involved in the murders of the prominent Republican politicians George Mandel and Jean Zay.

Mouvement Social Révolutionnaire (MSR) One of the most prominent collaborationist organisations, the Mouvement Social Révolutionnaire was set up in September 1940 by Eugène Deloncle, the former *Cagoulard*, and largely drew its support from ex-CSAR members. Virulently antisemitic, the MSR engaged in several attacks on synagogues and might even have been behind the attempted assassination of Laval and Déat in 1941, although Deloncle had earlier indicated support for the Rassemblement National Populaire. In 1942, the MSR split, and Deloncle was dismissed.

Mouvements Unis de la Résistance (MUR) In early 1943 de Gaulle's close lieutenant Jean Moulin convoked representatives from the three principal resistance movements of the Unoccupied zone – Combat, Franc-Tireur and Libération Sud – to form the MUR. This organisation set about coordinating resistance activities, and became a part of the Conseil National de la Résistance. In 1944, it joined forces with several northern-based groupings to create the Mouvement de Libération Nationale (MLN).

Organisation Civil et Militaire (OCM) Enlisting support from army officers, not all of whom had relinquished their Pétainist ties, the OCM was founded in 1940 in the Unoccupied zone and initially advanced a programme which was both antisemitic and technocratic in its outlook. Almost decimated by the Germans in 1943–44, the OCM gravitated leftwards and, in 1944, helped found a short-lived political party, the Union Démocratique et Socialiste de la Résistance.

Parti Populaire Français (PPF) Established in 1936, by the ex-Communist Jacques Doriot, much debate centres on whether the PPF was truly fascist before 1940. After the German invasion, the PPF re-emerged as the Mouvement Populaire Français and adopted an incontrovertibly fascist programme. One of the most extreme of all the collaborationist movements, it was always viewed with suspicion by Vichy, despite Doriot's avowed support for Pétain.

Rassemblement National Populaire (RNP) The brainchild of Marcel Déat, he hoped that the RNP, founded in February 1941, would become a single party drawing together all the supporters of collaboration. Although initially supported by the likes of Deloncle, the Paris collaborators were far too divided to rally behind any one organisation and the RNP's history was riven with factionalism. Vichy was always anxious about its influence and banned it from operating in the Unoccupied zone. Winning support among ex-Socialists, the RNP lost momentum, especially as Déat devoted his energies in other directions.

Abetz, Otto (1903–58) 'Ambassador' to France (1940–44), Abetz was an art teacher before busying himself in Franco-German youth rallies during the late 1920s, encountering the future collaborationist Jean Luchaire, marrying his secretary and later having an affair with his daughter. Inevitably, Abetz fell under the spell of Nazism, joining the SS in 1935 and the NSDAP in 1937. A member of the Ribbentrop Bureau, he was expelled from France in 1939 for war-mongering; his appointment as ambassador in August 1940 was meant as a snub to the French. Charged with conducting diplomatic relations with Vichy, he enjoyed good relations with Laval and did much to promote a 'divide and rule' policy among the Paris collaborationists, although he was never trusted by Berlin, which recalled him in December 1942. Back in France the following December, he was arrested in 1945 and sentenced to 20 years hard labour by a Paris court in 1949. Released in 1954, and working as a journalist, he died in a car accident almost certainly perpetrated by members of the Resistance.

Baudouin, Paul (1894–1964) A former inspector of finance, who served in several interwar cabinets, in March 1940 Baudouin relinquished his post as director of the Bank of Indochina to become under-secretary of state in Reynaud's government, being promoted to foreign minister on 5 June, a job he maintained in Pétain's first cabinet of 16 June. In favour of an armistice, it was Baudouin who proposed Vichy as a seat for the new government. Enjoying little success in encouraging collaboration, his position was usurped by Laval who, on 28 October 1940, became foreign minister, Baudouin reverting to secretary of state. Unsurprisingly, Baudouin was one of the plotters who overthrew Laval on 13 December 1940. Briefly serving under Flandin, he spent the remainder of the war at the Bank of Indochina. Arrested in 1944, he served three years of a five-year sentence, before re-establishing himself as a financier.

Blum, Léon (1872–1950) A lawyer by training, Blum became head of the Socialist Party and edited the left-wing paper, *Le Populaire*. In 1936–37, he led the Popular Front government which initiated sweeping social and economic reforms which were bitterly resented by the right. Attacked for being a Jew, Blum relinquished pacifism after Munich, and in July 1940 voted against investing Pétain with dictatorial powers. Arrested by Vichy in September that year, he was sentenced to life imprisonment for having prepared France inadequately for war, even though he did not appear on trial at Riom until 1942. He skilfully turned the tables on his accusers, thus halting the trials. Released in 1945, Blum relaunched *Le Populaire*, helped found UNESCO, and acted as prime minister in December 1946–January 1947.

Bousquet, René (1909–93) One of the Third Republic's most talented regional administrators, his sense of public service meant that he had little compunction in serving Vichy. He was prefect of the Marne in September 1940, regional prefect of Champagne in August 1941, and, on Laval's return to power in April 1942, became secretary-general for the police. A non-ideologue, unattracted to fascism or collaboration, Bousquet sought to emphasise French autonomy in both the Occupied and Unoccupied zones. When, in 1942, Germany demanded large quotas of Jews, Bousquet readily supported Laval's policy of exchanging foreign Jews, and personally oversaw deportations, including that of the Vél d'Hiv. In 1949, he was condemned to forfeit civil rights for a period of five years, but the sentence was not enforced as Bousquet claimed that in 1943 he had aided the Resistance, hiding Jews from the Germans. He thus entered business, sitting on the board of the Bank of Indochina, as well as several other large companies. He also counted several prominent politicians among his friends, including President Mitterrand, but ultimately such contacts did not save him from prosecution for 'crimes against humanity' in 1991. He was shot dead on 8 June 1993 by Christian Didier who claimed his action was revenge for the Vél d'Hiv.

Bouthillier, Yves (1901–77) A skilled technocrat and a believer in an authoritarian republic, in November 1938 Reynaud appointed Bouthillier secretary-general to the Ministry of Finance, in which capacity he undid Popular Front legislation, notably the 40-hour week. Appointed minister of finance on 5 June 1940, a post he retained in Pétain's first cabinet of 16 June, he campaigned for an Armistice and had the job of meeting Germany's huge financial demands. Angered at Laval's meddling in financial matters, he was one of the plotters who ousted this key minister on 13 December 1940. Laval rid himself of Bouthillier on his return to power in April 1942; yet the ex-minister still visited Vichy where Pétain valued his advice, and was involved in the marshal's fruitless scheme to initiate an authoritarian constitution in 1943. Imprisoned between 1947 and 1950, he returned to financial and public life.

Châteaubriant, Alphonse de (1877–1951) A prize-winning novelist, devout Catholic, and fanatical anti-Communist, in 1935 Châteaubriant became an open admirer of Hitler, believing that the dictator would forge a Christian Europe in the manner of Charlemagne. In 1940, he edited the collaborationist newspaper *La Gerbe*, and established the movement Groupe Collaboration which worked for closer Franco-German cultural contacts. Sentenced to death *in absentia*, he died in Austria in 1951, where he had been leading a clandestine existence.

Daladier, Edouard (1884–1970) Born in Carpentras in southern France, this baker's son went on to become a history teacher and leading Radical, being elected mayor of his home town in 1911. After distinguished war service, he was elected deputy for the Vaucluse in 1919, served in Herriot's 1924 cabinet, and became head of the Radical Party in 1927. Prime minister on the eve of the riots of 6 February 1934, Daladier urged his party to join the Popular Front. Prime minister again between March 1938 and March 1940, he signed the Munich Accords and led the Republic in a rightwards direction. Arrested by Vichy in September 1940, he was tried at Riom and spent the remainder of the war in French and German prisons. In 1946, he was re-elected deputy for the Vaucluse and became mayor of Avignon. De Gaulle's presidency of the Fifth Republic effectively ended Daladier's career.

Darlan, Jean-François (1881–1942) Son of a prominent Radical-Socialist senator, Darlan distinguished himself as a naval expert during the 1920s, becoming an admiral at the age of 48. In 1937, he was appointed Naval Commander, and became minister for the navy under Pétain. Despite his Republican credentials, Darlan was a vicious antisemite, a believer in an authoritarian regime and a virulent anti-Communist. In February 1941, he became Pétain's principal minister, promoted technocratic policies at home, and attempted to interest Germany in collaboration by offering French military bases in Syria (the Paris Protocols in June 1941). His foreign policy failures and the Riom trial fiasco partially led to Laval's return in April 1942, Darlan remaining as commander-in-chief of French forces. In November that year, he was in Algiers visiting his son, when the Allies landed. After much hesitation, he agreed to American plans to become head of French North Africa. He was assassinated on Christmas Eve 1942 by an unhinged gunman who was almost certainly working for someone else, probably the Free French or the British.

Darnand, Joseph (1897–1945)   Head of Vichy's infamous parallel police force, the *Milice*, Darnand was a distinguished First World War veteran who, in the 1920s, established a haulage company in his native Nice. There he progressed through a series of right-wing movements, although Darnand himself was no political thinker. In 1939, he enlisted for service and was taken prisoner the following year, only to break out of his POW camp. Returning to Nice, he set up the Service d'Ordre Légionnaire (SOL) which, in 1943, became the *Milice*, a paramilitary force designed to flush out resisters. Having joined the SS in 1943, in early 1944 he became Vichy's secretary for the maintenance of public order. In 1945, he was condemned to face the firing squad for treason.

Déat, Marcel (1894–1955)   A former Socialist, in the 1930s Déat drifted to the right and, in 1940, became a leading collaborator. A decorated war hero and teacher by profession, Déat became disillusioned with the Socialist Party in the 1930s; in 1933 he was expelled from its ranks and went on to found the Parti Socialiste de France which advocated economic planning and closer links with Germany. In May 1939, his newspaper *L'Œuvre* printed the headline 'Must one Die for Danzig?' In July 1940, he travelled to Vichy to persuade Pétain to establish a single party; when his efforts were rebutted, he established a powerbase in Paris where he wrote for *L'Œuvre*, criticising Vichy for its timidity, and founded the Rassemblement National Populaire with Deloncle. This failed to win the support of the collaborators, especially Doriot, and was not allowed to function in the southern zone. In March 1944, Germany bullied Vichy into granting Déat a ministerial post: minister for labour and national solidarity. He left with other members of the government for Sigmaringen, eventually taking refuge at a Catholic convent in Turin where he spent his remaining years.

Deloncle, Eugène (1890–1944)   Founder of the extreme right-wing terrorist organisation, the Cagoule, in 1940 Deloncle established the equally violent Mouvement Social Révolutionnaire which specialised in blowing up synagogues and stealing Jewish property. The following year he helped set up both the RNP and Légion des Volontaires Français contre le Bolchevisme. A man of violence, he was personally involved in the murder of Marx Dormoy, the former minister of the interior, and might have been behind the assassination attempt on Déat and Laval in August 1941. Expelled from the RNP, in 1942 he was also evicted from the MSR. Keeping his options open, he developed links with the Germans, Darlan and the British. Mystery surrounds his death on 7 January 1944 in a gun battle with either Gestapo agents, MSR supporters or Communist resisters.

Doriot, Jacques (1898–1945) A distinguished First World War veteran and militant trade unionist, in 1934 Doriot fell out with the Communist Party for urging a popular front against fascism before Moscow had given its approval. He went on to found the Parti Populaire Français in 1936, an embryonic fascist party which enjoyed working-class backing. In 1940, he was a staunch advocate of collaboration, but was also a supporter of Pétain, whose qualities he extolled in his newspaper, *Le Cri du Peuple*. The founder of the Légion des Volontaires Français contre le Bolchevisme, Doriot spent much of the Occupation fighting on the Eastern Front, where he eventually donned a German uniform, although Vichy always feared the PPF might become the foundation of an alternative Paris-based government. Travelling in Germany in March 1945, he was killed in an attack by two unidentified aircraft.

Flandin, Pierre-Etienne (1889–1958) Elected to parliament in 1913, Flandin became head of the right-wing Alliance Démocratique and served as prime minister in 1934–35. An ardent *Munichois*, in 1940 Flandin viewed Pétain as France's saviour, but disliked Laval, and, on 13 December 1940, was appointed Laval's successor. Distrusted by Abetz and cautious in his approach to collaboration, Flandin made way for Darlan on 8 February 1941. Flandin resurfaced in Algeria in November 1942, hoping to play a part in the emerging government there. Arrested in 1943, he was sentenced to a token 12 hours national indignity, and returned to head the Alliance Démocratique, although his Vichy background ensured he was never an influential figure in the Fourth Republic.

Frenay, Henri (1905–88) A professional soldier, Frenay was taken prisoner in 1940 but escaped to found the southern-based movement *Combat*; in 1942, he was behind the creation of the Mouvements Unis de la Résistance. Fiercely anti-Communist and from a bourgeois background, Frenay had several contacts with Vichy, but became ever more outspoken in his criticism of the regime. As a member of the Provisional Government, he was involved in the plans for the liberation of France and in 1946 was minister for deportees, prisoners of war and refugees. Thereafter, he retired from political life to live in Corsica.

Gamelin, Maurice (1872–1958) A career soldier and committed Republican, Gamelin became commander-in-chief of the French army in 1935 and attempted to overhaul the purely defensive strategy adopted by his predecessors, Pétain and Weygand. He advocated the deployment of mobile armour and initiated the Allied strategy whereby troops marched into Holland and Belgium in case of a German attack. Ineffectual as a commander-in-the-field, he overlooked the need for a strategic reserve and was replaced by Weygand on 17 May 1940. Arrested by Vichy and tried at Riom, he spent the war under German surveillance; afterwards, he was dubbed the man who 'lost the battle of France'.

Gaulle, Charles de (1890–1970) Born in Lille to upper-class parents, de Gaulle started life as a career soldier, fighting at Verdun in 1916, and becoming one of Pétain's *protégés* in the 1920s, and was later an advocate of mechanised warfare. A natural rebel, de Gaulle fell out with his mentor and refused to recognise defeat in 1940, fleeing to London where he broadcast to France on 18 June. Setting up the Free French, he became undisputed leader of the French Resistance overseas and oversaw the creation of the Provisional Government in Algiers. In 1944–46, he ruled France with wide-ranging powers while a new constitutional settlement was devised. Unhappy with the Fourth Republic, he retired to his home at Colombey-les-deux-Eglises, re-emerging at the time of the Algerian crisis in 1958 to become president of the Fifth Republic.

Giraud, Henri (1878–1949)   A distinguished soldier, in 1940 Giraud commanded the Seventh Army in its advance into Belgium. Taken prisoner by the Germans, he escaped two years later and offered his services to Vichy, and then to the Americans who, in the wake of Darlan's assassination, valued Giraud as an alternative to de Gaulle. Both men were named as presidents of the newly formed Comité Français de Libération Nationale, but it only took de Gaulle six months to brush aside the politically naive Giraud who was forced off the CFLN altogether in November 1943. In 1946, Giraud stood successfully for parliament and remained vice-president of the Conseil Supérieur de la Guerre until his death.

Henriot, Philippe (1889–1944)   A staunch Catholic and man of letters, in the interwar years Henriot was known as a fierce clericalist and anti-Socialist deputy. He was a natural supporter of Pétain and outspoken advocate of collaboration, joining the *Milice* in 1943. His skills as a writer ensured that he was appointed minister of information and propaganda in January 1944. Shot dead by the Resistance six months later, Henriot was granted a requiem mass at Notre Dame officiated by Cardinal Suhard, archbishop of Paris. The *Milice* responded to his death by murdering the Republican politicians Mandel and Zay.

Huntziger, Charles-Léon (1880–1941)   Born in Brittany, Huntziger was a career soldier, serving with distinction in both the colonies and the First World War, becoming a general in 1939. In charge of the Second Army in 1940, he was unable to withstand the German advance at Sedan, and soon became a champion of an armistice. Indeed, it was Huntziger who signed the Armistice at Rethondes on 22 June, and went on to represent Vichy at the Armistice Commission at Wiesbaden. In September 1940, he became minister of war and, after Laval's ousting from power on 13 December, became part of the triumvirate, with Darlan and Flandin, which briefly governed France. Although anti-British, in 1941 he became increasingly agitated by the collaborationist policies being pursued by Darlan. He died in an aeroplane crash when returning to Vichy in November 1941, a crash which some suggest might not have been an accident.

La Rocque, François de (1885–1946)   A decorated war hero and son of an aristocrat, in 1931 this fiercely nationalist soldier fronted the Croix de Feu and played a leading role in the riots of 6 February 1934. In 1936, the Popular Front's anti-league legislation forced him to turn the CF into the Parti Social Français. A fierce nationalist, he initially supported Pétain but detested the Germans. He subsequently worked for the Resistance and was arrested by the Gestapo in 1943. Rearrested by the Provisional Government, he died before his trial.

Laval, Pierre (1883–1945)   A lawyer by profession and initially a socialist, Laval broke with the left in the 1920s and gravitated to the centre-right, occupying the posts of both foreign minister and prime minister on several occasions before 1935, when the election of the Popular Front ousted him from power. Although no fascist, Laval was anti-communist and an admirer of dictatorship. An avowed appeaser, Laval opposed war in 1939 and supported a Pétain government in the hope that he could manipulate it. Rather, the marshal used him to steer through the destruction of the republican constitution in July 1940. Appointed deputy prime minister, Laval found that he was unable to interest the Germans in his plans for Franco-German *rapprochement*. Dismissed in December 1940, he was recalled in April 1942 to kick start collaboration, yet found that he was making an increasing number of concessions to the Nazis, including the handing over of Jews and French workers. Tried in 1945, he made a failed suicide bid on the day of his execution.

Menthon, François de (1900–84)   Of aristocratic birth, de Menthon was an economist and Christian Democrat who opposed the Armistice in 1940, going on to found the resistance movements Comité Général d'Etudes and Combat, eventually joining de Gaulle in Algeria in 1943. Named Commissaire de la Justice of the CFLN, he was minister of justice during the Provisional Government, and was France's principal prosecutor at the Nuremberg trials. A founder member of the Christian Democrat Mouvement Républicain Populaire, he served as a minister in the Fourth Republic. Defeated at the polls in 1958, he returned to academic life.

Michelet, Edouard (1899–1970)   Initially a supporter of Action Française, Michelet became a Christian Democrat, setting up the study circles Equipes Sociales, and is sometimes viewed as the first resister in France by dint of the written protest against the Armistice which he published in his native town of Brive on 17 June 1940. A member of Combat, he was arrested by Vichy in 1943, but survived Dachau. Elected an MRP deputy in 1946, he served as a minister under de Gaulle during the Fifth Republic.

Moulin, Jean (1899–1943)   A committed Republican and skilled civil servant, Moulin became de Gaulle's close lieutenant in France and was responsible for bringing together the various Resistance movements in 1943 before being betrayed to the Germans who tortured and murdered him. The youngest prefect in France, he was dismissed from his post by Vichy in November 1940 and gravitated to the Resistance, travelling to London in 1941. Controversy surrounds whether he was an early supporter of Pétain, or indeed a Communist agent; there is no evidence to support either supposition. In 1964, his symbolic importance was acknowledged when his ashes were transferred to the Panthéon, the resting place of French heroes.

Papon, Maurice (1910–)   A skilled civil servant, who served several Republican cabinets, in 1942–44 Papon was secretary-general of the Gironde *Préfecture*, in which capacity he oversaw the deportation of Jews. Desperately short of bureaucrats, the Provisional Government appointed Papon, who claimed resistance credentials, prefect of the Landes in 1944. He went on to serve the Fourth Republic in Algeria and Corsica before becoming prefect of the Paris police under de Gaulle (1958–68) and served as Giscard d'Estaing's budget minister. In 1983 he was charged with crimes against humanity and, following numerous legal delays, some orchestrated by his friend President Mitterrand, was condemned to a ten-year jail term in 1998.

Pétain, Philippe (1856–1951)   A hero of the First World War, the 'Victor of Verdun', France's military guru in the 1920s, and widely thought of as a prospective French leader in the 1930s, in June/July 1940 Marshal Pétain became head of the Vichy regime, pursuing a policy of so-called national renovation at home and collaboration with the Nazi occupier. Enjoying enormous popularity, he failed to see his own shortcomings and his policies did little to shield the French, as he himself claimed at his trial in 1945. Initially sentenced to death, the punishment was commuted to life imprisonment on the intervention of de Gaulle, and Pétain died in exile on the Ile d'Yeu. A small band of right-wing followers have ever since attempted to rehabilitate his reputation.

Pucheu, Pierre (1898–1944)   Of proletarian origins, Pucheu pursued a distinguished academic career before becoming an executive in the steel industry where he took an interest in far right politics. One of Vichy's technocrats, in the period February–June 1941 he was minister of industrial production and between July 1941 and April 1942 was minister of the interior. It was in this role that he handed over Communist hostages to be shot in retaliation for the assassination of German personnel. In 1943, he travelled to North Africa to offer his services to the Resistance but, under Communist pressure, was tried and executed in 1944 for his part in the hostage drama.

Reynaud, Paul (1878–1966)   An independent-minded politician belonging to the Alliance Démocratique, in the 1930s Reynaud championed de Gaulle's ideas for a professional army, before becoming justice and finance minister in the Daladier government (1938–40). A firm opponent of Munich, in March 1940 he was named prime minister but was unable to control defeatism within his cabinet, ceding power to Pétain on 16 June 1940. Arrested and tried by Vichy at Riom, Reynaud resumed his political career after the war, holding ministerial office under the Fourth Republic and advising de Gaulle on constitutional matters in 1958.

Sauckel, Fritz (1894–1946)   A Nazi in 1922, Gauleiter of Thuringia, in March 1942 Saukel became Hitler's Plenipotentiary for Labour and was thus in charge of enlisting foreign workers for the German war effort. An ardent Francophobe, having spent the First World War in a French POW camp, he negotiated the *Relève* and Service du Travail Obligatoire, and in 1944 was pressing Vichy for a further million workers. He was tried and hanged at Nuremberg in 1946.

Thorez, Maurice (1900–1964)   Secretary-general of the French Communist Party, in 1939 Thorez supported the Nazi–Soviet pact, yet maintained that the key enemy remained fascism. Enlisted in 1939, Daladier's prosecution of the Communists prompted him to desert, taking refuge first in Brussels and, ultimately, in Moscow where he led a secretive existence. Mistrusted by de Gaulle, who did not want him in London, in 1944 Thorez promised that his party had no intention of fermenting revolution and, during the Fourth Republic, he briefly served as deputy prime minister before ill health overtook him.

Touvier, Paul (1915–96) A devout Catholic and partisan of far right politics, Touvier was demobilised in 1940 whereupon he gravitated to the Légion Française des Combattants and eventually the *Milice*. Head of *miliciens* in the Savoy region, he was involved in the murder of several Jews. After the war, he was protected by fundamentalist Catholics and, in 1971, received a pardon from President Pompidou. A symbol of Vichy's antisemitism, he was indicted for 'crimes against humanity', and in 1994 was sentenced to life imprisonment.

Vallat, Xavier (1891–1972)   A veteran of the First World War, in which he lost both an eye and a leg, Vallat served as a right-wing Catholic deputy before becoming Pétain's minister for war veterans in 1940. The first president of the Légion Française des Combattants, in March 1941 he was named head of the Commissariat Général aux Questions Juives and set out to exclude Jews from all walks of French life. As much a Germanophobe as an antisemite, he was dismissed in March 1942. Thanks to his distinguished war service in 1914–18, he escaped a death sentence in 1947, and served two years of a ten-year jail term.

Weygand, Maxime (1867–1965)   A hero of the First World War, commander-in-chief of the French Army (1931–35), Weygand was recalled to replace the ill-fated Gamelin on 19 May 1940, but proved a devout pessimist who used his role to help bring about the collapse of the Third Republic. German pressure ensured his removal from Vichy to become High Commissioner of North Africa in September 1940 where he pursued an *attentiste* line, although he could not easily hide his hatred of the *Boche*. Dismissed by Darlan in November 1941, he was arrested by the Germans and spent the rest of the war in prison. He was tried and pardoned in 1948.

GUIDE TO FURTHER READING

PRIMARY MATERIALS

Because of the sensitivity of the Occupation, official French archives have only recently become available to researchers, and some documents still remain under lock and key, as Eric Conan and Henry Rousso recount in their *Vichy. Un passé qui ne passe pas* (Paris, Gallimard, 1994). This bureaucratic obduracy has meant historians have been very inventive in the types of source they have deployed, and the choices of materials in the present book have been selected to reveal something of that imagination: memoirs; unpublished diaries; legislation; speeches; newspaper articles; diplomatic papers; posters; radio broadcasts; oral testimony; trial depositions; novels; and film evidence.

At least, memoirs are plentiful. Virtually every one of the *dramatis personae* of the Vichy regime left behind their recollections of the Occupation, although these should be treated with caution as they were intended to portray their authors in the best possible light. Among the most candid are Henri du Moulin de Labarthète's *Les Temps des illusions. Souvenirs, juillet 1940–avril 1942* (Geneva, Le Cheval Ailé, 1946) and Joseph Barthélemy's *Ministre de la Justice. Mémoires* (Paris, Pygmalion, 1989). Few Vichy memoirs have been translated, an exception being the anglophobic *The Memoirs of Paul Baudouin* (London, Eyre & Spottiswoode, 1948). Equally numerous are resistance memoirs, although these too should be handled with caution. Some obvious ports of call are Charles de Gaulle, *War Memoirs* (3 vols, London, Collins, 1954–58), Henri Frenay, *The Night Will End* (London, Abelard Schuman, 1976), Paul Simon, *One Enemy Only. The Invader* (London, Hodder & Stoughton, 1942), in truth more an account of life in wartime Paris than a memoir, and Lucie Aubrac, *Outwitting the Gestapo* (Lincoln, NB, and London, University of Nebraska Press, 1993). Interestingly, the two key figures of the regime, Pétain and Laval, left no accounts of their time at Vichy, both because they had an aversion to writing. Nonetheless, Pétain's speeches and broadcasts are collected together in a definitive version by Jean-Claude Barbas, *Discours au Français, 17 juin 1940–20 août 1944* (Paris, Albin Michel, 1989); Laval's scribblings, in preparation for his trial, were published posthumously as *Pierre Laval parle* (Paris, La Diffusion du Livre, 1948). There exist numerous memoirs, too many to list here, of 'ordinary' French men and women, which give some impression of how the Occupation affected daily life, notably Jean Guéhenno's *Journal des années noires, 1940–1944* (Paris, Gallimard, 1947). One brilliant account is Micheline Bood, *Journal d'une lycéenne* (Paris, Gallimard, 1977) which recounts the dilemma of being a teenager at war. Hardly 'ordinary', Edouard Daladier kept a watch on affairs at Vichy in his *Prison Journal, 1940–1944* (Oxford, Westview Press, 1995). Pascal Jardin, son of the civil servant Jean Jardin, performs a similar task in *Vichy Boyhood. An Insider's View of the Pétain Regime* (London, Faber and Faber, 1975).

Collections of documents are numerous, although these are not generally found in English. The short volume by Dominique Remy, *Les Lois de Vichy* (Paris, Romillat, 1992) is exactly what its title suggests, while Pierre Milza provides a welter of evidence, much of it previously unpublished, in his *Sources de la France du XXe siècle de 1918 à nos jours* (Paris, Larousse, 1997). In 1957, the Hoover Institution on War published *France during the Nazi Occupation* (3 vols), but it should be noted that these documents were largely assembled by Laval's family. On propaganda, see the collection of essays and illustrations in Denis Peschanski, ed., *Le Propagande sous Vichy* (Paris, BDIC, 1991). Often overlooked, but critical for what Berlin and Abetz were thinking, are the *Documents on German Foreign Policy*, Series D, vols IX–XII. Michèle Cotta includes a large range of the Parisian collaborationist press in *La Collaboration* (Paris, Armand Colin, 1964) while Pascal Ory puts together several speeches in *La France allemande. Paroles du collaborationisme français, 1933–1945* (Paris, Gallimard, 1997). Jean-Pierre Azéma presents a much wider range of texts, including historical controversies, in his *La Collaboration, 1940–1944* (Paris, Presses Universitaires de France, 1975); Dominique Veillon does something similar in *La Collaboration. Textes et Débats* (Paris, Livre de Poche, 1984). Colin Nettelbeck assembles several literary sources in *Image and Identity. France and the Second World War* (London, Routledge, 1987).

Trial records also cast much light on the so-called 'dark years', although it is agreed that Pétain's own trial, published as the *Procès Pétain* by the *Haute Cour de Justice* in 1946, was more interesting for what issues were avoided than for those which were discussed. A sympathetic account of the trial, including lengthy extracts from the speeches, is to be found in Jules Roy, *The Trial of Marshal Pétain* (London, Faber and Faber, 1969). The voluminous documents contained in Louis Noguères, *Le Véritable Procès du maréchal Pétain* (Paris, Fayard, 1955) are also an attempt at rehabilitation. On the recent trials for 'crimes against humanity', François Bédarida presents *Touvier. Le Dossier de l'accusation* (Paris, Seuil, 1996) while Richard J. Golsan collates interviews, commentaries and texts in his *Memory, the Holocaust and French Justice. The Bousquet and Touvier Affairs* (Hanover, NH, University of New England, 1996) and in his *Memory and Justice on Trial. The Papon Affair* (New York, Routledge, 2000).

For more unusual documentation, see the extensive collection of oral testimonies assembled by Roderick Kedward in his *Resistance in Vichy France* (Oxford, Oxford University Press, 1978) and *In Search of the Maquis. Resistance in Rural France* (Oxford, Oxford University Press, 1993). Novels are not always classed as 'primary sources', but nonetheless offer excellent insights into the dilemmas posed by the Occupation. Something of the *exode* is glimpsed in Jean-Paul Sartre, *Iron in the Soul* (London, Hamish Hamilton, 1950); daily life in Paris and the workings of the black market are exposed in Jean Dutord, *Au bon beurre* (Paris, Flammarion, 1953); and Vercors (the pseudonym of Jean Bruller), *The Battle of Silence* (New York, 1968), originally published by the clandestine Editions de Minuit in 1942, recounts the awful choices posed by the billeting of a German soldier in a French family. Many anglophone novelists have attempted to recapture life under occupation, most unsuccessfully, but it does no harm to read Sebastian Faulks' *Charlotte Gray* (London, Virago, 1998). There are almost as many filmmakers as there are novelists who have taken the Occupation as a central theme, and to choose among their work is no easy matter. Ignoring the fact that Woody Allen's neurotic character dates his girlfriend in the eponymous *Annie Hall* by repeatedly taking her to see Marcel Ophuls' *The Sorrow and the Pity* (1971), this four-hour documentary on life in Clermont-Ferrand does repay viewing. Louis Malle's *Lacombe, Lucien* (1974) raised several ambiguities about resistance and collaboration; his *Au revoir, les enfants* (1987), the story of Jewish children hidden in a Catholic school, is less ambivalent. Among documentaries, see the impressive Claude Chabrol's *The Eye of Vichy* (1989).

INTERPRETING THE VICHY REGIME

Henry Rousso, *The Vichy Syndrome. History and Memory in France since 1944* (Cambridge, MA, Harvard University Press, 1989) is the starting point for any understanding of the way in which the French have remembered the 'dark years'. This may be supplemented with a special edition of *French Historical Studies*, vol. 19, no. 2, Autumn 1995, on the 'Vichy Syndrome', and the excellent chapter, 'Echoes of the Occupation', in R.D. Gildea, *France since 1945* (Oxford, Oxford University Press, 1995). For an introduction to the issue of Jewish memory, see Golsan cited above. Rousso gives a valuable perspective on the historiography of the regime, as do Jean-Pierre Azéma, 'Les historiens et Vichy', in Jean-Pierre Azéma and François Bédarida, eds, *Vichy et les Français* (Paris, Fayard, 1992) and Kim Munholland, 'Remembering Wartime France', in *French Historical Studies*, Spring, 1994, although both these essays are now a little dated. For a snapshot of current historical concerns, see Sarah Fishman, ed., *France at War. Vichy and the Historians* (Oxford, Berg, 2000).

THE THIRD REPUBLIC, 1934–40

A concise, up-to-date perspective of the 1930s is provided in Serge Berstein, *La France des années 30* (Paris, Armand Colin, 1988) which contrasts with the rather drab survey contained in Paul Bernard and Henri Dubief, *The Decline of the Third Republic, 1914–1938* (Cambridge, Cambridge University Press, 1990). Eugen Weber contributes a highly impressionistic overview of this crisis-strewn decade in his *The Hollow Years. France in the 1930s* (New York, Norton, 1994). That other doyen of American historians of France, Stanley Hoffmann, provides some brilliant commentaries on both the 1930s and Vichy in his *Decline or Renewal? France since the 1930s* (New York, Viking, 1974) On the Depression years, an excellent, albeit densely written account, is Julian Jackson, *The Politics of Depression in France, 1932–1936* (Cambridge, Cambridge University Press, 1985). The same author has also written by far the best history of the Popular Front, *The Popular Front in France, 1932–1936: Defending Democracy* (Cambridge, Cambridge University Press, 1988). On the vexed question as to whether France possessed its own fascists, a splendid introduction to the literature is contained in John Sweets, 'Hold That Pendulum', *French Historical Studies*, Summer, 1988. Aware of the main lines of debate, the reader can sample the protagonists themselves: René Rémond, *The Right Wing in France from 1815 to de Gaulle* (Philadelphia, Philadelphia University Press, 1969); Robert Soucy, *Fascism in France. The First Wave, 1924–1933* (Stanford, CA, 1987); Zeev Sternhell, *Neither Left Nor Right* (Stanford, CA, Stanford University Press 1987); and Kevin Passmore, *From Liberalism to Fascism. The Right in a French Province, 1928–1939* (Cambridge, Cambridge University Press, 1998). On

France's preparations for war, see Robert J. Young, *France and the Origins of the Second World War* (London, Macmillan, 1996) which may be supplemented by Anthony Adamthwaite, *Grandeur and Misery. France's Bid for Power in Europe, 1914–1940* (London, Arnold, 1995), more accessible than his narrowly diplomatic *France and the Coming of the Second World War* (London, Frank Cass, 1977). See, too, Peter Jackson, *France and the Nazi Menace* (Oxford, Oxford University Press, 2000) on the use of intelligence in formulating policy against Germany.

THE DEFEAT

Marc Bloch, *The Strange Defeat* (English trans., London, Oxford University Press, 1949) is the classic account of the débâcle, although it should be remembered that few historians would today agree wholeheartedly with his analysis. Another classic account is John Cairns, 'Along the Road back to France', *American Historical Review*, vol. 3, 1959, well ahead of its day and worth rereading now. A conspectus of the historiography is to be found in Andrew Shennan, *The Fall of France* (London, Pearson Education, 2000). Joel Blatt, ed., *The French Defeat of 1940. Reassessments* (Oxford, Berghan, 1998) does not really live up to its name as not all the essays are truly revisionist. See, too, the essays in Robert Boyce, ed., *French Foreign and Defence Policy, 1918–1940* (London, Routledge, 1998). Martin Alexander was one of the first historians to force a rethink of our understanding of the defeat, and argues a spirited defence of Gamelin in his *The Republic in Danger. General Maurice Gamelin and the Politics of French Defence, 1933–1940* (Cambridge, Cambridge University Press, 1993). On military strategy, the most convincing accounts are: Robert Doughty, *The Breaking Point. Sedan and the Fall of France* (Hamden, CO, Archon Books, 1990); Jeffrey Gunsburg, *Divided and Conquered. The French High Command and the Defeat of the West* (Westport, CT, Greenwood Press, 1979); and Robert Young, *In Command of France. French Policy and Military Planning, 1933–1939* (Cambridge, MA, Harvard University Press, 1979). Alistair Horne has provided the most readable commentary of the defeat in *To Lose a Battle. France 1940* (London, Macmillan, 1969), although this accepts that there was something fundamentally amiss in the French body politic at this time. French historians themselves have not rushed to tackle the collapse, but Robert Frankenstein, *Le Prix du réarmement français, 1935–1939* (Paris, Publications de la Sorbonne, 1982) is now a standard work, while Jean-Pierre Azéma's essays for *Le Monde* to commemorate the fiftieth anniversary of the defeat, are collected together in *1940. L'année terrible* (Paris, Seuil, 1990). It is, though, a Frenchman who has contributed the most adventurous interpretation of that fateful year, in part to satisfy his own curiosity as to why his country fell so quickly. See Jean-Louis Crémieux-Brilhac, *Les Français de l'an 40* (2 vols, Paris, Gallimard, 1990–91).

VICHY

The best overall study of wartime France remains Robert O. Paxton, *Vichy France. Old Guard and New Order* (New York, Alfred A. Knopf, 1972), although this has recently been run close by Philippe Burrin, *Living with Defeat* (London, Arnold, 1996) and Julian Jackson, *France, 1940–1944. The Dark Years* (Oxford, Oxford

University Press, 2001). Jean-Paul Azéma, *From Munich to the Liberation* (Cambridge, Cambridge University Press, 1985), Jean-Paul Cointet, *Histoire de Vichy* (Paris, Perrin, 1996), Yves Durand, *La France dans la 2e guerre mondiale* (Paris, Armand Colin, 1989) and Ian Ousby, *Occupation. The Ordeal of France, 1940–1944* (London, John Murray, 1998) are all worth reading, and contain their own bibliographies. Robert Aron, *The Vichy Regime* (London, Putnam, 1958) should now be regarded a primary source. For detailed essays on virtually every aspect of wartime France, see the collected volumes edited by Jean-Paul Azéma and François Bédarida, eds, *La France des années noires* (2 vols, Paris, Seuil, 1993) and *Vichy et les Français* (Paris, Fayard, 1992). The best succinct account is H.R. Kedward, *Occupied France. Collaboration and Resistance* (Oxford, Basil Blackwell, 1985).

On Pétain, the two key biographies are Marc Ferro, *Pétain* (Paris, Fayard, 1987) and Richard Griffiths, *Marshal Pétain* (London, Constable, 1994, 4th edn); the present author has also written a short synthesis, *Pétain* (London, Addison Wesley Longman, 1997). On Pétainism, see Pierre Servent, *Le Mythe Pétain. Verdun ou les tranchées de la mémoire* (Paris, Payot, 1992) and the following two essays: H.R. Kedward, 'Patriots and Patriotism in Vichy France', *Transactions of the Royal Historical Society*, vol. 32, 1982, and Richard Vinen, 'Pétain's Hollow Crown', in *History Today*, June 1994.

For a general introduction to the *National Revolution*, see Michèle Cointet's misleadingly titled, *Vichy et le fascisme* (Brussels, Editions Complexe, 1988). On individual aspects of this project, W.D. Halls, *The Youth of Vichy France* (Oxford, Clarendon Press, 1981) has written the best overview of educational and youth policies; the same author has also produced arguably the most thorough coverage of religious affairs in his *Politics, Society and Christianity in Vichy France* (Oxford, Berg, 1995), although this may be usefully supplemented by Renée Bédarida, *La Vie quotidienne des catholiques sous Vichy* (Paris, Hachette, 1999) and Michèle Cointet, *L'Eglise sous Vichy* (Paris, Perrin, 1998). On gender during the Occupation, amazingly a much neglected subject for many years, there is now a wealth of impressive material: see, especially, Célia Bertin, *Femmes sous l'occupation* (Paris, Stock, 1993); Hannah Diamond, *Women and the Second World War in France* (London, Longman, 1999); Sarah Fishman, *We Will Wait: Wives of French Prisoners of War, 1940–1945* (New Haven, CT, Yale University Press, 1992); C. Muel-Dreyfus, *Vichy et l'éternel féminin* (Paris, Seuil, 1996); Miranda Pollard, *The Reign of Virtue. Mobilizing Gender in Vichy France* (Chicago, IL, Chicago University Press, 1998); Fabrice Virgili, *La France 'virile'. Les femmes tondues à la Libération* (Paris, Payot, 2000); and a special issue of *Modern and Contemporary France* (1999). We still await a synthesis of Vichy's economic policies, but Richard Kuisel provides a good introduction in his *Capitalism and the State in Twentieth-Century France* (Cambridge, Cambridge University Press, 1980). The fraudulent nature of the regime's corporatism is exposed in Isabel Boussard, *Vichy et la corporation paysanne* (Paris, FNSP, 1980) and Jean-Paul Le Crom, *Syndicats, nous voilà, Vichy et le corporatisme* (Paris, Atelier, 1995). Inevitably much has been written about repression under Vichy, especially the Jews. Here, the groundwork was conducted by Michael Marrus and Robert O. Paxton in their *Vichy France and the Jews* (New York, Basic Books, 1981) and Serge Klarsfeld, *Vichy-Auschwitz: le rôle de Vichy dans la solution finale de la question juive en France* (2 vols, Paris, Fayard, 1985). For a concise view of the regime's antisemitism, see Paul Webster's eminently readable *Pétain's Crime* (London, Papermac, 1990). On more general aspects of repression, see Jean-Marc Berlière and Denis Peschanski, eds, *La police française, 1930–1950* (Paris, Documentation française, 2000) and Denis Peschanski, *Vichy, contrôle et exclusion* (Brussels, Complexe, 1997). André Halimi, *La Délation sous l'occupation* (Paris, Editions Jean Moreau, 1983) tackles the phenomenon of informing on one's neighbours; André Lefébure, *Les Conversations secrètes des français sous l'occupation* (Paris, Plon, 1993) explores the workings of the *contrôle postal*; and Pierre Giolitto exposes the murky world of the *miliciens* in his *Histoire de la Milice* (Paris, Perrin, 1997).

So much has now been written about the way in which the French responded to the Occupation that it is difficult to know where to begin. The two pioneering studies by Pierre Laborie, *L'Opinion française sous Vichy* (Paris, Seuil, 1990) and John Sweets, *Choices in Vichy France* (New York, Oxford University Press, 1986) are probably the best departure points. Dominique Veillon chronicles a daily life of hardships in her *Vivre et survivre sous l'Occupation* (Paris, Payot, 1997) while Roger Austin explores the ineffectual nature of Vichy propaganda at a local level in his 'Propaganda and Public Opinion in Vichy France. The Department of Hérault', *European Studies Review*, vol. 13, no. 4, October 1983, pp. 455–82. On the way in which local areas reacted to Vichy, see especially Paul Jankowski, *Communism and Collaboration. Simon Sabiani and Politics in Marseille, 1919–1944* (New Haven, CT, Yale University Press, 1989), Pierre Laborie, *Résistants, Vichyssois et autres. L'évolution de l'opinion et des comportements dans le Lot* (Paris, CNRS, 1980), Pierre Rigoulet, *L'Alsace Lorraine pendant la guerre, 1939–1945* (Paris, Presses Universitaires de France, 1997), Robert Zaretsky, *Nîmes at War* (Philadelphia, PA, Philadelphia University Press, 1995), and the many essays on specific regions in Azéma and Bédarida, *Vichy et les Français*, cited above.

COLLABORATION AND COLLABORATIONISM

Jean-Baptiste Duroselle gives a good overview of Vichy's foreign policy initiatives in his *L'Abîme* (Paris, Imprimerie Nationale, 1983) while Ernst Jaëkel, *Frankreich in Hitlers Europa* (Stuttgart, Deutsches Verlags-Anstalt, 1966) looks at how these efforts were scorned in Berlin. On the leading Vichy collaborators, see Geoffrey Warner, *Pierre Laval and the Eclipse of France* (London, Weidenfeld & Nicolson, 1968), still the best book on the subject, and Henri Coutau-Bégarie and Claude Huan, *Darlan* (Paris, Fayard, 1989), although this overly sympathetic account of the admiral should be read in conjunction with Robert Paxton, 'Un amiral entre deux blocs', in *Vingtième Siècle*, vol. 36, October–December, 1992, pp. 3–19. Martin Thomas, *The French Empire at War, 1940–1945* (Manchester, Manchester University Press, 1998) is good for colonial matters, while his namesake, R.T. Thomas, pursues Vichy's fruitless dialogue with London in *Britain and Vichy, 1940–1942* (London, Macmillan, 1979). On the world of the collaborationists, Bertram Gordon, *Collaborationism in France during the Second World War* (Ithaca, NY, Cornell University Press, 1980), Gerald Hirschfeld and Patrick Marsh, eds, *Collaboration in France* (Oxford, Berg, 1989) and Pascal Ory, *Les Collaborateurs* (Paris, Seuil, 1976) constitute a good introduction, but should be read alongside Stanley Hoffmann's groundbreaking article, 'Collaborationism in France', *Journal of Modern History*, vol. 40, no. 3, September 1968, pp. 375–95. On individual *collabos*, see Jean-Paul Brunet, *Jacques Doriot* (Paris, Balland, 1986), Philippe Burrin, *La Dérive fasciste: Doriot, Déat, Bergery, 1933–1945* (Paris, Seuil 1986) and Claude Lévy, *Jean Luchaire et 'Les Nouveux Temps'* (Paris, Armand Colin, 1974).

RESISTANCE

A pithy introduction to the world of resistance is provided in Jean-François Murraciole, *Histoire de la résistance en France* (Paris, PUF, 1996, 2nd edn) which tackles themes amplified in Kedward's *Resistance in Vichy France* and his *In Search of the Maquis*, both cited above. On the Free French, see Jean-Louis Crémieux-Brilhac's magisterial *La France libre* (Paris, Seuil, 1997). Among the hundreds of de Gaulle biographies, three stand out in the crowd: Julian Jackson, *De Gaulle* (London, Cardinal, 1989); Jean Lacouture, *De Gaulle* (2 vols, London, Harper Collins, 1990); and Andrew Shennan, *De Gaulle* (London, Longman, 1994). On Jean Moulin, there is Daniel Cordier's *Jean Moulin. L'inconnu du Panthéon* (3 vols, Paris, Lattès, 1989–93), which should be accompanied by Pierre Péan, *Vies et morts de Jean Moulin* (Paris, Fayard, 1998). On de Gaulle's *bête noire*, both Jean-Pierre Azéma et al., *Le Parti communiste français des années sombres, 1938–1941* (Paris, Seuil, 1986) and Serge Courtois, *Le PCF dans la guerre* (Paris, Ramsay, 1980) give an introduction to the debates surrounding the Communists during the Occupation. Something of the SOE's activities in France are recounted in M.R.D. Foot, *SOE in France* (London, HMSO, 1966), although this is very much an official history. On the *maquis*, see the many pieces by Kedward, in particular his exploratory essay 'The Maquis and the Culture of the Outlaw', in H.R. Kedward and R.S.P. Austin, eds, *Vichy France and the Resistance. Culture and Ideology* (London, Croom Helm, 1985), pp. 232–51, which also contains several other useful chapters. On gender and resistance, the following are worth consulting: M. Rossiter, *Women in the Resistance* (New York, Praeger, 1986); Paula Schwartz, 'Partisans and Gender Politics in Vichy France', *French Historical Studies*, Spring, 1989; and M.C. Weitz, *Sisters in the Resistance* (Toronto, Wiley, 1995). On the Liberation, Hilary Footitt and John Simmonds, *France 1943–1945* (Leicester, Leicester University Press, 1988) provide a good overview; specific aspects are tackled in H.R. Kedward and Nancy Woods, eds, *Liberation: Image and Event* (Oxford, Berg, 1995) and G. Madjarian, *Conflits, pouvoirs et société à la libération* (Paris, Union Générale des Editions, 1980). Remarkably, the most comprehensive study of the purges is still Peter Novick, *The Resistance versus Vichy. The Purge of Collaborators in Liberated France* (London, Chatto & Windus, 1968), better than Milton Dank, *The French against the French* (Philadelphia, PA, Philadelphia University Press, 1974) and H.R. Lottmann, *The People's Anger: Justice and Revenge in Post-Liberation France* (New York, Viking, 1986). For the politics of postwar reconstruction, Andrew Shennan's *Rethinking France. Plans for Renewal* (Oxford, Clarendon Press, 1989) displays the variety of schemes for revival.

REFERENCE WORKS

Several reference works are of use: Donna Elsveth, *France under the Nazi Occupation. An Annotated Bibliography* (Westport, CT, Greenwood Press, 1995);

Bertram Gordon, *Historical Dictionary of World War II France* (London, Aldwych Press, 1998); and P.H. Hutton, *Historical Dictionary of the French Third Republic* (2 vols, London, Aldwych Press, 1986). All were invaluable in putting together the present book, especially the glossary, yet by far the best reference tool is the handsomely produced volume by Michèle and Jean-Paul Cointet, *Dictionnaire historique de la France sous l'occupation* (Paris, Tallandier, 2000).

The world wide web is in a state of constant flux but one Vichy site, that produced by Simon Kitson, remains a constant: http://www.artsweb.bham.ac.uk/artsFrenchStudies/Kitson/Vichy/Vichyres/index.htm.

REFERENCES

PRIMARY SOURCES

Barthélemy, J. (1989) *Ministre de la justice. Mémoires*. Paris: Pygmalion.
Baudouin, P. (1948) *Neuf mois au gouvernement, avril–décembre 1940*. Paris: La Table Ronde.
Bloch, M. (1946) *L'Etrange défaite*. Paris. English translation (1949). London: Oxford University Press.
Bouthillier, Yves (1950–51) *Le Drame de Vichy* (2 vols). Paris: Plon.
Carcopino, J. (1953) *Souvenirs de sept ans, 1937–1944*. Paris: Flammarion.
Chambrun, R. de (1990) *Mes combats pour Pierre Laval*. Paris: Perrin.
Déat, M. (1989) *Mémoires politiques*. Paris: Denoël.
Duhamel, G. (1930) *Scènes de la vie future*. Paris: Denoël.
Gaulle, C. de (1934) *Vers l'armée de métier*. Paris: Plon.
Gaulle, C. de (1954–58) *War Memoirs* (3 vols). London: Collins.
Gillouin, R. (1966) *J'étais l'ami du maréchal Pétain*. Paris: Plon.
Girard, L.-D. (1948) *Montoire. Verdun diplomatique*. Paris: André Bonne.
Moulin de Labarthète, H. du (1946) *Le Temps des illusions. Souvenirs juillet 1940–avril 1942*. Geneva: Le Cheval Ailé.
Pétain, P. (1940) 'L'Education nationale', in *La Revue des Deux Mondes*, 15 August.
Rebatet, L. (1942) *Les Décombres*. Paris: Denoël.
Reynaud, P. (1947) *La France a sauvé l'Europe*. Paris: Flammarion.
Rougier, L. (1946) *Mission secrète à Londres. Les accords Pétain-Churchill*. Geneva: Le Cheval Ailé.
Sartre, J.-P. (1950) *Iron in the Soul*, Vol. 3: *The Roads to Liberty*. London: Hamish Hamilton.
Simon, P. (1942) *One Enemy Only: The Invader*. London: Hodder & Stoughton.
Tracou, J. (1948) *Le Maréchal aux liens*. Paris: Editions André Bonne.

SECONDARY SOURCES

Abrahams (1991) 'Haute Savoie at War, 1939–1945'. Cambridge: unpublished PhD thesis.
Adamthwaite, A. (1977) *France and the Coming of the Second World War*. London: Frank Cass.
Alexander, M.S. (1993) *The Republic in Danger. General Maurice Gamelin and the Politics of French Defence, 1933–1940*. Cambridge: Cambridge University Press.
Alexander, M.S. (1998) 'In Defence of the Maginot Line', in R. Boyce (ed.), *French Foreign and Defence Policy, 1918–1940*. London: Routledge.
Amouroux, H. (1976–) *La Grande Histoire des Français sous l'Occupation* (10 vols). Paris: Robert Laffont.
Aron, R. (1954) *Histoire de Vichy*. Paris: Fayard.

Aron, R. (1959) *Histoire de la libération de la France*. Paris: Fayard.

Atkin, N. (1999) 'Renewal, Reaction and Resistance: 1940–1944', in M.S. Alexander (ed.), *French History since Napoleon*. London: Arnold.

Atkin, N. (2000) 'Seduction and Sedition. Otto Abetz and the French, 1918–1940', in M. Cornick and C. Crossley (eds), *Problems in French History. Essays in Honour of Douglas Johnson*. London: Palgrave.

Austin, R.S.P. (1981) 'The Educational and Youth Policies of the Vichy Government in the Department of the Hérault, 1940–1944'. Manchester: unpublished PhD thesis.

Azéma, J.-P. (1975) *La Collaboration*. Paris: Presses Universitaires de France.

Azéma, J.-P. (1992) 'Vichy et les historiens', in J.P. Azéma and F. Bédarida (eds), *Vichy et les Français*. Paris: Fayard.

Azéma, J.-P. and Bédarida, F. (eds) (1992) *Vichy et les Français*. Paris: Fayard.

Azéma, J.-P. and Bédarida, F. (eds) (1993) *La France des années noires* (2 vols). Paris: Seuil.

Baruch, M.-O. (1997) *Servir l'Etat français*. Paris: Fayard.

Berstein, S. (1988) *La France des années 30*. Paris: Armand Colin.

Brunet, J. (1986) *Doriot*. Paris: Balland.

Bunting, M. (1995) *The Model Occupation. The Channel Islands under German Rule*. London: Harper Collins.

Burrin, P. (1986) *La Dérive fasciste. Doriot, Déat, Bergery, 1933–1945*. Paris: Seuil.

Burrin, P. (1993) 'Le collaborationisme', in J.-P. Azéma, and F. Bédarida (eds), *La France des années noires* (2 vols). Paris: Seuil.

Burrin, P. (1995) *La France à l'heure allemande*. Paris: Seuil.

Caron, V. (1999) *Uneasy Asylum. France and the Jewish Refugee Crisis, 1933–42*. Stanford, CA: Stanford University Press.

Carswell, R. (1999) 'The Press in Wartime France, 1940–1944'. London: unpublished MA thesis.

Chadwick, K. (1994) 'Alphonse de Châteaubriant, Collaborator on Retrial', in *French Historical Studies*, vol. 18, Fall.

Chadwick, K. (1998) 'A Broad Church. French Catholics and National Socialist Germany', in N. Atkin and F. Tallett (eds), *The Right in France, 1789–1997*. London: I.B. Tauris.

Cobb, R. (1982) *French and Germans. Germans and French*. Hanover, NH: University of New England Press.

Cointet, J.P. (1993) *Pierre Laval*. Paris: Fayard.

Cointet, J. and Cointet, M. (1987) *La France à Londres*. Brussels: Complexe.

Cointet, J. and Cointet, M. (eds) (2000) *Dictionnaire historique de la France sous l'occupation*. Paris: Tallandier.

Cointet, M. (1987) *Vichy et le fascisme*. Brussels: Complexe.

Cointet, M. (1989) *Le Conseil national de Vichy, 1940–1944*. Paris: Klincksieck.

Cointet, M. (1993) *Vichy capitale, 1940–1944*. Paris: Perrin.

Cordier, D. (1989–93) *Jean Moulin. L'inconnu du Panthéon*. Paris: Lattès.

Coutau-Bégarie, H. and Huan, C. (1989) *Darlan*. Paris: Fayard.

Crémieux-Brilhac, J.-L. (1990–91) *Les Français de l'an 40* (2 vols). Paris: Gallimard.

Crémieux-Brilhac, J.-L. (1997) *La France Libre*. Paris: Seuil.

Dard, O. (1998) *La Synarchie*. Paris: Perrin.

Delarue, J. (1968) *Trafics et crimes sous l'occupation*. Paris: Fayard.

Delperrié de Bayac, J. (1969) *Histoire de la Milice*. Paris: Fayard.

Diamond, H. (1999) *Women and the Second World War in France*. London: Longman.

Douzou, L. (1995) *Libération Sud*. Paris: Odile Jacob.

Dreyfus, F. (1990) *Histoire de Vichy*. Paris: Fayard.

Duquesne, J. (1966) *Les Catholiques français sous l'occupation*. Paris: Grasset.

Durand, Y. (1973) *Vichy, 1940–1944*. Paris: Bordas Poche.

Durand, Y. (1980) *La Captivité. Histoire des prisonniers de guerre français*. Paris: FNCPGCATM.

Durand, Y. (1989) *La France dans la Seconde Guerre Mondiale*. Paris: Armand Colin.

Duroselle, J.-B. (1981) *L'Abîme*. Paris: Imprimerie Nationale.

Flonneau, J.-M. (1992) 'L'évolution de l'opinion publique', in J.P. Azéma and F. Bédarida (eds), *Vichy et les Français*. Paris: Fayard.

FNSP (1972) *Le Gouvernement de Vichy, 1940–1942*. Paris: FNSP.

Frank, R. (1992) 'Double jeu ou double langage?', in J.P. Azéma and F. Bédarida (eds), *Vichy et les Français*. Paris: Fayard.

Froment, Pierre (1994) *René Bousquet*. Paris: Fayard.

Funk, A. (1992) *Hidden Ally. The French Resistance, Special Operations and the Landings in Southern France, 1944*. New York: Greenwood Press.

Gildea, R.D. (1995) *France since 1945*. Oxford: Oxford University Press.

Gordon, B.M. (1978) *Collaborationism in France during the Second World War*. Ithaca, NY: Cornell University Press.

Gordon, B.M. (1996) 'Ist Gott Französisch? Germans, Tourism and Occupied France, 1940–1944', in *Modern and Contemporary France*, vol. 4, no. 3.

Gordon, B.M. (ed.) (1998) *Historical Dictionary of World War II France*. London: Aldwych Press.

Griffiths, R. (1970) *Marshal Pétain*. London: Constable.

Gunsburg, J. (1979) *Divided and Conquered. The French High Command and the Defeat of the West*. Westport, CT: Greenwood Press.

Halls, W.D. (1981) *The Youth of Vichy France*. Oxford: Clarendon Press.

Halls, W.D. (1995) *Politics, Society and Christianity in Vichy France*. Oxford: Berg.

Hoffmann, S. (1968) 'Collaborationism in France', in *Journal of Modern History*, vol. 40, no. 3.

Hoffmann, S. (1974) *Decline or Renewal? France since the 1930s*. New York: Viking.

Horne, A. (1969) *To Lose a Battle. France 1940*. London: Macmillan.

Ingram, N. (1991) *Pacifism in France, 1918–1940*. Cambridge: Cambridge University Press.

Jackson, J. (1990) *De Gaulle*. London: Cardinal.

Jackson, J. (1999) '1940 and the Crisis of Interwar Democracy in France', in M.S. Alexander (ed.), *French History since Napoleon*. London: Arnold.

Jackson, J. (2001) *France, 1940–1944. The Dark Years*. Oxford: Oxford University Press.

Jaëckel, E. (1966) *Frankreich in Hitlers Europa*. Stuttgart: Deutches Verlags-Anstalt.

Johnson, D. (1970) 'Léon Blum', in *History*, July.

Kaspi, A. (1976) 'Le Centre de Documentation Juive Contemporaine', in *Revue d'Histoire Moderne et Contemporaine*, April–June.

Kedward, H.R. (1978) *Resistance in Vichy France*. Oxford: Oxford University Press.

Kedward, H.R. (1982) 'Patriots and Patriotism in Vichy France', in *Transactions of the Royal Historical Society*, 5th series, vol. 32.

Kedward, H.R. (1984) 'The French Resistance', in *History Today*, June.

Kedward, H.R. (1985a) *Occupied France. Collaboration and Resistance, 1940–1944*. Oxford: Basil Blackwell.

Kedward, H.R. (1985b) 'The *Maquis* and the Culture of the Outlaw', in H.R. Kedward and R. Austin (eds), *Vichy France and the Resistance. Culture and Ideology*. London: Croom Helm.

Kedward, H.R. (1993) *In Search of the Maquis. Resistance in Rural France, 1942–1944*. Oxford: Oxford University Press.

Kitson, S. (1995) 'The Police in the Liberation of Paris', in H.R. Kedward and N. Wood (eds), *The Liberation of France. Image and Event*. Oxford: Berg.

Klarsfeld, S. (1982–85) *Vichy-Auschwitz* (2 vols). Paris: Fayard.

Laborie, P. (1990) *L'Opinion publique sous Vichy*. Paris: Fayard.

Larkin, M. (1988) *France since the Popular Front*. Oxford: Clarendon Press.

Levisse-Touzé, C. (1995) *Paris libéré, Paris retrouvé*. Paris: Gallimard.

Lévy, C. (1974) *Jean Luchaire et 'Les Nouveaux Temps'*. Paris: Armand Colin.

Macmillan, J.F. (1992) *Twentieth-Century France*. London: Arnold.

Marrus, M. and Paxton, R.O. (1981) *Vichy France and the Jews*. New York: Basic Books.

Michel, H. (1962) *Pensées de la Résistance*. Paris: PUF.

Michel, H. (1966) *Vichy: Année 1940*. Paris: Robert Laffont.

Montclos, X. de (1982) *Eglises et chrétiens dans la Deuxième guerre mondiale. La France*. Lyon: Presses Universitaires de Lyon.

Muel-Dreyfus, F. (1996) *Vichy et l'éternel féminin*. Paris: Seuil.

Munholland, K. (1994) 'Remembering Wartime France', in *French Historical Studies*, Spring.

Muracciole J.-F. (1996) *Histoire de la résistance en France*. Paris: Presses Universitaires de France.

Ory, P. (1976) *Les Collaborateurs*. Paris: Seuil.

Passmore, K. (1997) *From Liberalism to Fascism. The Right in a French Province, 1928–1939*. Cambridge: Cambridge University Press.

Paxton, R.O. (1972) *Vichy France. Old Guard and New Order, 1940–1944*. New York: Alfred A. Knopf.

Paxton, R.O. (1993) 'La Collaboration d'état', in J.–P. Azéma and F. Bédarida (eds), *La France des années noires (2 vols)*. Paris: Seuil.

Péan, P. (1994) *Une jeunesse française François Mitterrand, 1934–1947*. Paris: Fayard.

Péan, P. (1998) *Vies et morts de Jean Moulin*. Paris: Fayard.

Peschanski, D. (ed.), (1990) *La Propagande de Vichy*. Paris: BDIC.

Peschanski, D. (1998) *Vichy. Contrôle et exclusion*. Brussels: Complexe.

Rajsfus, X. (1995) *La Police de Vichy*. Paris: Fayard.

Raymond, G. (1975) *Une certaine France. L'Antisémitisme, 40–44*. Paris: Balland.

Réau, E. du (1993) *Edouard Daladier*. Paris: Fayard.

Rémond, R. (1969) *The Right Wing in France from 1815 to de Gaulle*. Philadelphia: Philadelphia University Press.

Rigoulot, P. (1997) *L'Alsace Lorraine pendant la guerre, 1939–1945*. Paris: Presses Universitaires de France.

Rossignol, D. (1991) *Histoire de la propagande, 1940–1944*. Paris: Presses Universitaires de France.

Rousso, H. (1980) *Un château en Allemagne*. Paris: Ramsay.

Rousso, H. (1987) *La Collaboration*. Paris: Editions MA.

Rousso, H. (1989) *The Vichy Syndrome. History and Memory in France since 1944*. Cambridge, MA: Harvard University Press.

Sadoun, M. (1982) *Les Socialistes sous l'occupation*. Paris: FNSP.

Schwarz, P. (1989) 'Partisans and Gender Politics in Vichy France', in *French Historical Studies*, Spring.

Shennan, A.S. (1985) *Rethinking France*. Oxford: Clarendon Press.

Shennan, A. (1993) *De Gaulle*. London: Longman.

Soucy, R. (1986) *Fascism in France. The First Wave, 1924–1933*. Stanford, CA: Stanford University Press.

Sternhell, Z. (1986) *Neither Left nor Right*. Stanford, CA: Stanford University Press.

Stolfi, R. (1970) 'Equipment for Victory in 1940' in *History*, June.

Sweets, J. (1986) *Choices in Vichy France*. New York: Oxford University Press.

Sweets, J. (1989) 'La Police et la population dans la France de Vichy', in *Revue d'Histoire de la Deuxième Guerre Mondiale*, vol 39, July.

Taylor, L. (1997) 'The Black Market in Occupied Northern France, 1940–44', in *Contemporary European History*, vol. 6, no. 2.

Thomas, M. (1998) *The French Empire at War*. Manchester: Manchester University Press.

Thomas, R.T. (1979) *Britain and Vichy, 1940–1942*. London: Macmillan.

Veillon, D. (1990) *La Mode sous l'occupation*. Paris: Payot.

Veillon, D. (1995) *Vivre et survivre en France, 1939–1947*. Paris: Payot.

Veillon, D. and Flonneau, J.-M. (eds) (1996) *Le Temps des restrictions en France, 1939–1949*. Paris: IHTP.

Vinen, R. (1994) 'Pétain's Hollow Crown', in *History Today*, June.

Vinen, R. (1996) *France, 1934–1970*. London: Macmillan.

Warner, G. (1968) *Pierre Laval and Eclipse of France*. London: Weidenfeld & Nicolson.

Weber, E. (1994) *The Hollow Years. France in the 1930s*. New York: Norton.

Wiewiorka, O. (1995) *Défense de la France*. Paris: Seuil.

Wolf, D. (1969) *Doriot*. Paris: Fayard.

Zaretsky, R. (1995) *Nîmes at War*. Philadelphia, PA: Philadelphia University Press.

INDEX

General Editors: Clive Emsley & Gordon Martel

The series was founded by Patrick Richardson in 1966. Between 1980 and 1996 Roger Lockyer edited the series before handing over to Clive Emsley (Professor of History at the Open University) and Gordon Martel (Professor of International History at the University of Northern British Columbia, Canada and Senior Research Fellow at De Montfort University).

MEDIEVAL ENGLAND

The Pre-Reformation Church in England 1400–1530 (Second edition)
Christopher Harper-Bill   0 582 28989 0

Lancastrians and Yorkists: The Wars of the Roses
David R Cook   0 582 35384 X

TUDOR ENGLAND

Henry VII (Third edition)
Roger Lockyer & Andrew Thrush   0 582 20912 9

Henry VIII (Second edition)
M D Palmer   0 582 35437 4

Tudor Rebellions (Fourth edition)
Anthony Fletcher & Diarmaid MacCulloch   0 582 28990 4

The Reign of Mary I (Second edition)
Robert Tittler   0 582 06107 5

Early Tudor Parliaments 1485–1558
Michael A R Graves   0 582 03497 3

The English Reformation 1530–1570
W J Sheils   0 582 35398 X

Elizabethan Parliaments 1559–1601 (Second edition)
Michael A R Graves   0 582 29196 8

England and Europe 1485–1603 (Second edition)
Susan Doran   0 582 28991 2

The Church of England 1570–1640
Andrew Foster   0 582 35574 5

STUART BRITAIN

Social Change and Continuity: England 1550–1750 (Second edition)
Barry Coward   0 582 29442 8

James I (Second edition)
S J Houston

0 582 20911 0

The English Civil War 1640–1649
Martyn Bennett

0 582 35392 0

Charles I, 1625–1640
Brian Quintrell

0 582 00354 7

The English Republic 1649–1660 (Second edition)
Toby Barnard

0 582 08003 7

Radical Puritans in England 1550–1660
R J Acheson

0 582 35515 X

The Restoration and the England of Charles II (Second edition)
John Miller

0 582 29223 9

The Glorious Revolution (Second edition)
John Miller

0 582 29222 0

EARLY MODERN EUROPE

The Renaissance (Second edition)
Alison Brown

0 582 30781 3

The Emperor Charles V
Martyn Rady

0 582 35475 7

French Renaissance Monarchy: Francis I and Henry II (Second edition)
Robert Knecht

0 582 28707 3

The Protestant Reformation in Europe
Andrew Johnston

0 582 07020 1

The French Wars of Religion 1559–1598 (Second edition)
Robert Knecht

0 582 28533 X

Phillip II
Geoffrey Woodward

0 582 07232 8

The Thirty Years' War
Peter Limm

0 582 35373 4

Louis XIV
Peter Campbell

0 582 01770 X

Spain in the Seventeenth Century
Graham Darby

0 582 07234 4

Peter the Great
William Marshall

0 582 00355 5

EUROPE 1789–1918

Britain and the French Revolution
Clive Emsley

0 582 36961 4

Revolution and Terror in France 1789–1795 (Second edition) *D G Wright*	0 582 00379 2
Napoleon and Europe *D G Wright*	0 582 35457 9
The Abolition of Serfdom in Russia, 1762–1907 *David Moon*	0 582 29486 X
Nineteenth-Century Russia: Opposition to Autocracy *Derek Offord*	0 582 35767 5
The Constitutional Monarchy in France 1814–48 *Pamela Pilbeam*	0 582 31210 8
The 1848 Revolutions (Second edition) *Peter Jones*	0 582 06106 7
The Italian Risorgimento *M Clark*	0 582 00353 9
Bismark & Germany 1862–1890 (Second edition) *D G Williamson*	0 582 29321 9
Imperial Germany 1890–1918 *Ian Porter, Ian Armour and Roger Lockyer*	0 582 03496 5
The Dissolution of the Austro-Hungarian Empire 1867–1918 (Second edition) *John W Mason*	0 582 29466 5
Second Empire and Commune: France 1848–1871 (Second edition) *William H C Smith*	0 582 28705 7
France 1870–1914 (Second edition) *Robert Gildea*	0 582 29221 2
The Scramble for Africa (Second edition) *M E Chamberlain*	0 582 36881 2
Late Imperial Russia 1890–1917 *John F Hutchinson*	0 582 32721 0
The First World War *Stuart Robson*	0 582 31556 5

EUROPE SINCE 1918

The Russian Revolution (Second edition) *Anthony Wood*	0 582 35559 1
Lenin's Revolution: Russia, 1917–1921 *David Marples*	0 582 31917 X
Stalin and Stalinism (Second edition) *Martin McCauley*	0 582 27658 6
The Weimar Republic (Second edition) *John Hiden*	0 582 28706 5
The Inter-War Crisis 1919–1939 *Richard Overy*	0 582 35379 3

Fascism and the Right in Europe, 1919–1945
Martin Blinkhorn   0 582 07021 X

Spain's Civil War (Second edition)
Harry Browne   0 582 28988 2

The Third Reich (Second edition)
D G Williamson   0 582 20914 5

The Origins of the Second World War (Second edition)
R J Overy   0 582 29085 6

The Second World War in Europe
Paul MacKenzie   0 582 32692 3

The French at War, 1934–1944
Nicholas Atkin   0 582 36899 5

Anti-Semitism before the Holocaust
Albert S Lindemann   0 582 36964 9

The Holocaust: The Third Reich and the Jews
David Engel   0 582 32720 2

Germany from Defeat to Partition, 1945–1963
D G Williamson   0 582 29218 2

Britain and Europe since 1945
Alex May   0 582 30778 3

Eastern Europe 1945–1969: From Stalinism to Stagnation
Ben Fowkes   0 582 32693 1

Eastern Europe since 1970
Bülent Gökay   0 582 32858 6

The Khrushchev Era, 1953–1964
Martin McCauley   0 582 27776 0

NINETEENTH-CENTURY BRITAIN

Britain before the Reform Acts: Politics and Society 1815–1832
Eric J Evans   0 582 00265 6

Parliamentary Reform in Britain c. 1770–1918
Eric J Evans   0 582 29467 3

Democracy and Reform 1815–1885
D G Wright   0 582 31400 3

Poverty and Poor Law Reform in Nineteenth-Century Britain, 1834–1914:
From Chadwick to Booth
David Englander   0 582 31554 9

The Birth of Industrial Britain: Economic Change, 1750–1850
Kenneth Morgan   0 582 29833 4

Chartism (Third edition)
Edward Royle   0 582 29080 5

Peel and the Conservative Party 1830–1850
Paul Adelman   0 582 35557 5

Gladstone, Disraeli and later Victorian Politics (Third edition)
Paul Adelman   0 582 29322 7

Britain and Ireland: From Home Rule to Independence
Jeremy Smith   0 582 30193 9

TWENTIETH-CENTURY BRITAIN

The Rise of the Labour Party 1880–1945 (Third edition)
Paul Adelman   0 582 29210 7

The Conservative Party and British Politics 1902–1951
Stuart Ball   0 582 08002 9

The Decline of the Liberal Party 1910–1931 (Second edition)
Paul Adelman   0 582 27733 7

The British Women's Suffrage Campaign 1866–1928
Harold L Smith   0 582 29811 3

War & Society in Britain 1899–1948
Rex Pope   0 582 03531 7

The British Economy since 1914: A Study in Decline?
Rex Pope   0 582 30194 7

Unemployment in Britain between the Wars
Stephen Constantine   0 582 35232 0

The Attlee Governments 1945–1951
Kevin Jefferys   0 582 06105 9

The Conservative Governments 1951–1964
Andrew Boxer   0 582 20913 7

Britain under Thatcher
Anthony Seldon and Daniel Collings   0 582 31714 2

INTERNATIONAL HISTORY

The Eastern Question 1774–1923 (Second edition)
A L Macfie   0 582 29195 X

India 1885–1947: The Unmaking of an Empire
Ian Copland   0 582 38173 8

The Origins of the First World War (Second edition)
Gordon Martel   0 582 28697 2

The United States and the First World War
Jennifer D Keene   0 582 35620 2

Anti-Semitism before the Holocaust
Albert S Lindemann   0 582 36964 9

The Origins of the Cold War, 1941–1949 (Second edition)
Martin McCauley
0 582 27659 4

Russia, America and the Cold War, 1949–1991
Martin McCauley
0 582 27936 4

The Arab–Israeli Conflict
Kirsten E Schulze
0 582 31646 4

The United Nations since 1945: Peacekeeping and the Cold War
Norrie MacQueen
0 582 35673 3

Decolonisation: The British Experience since 1945
Nicholas J White
0 582 29087 2

The Origins of the Vietnam War
Fredrik Logevall
0 582 31918 8

The Vietnam War
Mitchell Hall
0 582 32859 4

WORLD HISTORY

China in Transformation 1900–1949
Colin Mackerras
0 582 31209 4

Japan faces the World, 1925–1952
Mary L Hanneman
0 582 36898 7

Japan in Transformation, 1952–2000
Jeff Kingston
0 582 41875 5

US HISTORY

American Abolitionists
Stanley Harrold
0 582 35738 1

The American Civil War, 1861–1865
Reid Mitchell
0 582 31973 0

America in the Progressive Era, 1890–1914
Lewis L Gould
0 582 35671 7

The United States and the First World War
Jennifer D Keene
0 582 35620 2

The Truman Years, 1945–1953
Mark S Byrnes
0 582 32904 3

The Korean War
Steven Hugh Lee
0 582 31988 9

The Origins of the Vietnam War
Fredrik Logevall
0 582 31918 8

The Vietnam War
Mitchell Hall
0 582 32859 4